CW00706803

Memoirs Of Mrs. Siddons, 2...

James Boaden

Act ①

① madhouse visit
Isabella
success - Solonnana

Brereton loves her
then She accidentally stabs him
He forgives her
she throws him off
He spreads rumours about her
refuses to come to her defence on stage
She has to 'carry the house'

Royal interest — question — Solonns mania
Lady M - will she do it?
she's afraid

2 visit madhouse
Lady M blows roof off stage
& escape from madhouse.

ACT 2 —> painting. Mr Lawrence
She takes her image into her own hands
She is sick of portrait painters
—> De Montfort

Nabu Public Domain Reprints:

You are holding a reproduction of an original work published before 1923 that is in the public domain in the United States of America, and possibly other countries. You may freely copy and distribute this work as no entity (individual or corporate) has a copyright on the body of the work. This book may contain prior copyright references, and library stamps (as most of these works were scanned from library copies). These have been scanned and retained as part of the historical artifact.

This book may have occasional imperfections such as missing or blurred pages, poor pictures, errant marks, etc. that were either part of the original artifact, or were introduced by the scanning process. We believe this work is culturally important, and despite the imperfections, have elected to bring it back into print as part of our continuing commitment to the preservation of printed works worldwide. We appreciate your understanding of the imperfections in the preservation process, and hope you enjoy this valuable book.

met Joanna Bailey — interview — a new role

her ?husband spent her money.

her new 'servant' tends to her —
running from workhouse.
will ??? reveal her?

Perfect Storm

Butler a g → May fails
Plays Mrs Halle

Miss Carpenter with → Sirena ??
Laurence suicide?
Brother → as well.

Butler → Orra — gothic of Colonin
life

Crabtree → scandal.

Farce — but Clara escapes from it
while Siddons is trapped

Lady M → she scares the shit out
of Kemble

TROLLED ON DEATH — She is scared of her own rage
OF DAUGHTER — refuses Orra. system
(Too much rage) breaks
down

Rules for female artists. They can't be ruthless.
re Catherine de Medici
outrage

She kept Clara
but got improved

Plan
her to
let go
when
heart
is
on

OF

MRS. SIDDONS.

INTERSPERSED WITH

ANECDOTES OF AUTHORS AND ACTORS.

By JAMES BOADEN, Esq.

"Siddons!---whose learned theatre disdains
Melodious trifles, and enervate strains,
And blushes on her injured stage to see
Nonsense well-tun'd, and sweet stupidity,---
Unrivall'd as thy merit be thy fame,
And thy own laurels shade thy envy'd name!"
Apud TICKELL.

SECOND EDITION.

IN TWO VOLUMES.
VOL. II.

LONDON:

HENRY COLBURN AND RICHARD BENTLEY,
NEW BURLINGTON STREET.

1831.

R.92.675

CONTENTS

OF

THE SECOND VOLUME.

CHAPTER XII.

CHAPTER XIII.

CHAPTER XIV.

CHAPTER XV.

Preliminary Observations .. Mrs. Siddons at length performs Lady Macbeth .. Real History of Duncan and Macbeth .. The Tyrant's Pilgrimage to Rome .. What it would probably have suggested to Shakspeare .. Mrs. Siddons's entrance with the Letter .. The first Scene gone through critically .. Remarks continued ·· Omission of the Lady after the Murder of Duncan .. Its Propriety questioned .. The Banquet Scene .. Theory of Somnambulism .. Their Majesties commanded Macbeth immediately .. Lady Macbeth an exclusive Possession to Mrs. Siddons .. The Electra of the Greek Drama, if studied and written by Shakspeare,

CHAPTER XVI.

CHAPTER XVII.

CHAPTER XVIII.

CHAPTER XIX.

CHAPTER XX.

CHAPTER XXI.

ERRATA.—VOL. II.

Page 85, read he *tells* her.

148, read *souvent*

154, for stories, read *stores*.

MEMOIRS

OF

MRS. SIDDONS.

CHAPTER XII.

AS ACTED BY HIM. — MR. KEMBLE IN HAMLET. — A RE-
CENTLY DISCOVERED COPY OF THAT PLAY. — MRS. SID-
DONS VISITS DR. JOHNSON.

THE management of Drury Lane Theatre, in allowing Mrs. Siddons an extra night in the month of March, 1783, had in fact given but little out of their own funds, though, from the great extent of her fashionable connexion, they put the actress in the receipt of a large accession to her esta-blished salary. On this night seven rows of the pit were laid into the boxes, and her *book*, as it lay open in the lobby, was literally the Court Guide.

The benefit produced to Mrs. Siddons, no less a sum than £650, but then Lady Spencer gave 90 guineas for her side box, and Lady Aylesbury a Bank note of £50, for an upper box.

A desire to preserve all reasonable continuity in this narrative, has compelled me to omit, in the series of dramatic events, some that claim this supplemental record. On the 14th of January expired a very *prominent* character, the delight of former times, whose cognomen was the sign of merriment, and the prelude of harmony. The reader, to be sure, anticipates the person of Old Cervetto, who, at the age of one hundred and two, resigned all the noisy honours of his *nose*. He played the double bass in the band for many years, and was the father of the great violoncello player. He came to England in the year of the hard frost, and was then an old man.

I am afraid his successors in the orchestra have been but slightly accomplished to succeed him; but under the original call for nosy, or *nozée*, his fame yet survives, though that of the trunk-maker excites no longer noise among us.

Mr. Cumberland has a name in the drama, which demands attention to every effort not very much below himself. The *Mysterious Husband*, acted at Covent Garden, on the 28th of January, is in many respects one of his best productions. Before the play went into rehearsal, he brought it to Henderson's house to read it to him. Mrs. Henderson, with a very natural feeling, exclaimed to him, " Well, Mr. Cumberland, I hope at last you will allow Mr. Henderson to be *good for something* on the stage." " Madam," replied the poet, " *I can't afford it*—a VILLAIN he *must be*." And, to be sure, of all the *causeless* depravity, in the great moral massacre of the English tragedy, the character of Lord Davenant, in the present play, affords the completest specimen. It seems to have been suggested by Lord Orford's mysterious *Mother*, which had been printed in 1768 at Strawberry Hill, and presented to his friends, with the express stipulation, that neither Garrick, nor Dr. Johnson, should be permitted to read it. The Doctor would call this a " very " *angry*, but *unnecessary* prohibition." It would severely mortify Mr. Garrick, who, however idly, hoped for universal esteem.

I do not wonder that Walpole, when, in 1781, he consented to a publication of this play from his own copy, pronounced a subject so horrid unsuited to the stage; and it should be remembered, that, in horrors, the *Mysterious Mother* greatly transcends either Phædra or Jocasta. But the nervous dignity of its composition will for ever delight in the closet. Yet, when we have in the mind's eye, such an actress as Mrs. Siddons, it is impossible to read some of its passages without attempting to conceive the astonishing effect they must receive from her *look* and *utterance*. The fifth scene of the first act, where an artful friar is endeavouring to worm out the cause of her remorse, that he may be master of her wealth, offers a few points that are irresistible, among many that are fine.

> " *Bened.*   The church could seal
>   Your pardon, but you scorn it.   In your pride
>   Consists your danger.   Yours are pagan virtues.
> *Countess.*   Father, my *crimes* are pagan: my belief
>   Too orthodox to trust to erring man."

When the reader, who has known this magician in her strength, has a little considered the effect of *one word* in this reply, he may be disposed to go on with her in a speech so calculated for her powers.

> " What! shall I, foul with guilt, and self-condemn'd,
>   Presume to kneel, where angels kneel appal'd,

And plead a *priest's certificate* for pardon ?
While HE, perchance, before my blasted eyes
Shall sink to woes endless unutterable,
For having *fool'd* me into that presumption.
Bened. Is HE to blame, *trusting* to what he grants ?
Countess. Am I to blame, NOT trusting what he grants ?"

Nor is the power of the poet at all weakened to the very end of the first act; where, with some of the *forms,* and more of the *spirit,* he adopts the interrogative style of Cato to Labienus in the ninth book of Lucan. Of its *forms* in the outset :

"*Countess.* Good father, wherefore ? what should I inquire ?
Must I be taught of him, that guilt is woe ?
That innocence alone is happiness ?"

Of its *spirit* about the middle of her speech :

" We want no preacher to distinguish vice
From virtue. At our birth the god reveal'd
All conscience needs to know."*

---

* " Quid quæri, Labiene, jubes ? an liber in armis
Occubuisse velim, potius quam regna videre ?
An noceat vis ulla bono ?" &c.

—— —— —— —— ——

" Nil agimus nisi sponte dei, non vocibus ullis
Numen eget, dixitque semel nascentibus autor
Quicquid scìre licet."

Pharsal, Lib. IX.

Rowe, though even *alarmingly* paraphrastical, has done this whole speech of Cato, with the vigour and majestic ease of Dryden himself.

As Mr. Cumberland chose a slighter degree of
incest for the subject of his play, I wish he had
not written it in prose, and that with the dexterity
of Walpole, he had thrown the occurrence back
a few centuries. In hearing or reading the vices
of another and distant age, we have a twofold
consolation : an involuntary suspicion that the
facts may never have been true ; and a voluntary
belief, that our own times exhibit nothing like
them.

A slight sketch of the interest will illustrate
and justify this remark. Davenant, already a
widower, marries the daughter of Sir Edmund
Travers ; she had a former attachment, but his
lordship gets his rival a ship, and sends him upon
a distant discovery, perhaps to the North Pole.
In a ramble to Spa, Davenant meets with the
sister of this very Captain, and under another
name marries her. After a short cohabitation he
quits her, and from Paris transmits to her an account of his own death. The second wife, conceiving herself a widow, comes to England, and
marries clandestinely the son of Davenant. On
the morning of her marriage, she accidentally
sees her first husband, his father. The circumstances are at length disclosed by Lady Davenant, to the " *precious* villain," her husband, who,
from desperation destroys himself; and so re-
moves the only bar to the happiness of the survi-

vors. Yet the sort of happiness is not enviable, and should be preserved as a *dramatic* rarity. Dormer, the discoverer, comes back to take the command of the real Lady Davenant, and the son has to forget, if possible, that his father was born before him.

Henderson was amazingly terrible with all these horrors about him; and Miss Younge delightful in the suffering and excellent Lady Davenant. She had a *sensible* patience in her composition, a dignity in misfortune quite unaffected: and in all her range, and it was a very wide one, never shone more than in the meek endurance of a brutal or profligate husband. This it was that almost rendered her *sublime* in the Countess of Narbonne. Sir Edmund Travers, a character of odd humour, acted by Yates in this play, shewed a peculiar comedy, which we now happily preserve in Dowton: from its chasteness it will combine with tragedy, at a proper distance from the catastrophe.

On the following night, Mr. Pratt, whose *Fair Circassian* has been mentioned, followed up his serious success by a comic failure; it was called the *School for Vanity*. Among the extraordinary events, a baronet is saved from *drowning* by an alderman! of the name of Ingot. Such an incident passed even dramatic credibility. " For the " water swells a man, and what a thing should I

" have been when I had been swoln! I should
" have been a mountain of mummy."

Miss Farren performed a very tender orphan,
named Ophelia, and Miss Philips, (her *real* fate
too,) had a swain insensible to her beauty; a
song thrown into the part was much admired;
but the school *broke up* for a long vacation, when
the tiresome lesson of *vanity* ended.

Miss E. Kemble, another sister of Mrs. Siddons, made an appearance in Portia, notwithstanding " her greater" had done so little in it
seven years before. This lady more resembled
Mrs. Siddons in her person and countenance than
Miss Kemble did, and was certainly a better
actress. However, she was not brought so forward in the arrangements of the theatre; and, if
I am correct, only once repeated Portia, and then
was untroubled by the call-boy for the rest of the
season. Her elder sister, Frances, beside the
tragic *seconds* to the Siddons, was one night tried
in *Beatrice;* but the audience were rather cruel,
for their censure anticipated the first sentence
pronounced by her.

The reader will easily imagine that these ladies
could not expect to be received upon the footing
of their actual merits. They were thwarted by
the fears of the whole dramatic body. If the
influence of Mrs. Siddons equalled her *talent*, what
was to be expected but an invasion of her whole

family, male and female, which as it was certainly numerous, would swallow up all business worth doing in the theatre? At Drury Lane Theatre, it was now known that Mr. Kemble might be expected, and that from his provincial success, he would occupy the first place in tragedy or none. When we consider, therefore, the *jealousy* peculiar to this profession, and the *interest* equally peculiar that it excites in others, we can see no inconsiderable numbers, among the frequenters of the play-house, strongly prejudiced against the family.

It is very natural for a lady addicted to dramatic composition, to look to the authors of her own sex with partiality. It is thus we see the Bold Stroke for a *Wife*, of Mrs. Centlivre, suggesting to Mrs. Cowley a Bold Stroke for a *Husband*—a comedy which she brought out at Covent Garden Theatre on the 25th of February, 1783. This play labours with two distinct interests, which a very little attention might have woven into each other. One of them is the common girlish expedient of *disgusting* a variety of known suitors in favour of one unknown. The pleasantest point here, was the father locking the daughter up, and upon his leaving the room, her lover starting suddenly from his concealment.

The girl upon her surprise, screams aloud; while the father is heard on the stairs to say, " Aye, " aye, you may *scream*, but there you shall stay, " Miss," or something like it. The other is the trite expedient (I mean on the stage, for in real life, nothing perhaps of the sort ever occurred,) of a neglected wife going *en cavalier* to her husband's mistress, to learn *how to captivate*. The mistress naturally falling in love with this wife, who can play to the life any part but her own, in her fondness, possesses her of all the *conveyances* which her husband had made to the prejudice of his family.

It is a common observation that the writings of the ladies do not shun the broadest latitude taken by the other sex; and so indifferent, for the most part, do they seem to their peculiar interests, that they luxuriate in the description of a gay agreeable profligate. They would inspire constancy, but they paint the rover: in their most perfect characters the heart always pants for pleasure. But this I learn is the *creed*, as well as practice, among the dramatists of the fair sex. The female friend who sketches the character of Mrs. Behn, speaks out upon the subject. " She " was a woman of SENSE, and *consequently* a lover " of pleasure." We have had four ladies eminent among our comic writers—Behn, Centlivre, Cowley, and Inchbald; and a not very rigid moralist would strike out much from the writings of each of them.

I presume an admirer of either lady, who had composed and addressed a poem called the *Comic Muse* would have incurred no blame. Russel, the author of a History of Modern Europe, and other ingenious works, now published a poem called the *Tragic Muse*, with which he complimented Mrs. Siddons. He was severely reproved by the critics for " wasting his verse " upon excellence that was in its nature *fugitive*, " the METEOR of the moment." A more liberal feeling might have applauded even an endeavour to give some little fame beyond the memories of cotemporary admirers. There is something grateful in the very notion, that verse is trying to *repay* some of the charm it has derived from the organs of the actress. And surely if in the language of either Cibber, or Lloyd, or Sheridan, the art of the great actor leaves no memorial, unlike every other effort of genius, we are doubly called upon to perpetuate what we can of gifts so singularly circumscribed; not as some would represent them, the mere *mimicry* of man, but arising out of the most vivid imagination of his nature, passions, and habits, and a power of *becoming* steadily all that the fancy suggests, as constituting any individual existence.

Mrs. Siddons having acted for the benefits of

the four leading actors in tragedy, Messrs. Smith, Palmer, Bensley and Brereton during her first brilliant season, on the 19th of May, performed Shore for the Theatrical Fund. This was followed by a repetition of Zara on her sister's night; and on the 5th of June, with Isabella, for the twenty-third time, the doors of Drury Lane play-house

" Shut up in measureless content."

In looking to the comparative popularity of the characters acted by Mrs. Siddons, the triumph was unquestionably with Southerne's Isabella, which she played twenty-two times in her first season. Rowe to his Jane Shore and Calista, had of each fourteen performances; Otway's exquisite Belvidera had thirteen repetitions; Murphy, eleven for his Grecian Daughter; Congreve's Zara was acted thrice, and she kept her friend Hull's Fatal Interview alive till the author's third day; neither his own merits, nor those of his heroine, could do more for this weak imitation of Lillo in *prose*. We are here presented with the astonishing total of eighty performances in one season, of characters full of emotion and fatigue, an effort beyond any parallel, and as to excellence beyond all praise.

Nor was any rest allowed our charming actress.

On the 9th of June, in company with the Brere-
tons, she set off post for Ireland; the party took
up F. Aickin by the way, and pursued their
journey to the sister kingdom. She was now
anxious to join her brother, Mr. Kemble, who
had already signed an article for three years with
the proprietors of Drury Lane Theatre.

We have now leisure to turn ourselves, to look
at the Haymarket, with its grand and little
theatres; and as all foreign concerns, to this or
any other work, should be out of the way as
speedily as possible, we shall look first at that
shameless prodigy the Opera House. A few
months only are past, since I read some motion
or other respecting the late proprietor, Mr. Tay-
lor; I have now under my eye a notice, heading
the bill of the night, in the year 1783, calling his
creditors together, to meet the trustees of the
concern. He was then in such a state as to be
utterly unable to go on; but, on " a certain
" ground," he permitted the performers to continue the entertainments for their *own* advantage,
from the 22nd of May to the end of the season.
The nobility and gentry had already given one
subscription for the relief of the deluded artists,
who had come over in the fair exercise of
first rate talents; and a second was now set on
foot, at five guineas for twelve operas. I have
brought these two facts together, that the reader

may reflect upon the mysteries of EQUITY, by which a shuffling concern can thus be kept litigiously alive for FORTY years together.

In the season of 1782-3, the Opera was crowded to excess. One o'clock in the morning did not see the Haymarket clear of the carriages, and the stage had every fascination both in the serious and comic opera. Pacchierotti, the most pathetic singer in the world, was executing the divine music of Sarti—perhaps not fully supported as to a first woman—for neither Carnevale nor Morigi had sufficient power for so great a master, and they slighted the recitativo, a thing inexcusable indeed in Italians, who know its value. But what so seldom happens, the comic opera was now quite equal in attraction to the serious. The graceful hilarity and taste of Viganoni were seconded by a prima buffa, whom no time has approached in all the requisites, I mean the Allegranti. In Ballet there was Le Picq and Slingsby, and for their ladies Rossi; and *Theodore*, who was the Allegranti of the dance. The house itself, too, had been enlarged, and rendered splendid beyond every thing known. His present Majesty, then Prince of Wales, graced it frequently by his presence, with other branches of his illustrious family, and the principal nobility had boxes; and yet, from the hard and dogged vulgarity of one man, who had got into the property, nothing but disgrace and ruin attended the concern.

The *little* manager, as he delighted to style himself,* but who occupied no small space in the eye of taste, was this season induced to beautify his pigmy palace. The friendly journals celebrated his ballustrades and his pillars, his paper and his paint, not forgetting his frontispiece, with its new motto, of which the ominous word *serpentem* was omitted, and the spectator read only:

" Spectas, et tu spectabere."

Our recent encampments all over the country suggested a military allusion on his opening. As an article, certainly from Colman, it merits preservation. He begins with his triumph in the recent publication of the art of poetry.

INTELLIGENCE EXTRAORDINARY.

(From the Camp just forming in the Haymarket.)

Town Major Colman, who has just given the public a very elegant *Theory of his Art*, will reduce it into *practice*, by opening the summer campaign with some of the best troops that can be mustered from the two garrisons which have been on duty during the course of the winter, as well as others from country cantonments.

The following is the disposition of the encampment :—

---

* " *Small* though his talents, smaller than his *size*,
  Beneath your smiles his *little* Lares rise."

  Prol. at opening.

Major General Palmer is to head the *principal division*, in which he is to be supported by Colonels Aickin, Bensley, Bannister, jun. &c.

The *Hah! hah!* Pioneers to consist of Captains Edwin, Parsons, Wewitzer, Baddeley, Massey, and R. Palmer.

This *corps* will likewise be joined by Captain *Wilson*, who, in consequence of many *gallant* engagements had received a *violent* contusion in his *leg*, but is now so well recovered as to be able to *stand* to his duty.

The *heavy* cavalry will be led by the *Webbes*, two officers of as much *personal weight* as any in the field.

The *light* troops by Mrs. Bulkeley, Mrs. Wilson, Mrs. Wells, Miss Hale, &c.

Necessary woman to the *Buskin* and *Sock* Heroines, Mrs. Poussin.

The *band* of *music* to be composed of Messrs. Bannister, Brett, Wood, Mrs. Bannister, and Miss George from the *pipe* office, Oxford.

Besides the above band, several *out-door trumpeters* will occasionally entertain the town with the celebrated anthem of *Te dominum theatri laudamus*.

Chasseurs and *Light Infantry*, Master and Miss Byrne, &c. &c.

For an account of the names of the *Artillery*, that is to say, thunder and lightning men, rain showerers, camp-shifters, &c. vide the *orderly* books of the company.

N.B. The *site* of the old Camp is considerably enlarged, by removing the pallisados, &c. The *tents* are all new painted; and the whole encampment, under the direction of the able engineer *Rooker*, cuts a very brilliant and soldier-like appearance.

And thus, in those days, a manager could shew his *company*, before and behind the curtain, that

he had the *right* of WIT to entertain them; and
affirm his judgment as to the efforts of other
authors by his own powers of performance.

Colman knew how contemptible the new theatrical disease was, of *altering* boxes and avenues,
and calling the thing a *new theatre*. Though he
felt himself, according to the laws of proportion,
bound to vie with his antagonists in this vanity of
the art, he yet taught his own audiences to laugh
at it on his first night of opening :—

> " What tho' our house be three score years of age,
> Let us new-vamp the box, new-lay the stage ;
> Long paragraphs shall paint, with proud parade,
> The gilded front, and airy ballustrade ;
> While on each post the flaming bill displays,
> Our *old* NEW THEATRE, and *new* OLD PLAYS."

The Miss George alluded to proved a very
pleasing singer and very respectable actress. One
of the earliest novelties produced by the manager,
was a comedy called *A Friend in Need is a Friend
Indeed !*—a first and only dramatic attempt by Mr.
D. O'Brien, so well known as the zealous friend
of Charles Fox. It produced some public altercation between Mr. Colman and the author, and
eight nights performance but slightly connected
with each other. A *ninth* night was at length
yielded by the manager, to verify the *title*, and
then this *rara avis* suddenly disappeared. *O'mi-*

cron Brien yielded to *O'mega* Keefe. The *Young Quaker* of the latter, the loves of Reuben Sadboy and Dinah Primrose, amused the town and seem to have strongly interested the manager, for he wrote both prologue and epilogue *himself*.

O'Keefe wrote a trifle in two acts for the birth-day of the Prince of Wales, (our present most gracious Sovereign,) called the Prince of Arragon; and the compliment paid is, that the royalty about him undeclared, he is preferred to the presumed Prince. The great personage to whom this tribute was paid always announced his rank in his appearance.

On the 19th of August, a comedy in two acts was brought out for Mrs. Bulkeley's benefit, called the *Lawyer;* who, as a critic of the day said, with as much *naïveté* as truth, drew *tears* from all present.

I cannot allow this season to close without stating the very singular pleasure I received from seeing, on the 12th of September, that master work of Jonson, the Fox, acted under the auspices of Mr. Colman. Bensley and Parsons were by nature fitted for Mosca and Corbaccio, and Palmer took, I thought, very kindly to Volpone. Bannister gave to Voltore more of the modern than the ancient advocate—but he excited a laugh at some well known excesses of our bar; affectations rendering oratorical imperfection violent absurdity. Mr. Gifford, the matchless editor of Jonson, remembers the representation to which I allude, and thus expresses himself. See his 3rd vol. p. 160. " Its last appearance, I believe, " was at the Haymarket, some time before the " death of the elder Colman, who made some " trifling alterations in the disposition of the " scenes. That it was not successful, cannot be " wondered at; the age of dramatic imbecility " was rapidly advancing upon us, and the stage " already looked to jointed-dolls, water-spaniels, " and peacock's-tails, for its main credit and sup- " port."

As far as his manly censure stigmatizes the degeneracy into which personal avarice has plunged what should be the seat of taste, I copy him with a feeling of respectful acquiescence; but I cannot think the representation of the *Fox* then unsuccessful. It was acted on Friday, the 12th of September, repeated on Saturday the 13th, and on the 15th, the theatre closed for the season with the last new comedy. It was a profitable season on the whole. With the thermometer at 82, an additional ventilator had rendered the house as pleasant, at least, as any other; and for once trusting entirely to Rooker for decorations, the little manager wrote nothing himself for the town but a few prologues.

Before I notice the winter theatres, I must recall

to the reader's recollection the very strange and
unmanly criticism, which had assailed that sister
of Mrs. Siddons, who acted with her in Jane
Shore and the Mourning Bride. The terms in
which our critic expressed himself savoured of
insane hatred. He challenged any one human
being to pronounce her other than the *most detestable* of actresses. While she was in Ireland,
he had not suffered her to enjoy the usual privileges of absence, but had kept up his vitupera-
tion, by a pretended report of what she was doing
in the sister kingdom.

I had the happiness to meet the late Mrs.
Twiss at her brother's, and can therefore speak,
on absolute knowledge, to her gentle manners,
and the loveliness of her person. I cannot doubt
that she stept with reluctance on board the packet,
that was to bring her back to the daily annoyance
of her London critic. Her merits of every kind
had, however, attracted the attention and secured
the friendship of George Steevens, Esquire, the
celebrated commentator on Shakspeare, and he
inflicted upon her unmanly assailant, one of the
severest punishments that can be borne, the
chastisement of genius. It bears his peculiar
stamp on every line of it. I am sure, at that
time, his *heart* governed his pen, at least, as much
as his justice. The fugitive efforts of Steevens
are innumerable, but they have never been col-

lected, however easily distinguished. The manner of this address to Woodfall is so temperate, the topics so well chosen and so feelingly touched, that I must lay it before the reader entire. It will, I hope, have an effect beyond its immediate object—future Rosciads and Clios, and other masqueraders of malignity, may thus be startled into reflection, and withhold the tortures of the press, which are here so keenly marked and so earnestly deprecated.

" MISS KEMBLE.

" Sir,

" Among the motives that divest criticism of its rigour, none has hitherto been reckoned more prevalent than our habitual tenderness to the fairsex. Even reviewers abate somewhat of their asperity, when they decide on the qualifications of a female writer : —

> ' Tempests themselves, high seas, and howling winds,
> The gutter'd rocks and congregated sands,
> (Traitors ensteep'd to clog the guiltless keel,)
> As having sense of beauty do omit
> Their mortal natures, letting go safely by
> The divine Desdemona.'

" I wish, Mr. Woodfall, I could add, that your theatrical agent had been influenced by similar considerations. His repeated and unaccountable severities respecting Miss KEMBLE, have shown that *he* at least is unaffected by any such ' com- ' punctious visitings of nature.' Throughout the course of last winter, as frequently as he found occasion to speak of this amiable girl, his remarks, rather wore the aspect of personal resentment than of impartial criticism. His malignity pursued her even into Ireland. He might have allowed Mrs. Siddons her just dividend of fame, without introducing comparisons between her and her sister; that is, between acting, which is the result of more than ten years practice, and the less experienced efforts of a young performer. Mrs. Siddons, I am sure, would return but cold acknowledgments for praise at the expence of one whose welfare is so intimately connected with her own. Neither does confirmed excellence require the sacrifice of all subordinate pretensions. It is by no means necessary to the brightness of the moon, that each inferior planet should be extinguished.

" But, perhaps, it will be said that every candidate for public favour is liable to public animadversion. It may be added, however, that critical, like legal justice, should be dealt out in exact proportion to offence, and not without regard to private character, especially, when the interests of a blamele s female are at stake. The severity,

even of Roman justice, allowed exclusive privileges
to the vestal. But the headlong author of the
playhouse articles in your paper, Sir, makes no
distinction in his usage of the abandoned wanton,
who seeks the stage as an asylum, when her vices
have disqualified her for every other way of life,
and the girl of unsullied manners, who becomes
an actress through the hope of deriving creditable
support from her profession. Surely, two characters so discriminated might expect an opposite
treatment. The first has, probably, lulled those
sensibilities which are tremblingly awake in the
second. Not driven by necessity from one trade
to the exercise of another, and, therefore, un-
hardened by degrees to censure, such a one feels,
severely feels, every sting of reproach, and is
agonized by the paragraph or critique, which a
hackneyed appendage to the scenes would peruse
without emotion.

" Nor does this cruel mode of passing a premature sentence on the disciples of the drama
operate only against their private happiness. A
degree of self-confidence is necessary toward
every undertaking ; but, when juvenile performers are completely humbled in their own
estimation, their solicitude for improvement is at
an end. Let me ask our critic what his own
feelings would suggest, were he of this forlorn

hope, and compelled to represent at night the very character in which he had been condemned without mercy in one of our Morning Papers. Must not then an innocent girl suffer yet more exquisitely from the same distress? Will she not think she hears the enemy's voice in every casual sound that disturbs the theatre, and find her powers irrecoverably blasted by the dread of yet more forcible disapprobation? Is there (I appeal to your own breast, Mr. Woodfall,) any thing so mean, so vile, as triumph over a defenceless unoffending woman? The money, in short, received by hirelings for exposing defects in a set of people, whose subsistence depends on their favour with the public, may almost be called *the price of blood;* for as Shylock well expresses it,—

> ' You take my life
> When you do take the means whereby I live.'

"To the effects which newspaper acrimony, and its immediate contrast, the applause of an audience have produced on Miss KEMBLE, your present correspondent, Sir, is no stranger. Her eyes have streamed over the severities of the Public Advertiser, and her exertions have been successful when encouraged by those who took the liberty of judging for themselves, without asking the author of *Theatrical Intelligence* whether censure or commendation was due to her performances.

" I must conclude, Mr. Woodfall, by acknowledging the general vigilance and acuteness of your theatrical *Argus*, though humanity obliges me to disapprove the unremitted malice with which he has persecuted a young lady whose elegance of manners, whose blameless character, and whose ambition and power to delight, support her claim to all the indulgence and protection a generous and candid public can afford.

" I am, Sir,

" Your most obedient servant.

" P.S. I wish, Mr. Woodfall, some of your numerous correspondents, who have paid attention to playhouse matters, would trace the literary persecution, which has been continued with a kind of conspiracy against the performers of both theatres, to its original source. About twenty years ago, the demerit of an actor could be understood only by those who saw him, or heard of him in conversation. I own I cannot help being desirous that the name of the first of our stage inquisitors should be divulged, like that of the brazen bull founder, for the information of posterity, that players yet unborn may know to whom they are indebted for the cruel treatment they are almost sure to experience in the course of their best endeavours to entertain the public."

" The words of Mercury are harsh after the " songs of Apollo," and, therefore, I do not insert Mr. Woodfall's addition to this powerful appeal. But so absolutely had he yielded to the forcible reasons of Steevens, that he expresses his own regret for the past; and as to the future, he promises that the imperfections of the ladies shall be touched, without any brutal violence to their sensibility.

Mrs. Siddons had succeeded in Dublin almost beyond expectation, for the Irish neither did, nor could be expected to resign at once their reigning favourite, Mrs. Crawford. She is believed to have carried away £1100 from Dublin, about £700 from Cork, and on touching her native shores £160 at Liverpool. It now therefore assumed the appearance of certainty, that she would reach a station more honourable than had yet been accorded to theatrical talent, and that her fortune would equally surpass what had ever been acquired by acting solely in this country.

The winter managers had not been indifferent even to the *male* part of this lady's family, and they had each of them engaged a Mr. Kemble from the Dublin Theatre. But the usual mode, by which distinction in families is preserved in real life, was disdained on this occasion. The elder brother alone was *Mr. Kemble*—the second should have attached the elucidation afforded by his Christian name. We have heard of those anomalies called " distinctions without a *differ-* " *ence.*" The difference as to these brothers was great indeed. The only resemblance was in the style of the features, for the countenance of Mr. Stephen Kemble was certainly handsome, though not dark, like that of his elder brother. But his figure was encumbered with flesh, there was nothing of the heroic in his proportion ; but had he personated Achilles, and shouted at the door of his tent, he had equally struck a terror through the army, and probably the whole city of Troy.

He appeared, on the 24th of September, at Covent Garden Theatre in the character of Othello, and thus by blackening his face parted with his only agreeable distinction. But he had nothing of the subtle and discriminating character of his family—at least it did not enter into his acting. He was a man of sense, and even of some literary attainment; but his declamation was coarse and noisy, and his vehement passion was too ungovernable for sympathy. Othello was, in one way, a fortune to him, for in the Desdemona of that evening, Miss Satchell, he found his *real* wife. Henderson's Iago was perhaps the crown of all his serious achievements—the part in which other actors were left by him in the most hopeless condition. It was all profoundly intellectual like the character. Any thing near this, I have never seen. A writer of great skill, though he does not agree with those who think Iago villanous without a sufficient motive, seems to me to be much too general when he finds it only in the love of power. He has two motives of no mean rank, professional ambition and jealousy. He has seen a counter-caster, a man with nothing but the *theory* of the soldier, put over his head ; and he suspects the gallant Moor to have injured him in his bed. He punishes preference, as inexpiable guilt, and suspicion in his nature goes the full length of cer-tainty. His invention combines all his enemies in one plan of exquisite revenge, and he cares not though it should involve the innocent with the guilty. But his *motives* are clearly defined in his mischiefs—he would destroy Cassio for his *office*, and Othello by that same *jealousy* which he had excited. No *moral* considerations thwart his designs, and among his means he has a *fool* for his purse-bearer. Iago has well estimated his powers of every kind, and descends from his proper sphere only for his sport or his profit. A master in all the arts of insinuation, his triumph is equally certain with the simple *Roderigo*, the brave convivial *Cassio*, and the noble *Moor*, " all-" sufficient" out of the territory of the passions.

The most perplexing difficulty in the art, is to

turn the inside of design *outward* to the spectators, and yet externally seem to be cordial and sincere and interesting among the victims—it demands an instant versatility, that yet must not savour of trick. You must hear his insinuations with curses, and yet confess that you also would have been deceived. Other Iagos were to be seen through at once—their success was incredible and impossible except upon *wilful* blindness.

I should notice upon the present occasion the very clever performance of Roderigo by Charles Bonner, then new to the London public—nothing could possibly come nearer to the manners of this silly gentleman. Shakspeare has afforded three striking instances of fatuity in courtship, Roderigo, Master Slender, and Sir Andrew Aguecheek; yet observe their marked distinctions, and recognise in the poet an invention that almost keeps pace with the prodigality of nature.

The impatience of English audiences to come to the great interest, has done some mischief in Othello—but enough was spared to shew Roderigo stand *tempering* between the finger and thumb of Iago, in that exquisite scene where the master works him from the design of drowning himself, to the more *necessary* evil of selling all his land. Eleven times does Iago recommend his pupil prey to "*put money in his purse.*" With the skill to

write as no other man ever thought of writing,
Shakspeare we may be sure had actors capable
of exhibiting perfectly all this mastery of art—to
make it untiring to the ear, as Henderson certainly did; and yet the injunction has only these
slight variations, " Put money in thy purse."
" Put *but* money in thy purse"—" *Fill* thy purse
" with money."   " *Make* all the money thou
" can'st."   " *Provide* thy money"—" Put money
" *enough* in thy purse."

In *level earnest recitation*, I think, Mr. Kemble
surpassed all men:—but in all the mellow varieties
of ingenious or humorous or designing conversation, where the art is to conceal the art, and the
most pungent effects are to flow in *oil* itself,
nothing has approached Mr. Henderson; and
now I fear we have less chance than ever of such
perfection,—the voice, in large theatres, is taken
out of the scale for these delicate inflexions of
tone.

But if the ambition of the family to occupy
the highest ranks seemed a little checked by the
rash enterprise of Mr. Stephen Kemble, the 30th
of the same month gave to Mrs. Siddons the full
triumph she had predicted, in the success of her
elder brother in the character of Hamlet.   I have
left myself little to remark in this place, having
gone already very minutely and critically into

that performance, and pointed out I hope with proper respect to other great men, the peculiar and original features of Mr. Kemble's Hamlet.*

I have never refused to myself, in these Memoirs, the pleasures of even discursive if relevant criticism; and on the present occasion, I feel strongly tempted to remark upon the recent appearance of a copy of Hamlet, previously unknown, and printed for N. L. (Nicholas Ling) and John Trundell, 1603. Among a variety of curious readings, arising from whatever cause, it has *one* affecting a very important point in the performance of Mr. Kemble. If the reader has honoured me by making the reference which I last pointed out, he will see on one side all *previous* Hamlets exclaiming to Horatio, Marcellus, and Bernardo, with regard to the Ghost, " Did you not *speak to* it ?" and he will find Mr. Kemble *alone* selecting his friend and school-fellow, Horatio, for this interesting demand, and in a solemn and tender tone of voice thus deliberately mixing up his *grief* with his curiosity.

" Did you not *speak* to it ?"

Now the copy just alluded to, if genuine Shakspeare, would put an end to this ingenious point

* See Memoirs of Mr. Kemble, vol. I. p. 88.

of my late friend, however applauded by Dr.
Johnson; for thus is the passage exhibited in
that impression of the play.

> " *Ham.*—Did you not speak to it ?
> *Hor.*—My lord WE did."

And thus, although the fuller and more correct
impression of the year following (1604,) made
Horatio take the replication entirely to himself,
" My lord, I did," yet Mr. Steevens would have
been greatly strengthened in the objection he
made to Mr. Kemble's emphasis, which rested on
what he thought would be *awkward* construction
if so spoken, namely, with the personal pronoun
preceding the negative.

> " Did YOU *not* speak to it ?"

The very use of the term *we* by Horatio would
have seemed to him to prove decisively that,
though it was better for Horatio to say " *I did*,"
than " *we* did," it never had entered the mind of
Shakspeare to build a *peculiar* and *endearing* question to Horatio, grounded on their college inti-
macy, and the suspicions that might have tinged
their evening or morning conferences at Wittemberg.

But had Mr. Kemble lived to enjoy this singular curiosity, he would, *perhaps*, triumphantly have affirmed, that a copy that possessed so many passages of absolute *guess* at the real text, and others of premises without their *conclusions*, if it were allowed to confirm the usage of a *word*, was an unsafe guide as to meaning. He would have quoted from it—

> " *Ham.*—O that this too much *griev'd* and *sallied* flesh
> Would melt to *nothing*, or that the *universall*
> *Globe of heaven* would turne al to a chaos."

And further on in the play—

> " *Ghost.*—O I find thee apt, and duller should'st thou be
> Then the fat weede which rootes it self in ease
> On Lethe wharffe : breife let me be."

Where the necessity of quickly hurrying the stolen matter together, has left the point antagonis'd out of the phrase ; for the reader knows it should stand—

> "And duller should'st thou be than the fat weed
> That roots itself in ease on Lethe wharf,
> *Would'st thou not stir in this?* Now, Hamlet, hear."

But the furtive rogues were bold indeed, when they audaciously gave us the following for the well-known address of the sovereign to Hamlet's two friends, whom he calls Rossencraft and Gilderstone.

" *King.*—Right noble friends, that our deere cousin Hamlet
Hath lost the very *heart* of all his *sence*,
It is most *right*, and we most sory for him."

But his Majesty, however earnestly he con-
jures the services of these courtiers, seems to
make light of them by the unfortunate employment of the difficult word *but*.

" Therefore we doe desire, even as you tender
Our care to him, and our great love to you,
That you will labour *but* to wring from him
The cause and ground of his distemperancie.
Doe this, the King of Denmarke shal be thankfull."

A comparison of this with original Shakspeare,
from the absence of all resemblance, except in
the *design* of the speaker, must confirm a suspicion that here our vamper of Hamlet used the
actual words of a very miserable play upon the
subject, which preceded the mighty performance
of Shakspeare several years; and was, Mr. Ma-
lone thinks, the work of *sporting* Kyd, as Ben
Jonson calls him, rather perhaps from his *name*
than his character. It would be, I confess, with
some feeling of alarm, that I should take up
Kyd's play, were it in existence, in the fear that
he might be entitled to any portion of our poet's
fame, for even a *first* and *rough* sketch of the
awful shade of Denmark. Yet it would be wrong

to withhold from Shakspeare's predecessor, who-
ever he was, the credit so justly his own of being
the most attentive observer of decorum. The
closet scene of the senior play is regulated with
the exactest propriety. Instead of bursting in
upon the conference between the Queen and her
son, held in the private chamber of her Majesty,
in the frightful armour worn by him when he
combated Norway, we are instructed to dress the
late King more suitably for such a place—" Enter
the Ghost *in his night gowne.*" He has also furnished his Queen with an explicit disclaimer
of all participation in the murder of her first
husband—

> " But as I have a soule, I sweare by heaven,
> I never knew of this most horride murder."

Nor should the familiar language in which it is
conveyed diminish our regard for so comfortable
an assurance. In the meanwhile, the controversy
between the poet's commentators may remain in
its full force, and her guilt or innocence be doubtful to the end of time, or end of the poet's fame,
which some may consider the same date.

It was now that Mrs. Siddons paid a visit to
Dr. Johnson. We have happily his own account
of it in a letter to Mrs. Thrale, dated October the
27th, 1783. From the abrupt commencement,

Mrs. Thrale seems to have been apprised either of the intention or the visit. " Mrs. Siddons in " her visit to me behaved with great modesty " and propriety, and left nothing behind her to " be censured or despised. Neither praise nor " money, the two powerful corrupters of man- " kind, seem to have depraved her. I shall be " glad to see her again. Mrs. Siddons and I " talked of plays, and she told me her intention " of exhibiting this winter the characters of " Constance, Katharine, and Isabella, in Shak- " speare."

When Mrs. Siddons came into the room, there happened to be no chair ready for her. "Madam," said Johnson, with a smile, " you who so often oc- " casion a want of seats to other people, will the " more easily excuse the want of one yourself." He inquired with which of Shakspeare's charac- ters she was most pleased? Upon her answering that she thought the character of Queen Katha- rine, in Henry the Eighth, the most natural—" I " think so too, Madam," said he; " and whenever " you perform it, I will once more hobble out to " the theatre myself."

Little as the Doctor could either see or hear in a theatre, I regret that he did not witness the performance of Katharine by Mrs. Siddons. John- son had told her that " her great predecessor, " Mrs. Pritchard, was in common life a vulgar

" idiot, who used to talk of her *gownd;* but that
" on the stage, she seemed to 'be inspired by
" gentility and understanding." Inspiration indeed! unless we are to suppose that in *private*
she condescended to slip slop, and erred, not
from ignorance, but carelessness and habit. I
have known great knowledge oddly enough tinged
by early laxity of pronunciation. The reader may
reflect how often, from those who must be aware
of the true word, he has heard a pantomime
called *pantomine.*

CHAPTER XIII.

THE ROYAL PATRONAGE OF MRS. SIDDONS. — THE ENTHU-
SIASM EXCITED BY THE GREAT ACTRESS ALWAYS REASON-
ABLE. — CATHERINE MACAULAY THE HISTORIAN. — HER
STATUE IN ST. STEPHEN'S, WALBROOK. — DR. GRAHAM
AND HIS BROTHER. — THE UNBROKEN LINE OF CARRIAGES
THAT PROCEEDED TO DRURY LANE THEATRE. — MRS. SID-
DONS TOUCHES SHAKSPEARE AT LENGTH. — THE ISABELLA
OF HIS MEASURE FOR MEASURE. — MORAL ENERGY OF
THAT CHARACTER. — MODERN CLOSE OF THAT PLAY. —
ABSURDITY OF THE STAGE DISCOVERY OF THE DUKE. —
MRS. SIDDONS'S GRACEFUL DIGNITY IN THE SECOND ACT.
— IMMEDIATELY COMMANDED BY THEIR MAJESTIES. — TA-
MERLANE. — O'KEEFE'S POOR SOLDIER. — PARTICULAR RE-
FERENCE TO THE MERITS OF HENDERSON. — DIFFERENT
STYLES OF HENDERSON AND KEMBLE. — MRS. CRAWFORD
ACTING LADY RANDOLPH, HENDERSON TOOK OLD NORVAL.
— HOME FRAMED HIS PLAY FROM THE BALLAD OF GIL
MORRICE, AND VOLTAIRE'S MEROPE. — THE CRESPHONTES
OF EURIPIDES. — THE GAMESTER OFFERS TO MRS. SIDDONS
THE OPPORTUNITY OF ACTING WITH HER BROTHER. —
GAMING NOT THE ONLY VICE IN THE PLAY. — BEAUTIES
OF THE AUTHOR, AND THOSE OF THE ACTRESS. — THE
PLAY BEAUTIFULLY ACTED IN ALL ITS PARTS. — MRS. SID-
DONS ACTS CONSTANCE IN KING JOHN. — HER DRESS IN
THAT CHARACTER. — ON THE NIGHT OF HER BENEFIT
SHE RESOLVES TO DISPUTE EVEN LADY RANDOLPH WITH
MRS. CRAWFORD. — THE IMPORTANCE OF A CONFIDANTE.
— LA CLAIRON AND MADEMOISELLE BRILLAND. — THE
GREAT POINT " WAS HE ALIVE ?" EXAMINED CRITICALLY.
TOURS DE FORCE MOST COMMONLY ERRONEOUS. — SPLEN-
DID PASSAGES IN HOME. — CRITICISM ON THE SCENERY. —
GENERAL SUPERIORITY OF MRS. SIDDONS. — HER DRESS.

THE reader will have observed the peculiar at-

tention paid to Mrs. Siddons last season by their
Majesties, who made a point of seeing her in all
the characters which she had sustained. The
honour of such patronage, so marked and persevering, was reserved for our great actress exclusively. A royal command introduced her second
season in the character of Isabella. The late
King was an excellent judge of acting, and might
be said to be well studied in the respective
schools of Quin and of Garrick. He here found
the dignified declamation of the old school combined with the exquisite pathos of the new. I
cannot doubt, however, that it was the exact
propriety of her utterance that led to the appointment of Mrs. Siddons to be reading preceptress
to the Princesses.

The honours paid by all ranks to the delightful
ornament of the stage, kept however in due
bounds—the enthusiasm neither became fanatical
nor profane—it placed a few indifferent pictures
and worse likenesses upon the walls of our dwell-
ing-houses, was most free and bounteous in presents of various kinds; but it stopped on this side
idolatry, and the drama yielded the votive palm
to speculative *politics*.

The republicans of the city, I remember, did
not rest here, as to the historian, Catherine Macaulay. She could discover that " the prelates

" of Charles the First paid *him* an *impious flattery*."
But I heard of no protest from the modern CLIO,
when *her* high priest, Dr. Wilson, set up her
statue in the parish church of St. Stephen, Walbrook; the fierce Moloch of *regicide* in the very
sanctuary of mercy.

> " Within his sanctuary itself their shrines
> Abominations—and with cursed things
> His holy rites and solemn feasts profan'd."
>   PARADISE LOST.

But our doting Doctor did still more : he dedicated a temple to his idol, for her *residence*, not to
her memory, and presented to her a mansion
called Alfred House. (Alfred, a patriot certainly,
but unluckily a *king*.) He furnished it with
splendor, supplied a long retinue of servants, and
stored the library with the literature of freedom.
At Alfred House she was enthroned on her returning birth-days, and incensed by odes recited by
gentlemen, and medals presented by our Doctor
himself. But one little *speck* presented itself to
the eye; the *celestial* Dr. Graham had restored
the fair historian to health, and was, therefore,
allowed to lay at her feet a copy of his *modest*
works. He approached, it appears, on her weak
side, for she finished by marrying his brother.
The *reverend* Doctor, as is usual in these cases of

literary devotion, " breathed one sigh of ineffec-
" tual tenderness," and set himself with reluctance entirely at *liberty*.

The attentions paid to Mrs. Siddons, as they
were reasonable and temperate, were quite un-
exceptionable and more lasting.

Of her performances now, it is only necessary
to repeat the order in which they succeeded each
other; namely, Shore, Euphrasia, Calista, and
Belvidera, and to add that her attraction did not
in the least decline; and that the rival theatre,
by whatever talents supported, and great indeed
they were, was doomed to see a long and unbroken line of splendid carriages, in a sort of
birth-day procession, slowly pass the foot of Bow-
street, which lent its space, too, at the close of the
night to the noble vehicles of those who were at
the other theatre.

In the midst of these triumphs, I will not omit
to mention one opportunity afforded Miss E.
Kemble of acting Rosalind, on the 16th of October. Lee Lewes wanted to play Touchstone,
in humble imitation of Woodward, but the result,
I believe, never transpired; and as to the lovely
Rosalind, she was smothered, whatever power
she possessed, except when Kemble himself
called upon her in the Black Prince, and the
New Way to Pay Old Debts. Her elder sister

kept her rank, but did not extend her range,
by acting with Mrs. Siddons in Alicia and
Almeria.

Mrs. Siddons had hitherto left Shakspeare un-
touched, and the first character which she acted
was selected as affording some relief to her frame,
really exhausted by the dreadful fatigues she had
undergone, with no other intermission than was
afforded by her travelling from place to place.
However honourable to her, the intimacies she
was compelled to cultivate with the noble, the
polite, or the learned of the sister kingdoms,
called for no slight efforts of those *spirits,* which
had it been practicable, should all have been
reserved for the theatre. The part, therefore, thus
considerately chosen was *Isabella* in Measure for
Measure, which she acted for the first time in
London on Monday the 3d of November.

They who judged only by the bustle and noise,
the rage or protracted sufferings of a heroine,
considered Isabella to call for something less than
the powers of this actress. But if *measure* is to
be given for *measure,* what lower talent could possibly express this " ensky'd and sainted virgin,"
whose inborn purity creates a dignity beyond
that of power, and a logic so firm and convincing,
that it even hides, at times, the poetical beauties

of its own diction. The *moral energy* of Isabella is, perhaps, unequalled in the volumes of Shakspeare. Portia's solemn eulogy upon *mercy* is nothing to the truly dramatic charm of what follows :—

> " O, it is excellent
> To have a giant's strength ; but it is tyrannous
> To use it like a giant.
>   Could great men thunder
> As Jove himself does, Jove would ne'er be quiet;
> For every pelting, petty officer
> Would use his heaven for thunder; NOTHING BUT thunder.—
> Merciful heaven !
> Thou rather with thy sharp and sulphurous bolt
> Split'st the unwedgeable and gnarled oak
> Than the soft myrtle : But man, proud man,
> Dress'd in a little brief authority,
> Most ignorant of what he's most assur'd,
> His glassy essence,—like an angry ape,
> Plays such fantastic tricks before high heaven,
> As make the angels weep."

The Duke, in this play is a character of great moral wisdom, and Shakspeare had, from the beginning, determined to unite him suitably to Isabel. But lest so much staid gravity and wisdom should be thought too aged for such a purpose, he makes, in the very outset, Friar Thomas throw out a suspicion, that his very retirement has *love* for its motive. This the Duke disclaims in good set terms—

> "*Duke.*—No! holy father; throw away that thought:
> Believe not that the dribbling dart of love
> Can pierce a complete bosom."

He yields at last to a wisdom and virtue fully proved, and worthy of the throne. The poet, at the close of the play, touches the subject very guardedly—

> " Dear Isabel
> I have a motion much imports your good;
> Whereto if you'll a willing ear incline
> What's mine is yours, and what is yours is mine."

It was at one time a good deal the fashion to end all comedies with a " call in the fiddles," or a " strike up pipers"—and our modern stage cooks could not permit Shakspeare to remain at the close, the master of his own creatures. See how awfully it is now managed.

> " For thee, sweet saint,—if for a brother sav'd,
> From that most holy shrine thou wert devote to,
> Thou deign to spare some portion of thy love,
> Thy duke, thy friar, tempts thee from thy vow."

and then we have the " spirit shining in its " *right orb*," blessing in course, " both prince " and people," and a royal maxim to boot—

> " To rule ourselves, before we rule mankind :"

all which, may, perhaps, come from the muse of Charles Gildon, but really is not worth inquiry.

I take the liberty to smile at the stage *discovery*
of the Duke in the last scene of this play, with all
his regal paraphernalia, with difficulty concealed
under the *outstretched* garments of the friar—as if
it was not the *man* who was recognized, but the
clothes. At this rate, let the machinist also con-
trive for him **a** *portable* chair of state, which may
safely be hooded with the robes, and a small globe
and sceptre ready for handling upon the seat,
that he may burst complete in the *full* blaze of
sovereignty upon the scared and unsuspecting
offenders.

Our most extraordinary actress performed the
first scene of the second act, before Angelo, with
the most perfect ease, grace, and impression, from
the first rebuff to her suit—

" I *had* a brother then—"(which by the way is *classical* idiom.)

through all the arguments deduced from fitness,
satire, or religious considerations. As her mind
quickened in the altercation, her figure seemed
to distend with the golden truths she delivered,
and malignant *possession* appeared alone able to
compel the resistance of the wretched Angelo.

Nor was she less remarkable in the scene with
her brother, where she stood before him, as a searching, scrutinizing spirit, to detect any quailing of
feeble resolution, any even momentary preference

of shameful life to lasting honour. I loved particularly the strong but tuneful accents of her
satisfaction—

> " There spake my brother ! there my FATHER'S GRAVE
> Did utter forth a voice."

But when the storm rose, upon his change of feeling, nothing could exceed the effect of her exclamations—

> " Take my *defiance !* die ! perish !"

After this scene, the part of Isabella is no more —
she has only to await her reward in the *safety* of
her brother, and the *passion* of the prince.

As I do not think the coincidence has been
hitherto pointed out, I may remark, that, in the
famous speculation of Claudio as to what, after
its separation from the body, may become of the
delighted spirit,—Shakspeare's—

> " And blown with restless violence round about
> The pendant world."

is clearly from Cicero, in somn. Scip. " Cor-
" poribus elapsi circum terram ipsam volutan-
" tur."

So desirous were the royal party to see anything
new from Mrs. Siddons, that, on the Wednesday

after its first performance, Measure for Measure was honoured by the presence of their Majesties. If the play of Shakspeare contained much that was complimentary to the public and private virtues of the *present* sovereign, the other Theatre, the previous night, offered the annual incense of Rowe's Tamerlane, to the memory of William the Third.

However Rowe might misconceive, certainly misrepresent, the character of Tamerlane, Bajazet was a most outrageous caricature of Louis the XIV. Of whom it may be bare justice to assert, that he reigned in the exact *spirit* of his people, and his reign is not more properly his than theirs. It is a concentration of the egotism, the ambition, the taste, the refinement, the gallantry, the luxury of the French nation.

I presume *tyrant* Aickin did not suffer much from this temporary invasion of his brutal rights by Stephen Kemble, who was not likely to tyrannize long in Bajazet. Henderson spoke Tamerlane beautifully—Wroughton was extremely affecting in Moneses — the ladies were highly respectable, and had Bajazet appeared in his *iron cage* during the evening, the shew had been perfect. After this piece was performed a first time, as we now have it, O'Keefe's delightful entertainment of the Poor Soldier, which while we are permitted the enjoyment of either the national humour or its music, cannot fail to amuse the people of the united kingdom.

However agreeable to me the brilliant success of Mrs. Siddons and Mr. Kemble, there was *one* other great artist, who was making such a display of masterly talent at this time, that it would be the height of injustice not to take a more than cursory notice of his efforts. I allude to Mr. Henderson, in whom resided nearly all the *critical* fame of Covent Garden Theatre. The high-erected deportment, the expressive action, the solemn cadence, the stately pauses of that great original tragedian, Kemble, with the magic of countenance and form to bear up his style, have by degrees won us from the school of ease and freedom, and variety, and warmth, and all the mingling proprieties of humour and pathos, as Shakspeare founded it, and as it was taught by the professor whom I have just named. The styles were certainly incompatible with each other. They were excellencies to be seen apart: no man I think ever seriously wished for Henderson and Kemble upon the stage together. Their voices would have harmonised as little as their manners. Neither could have been expected to concede at all to the other. Henderson would never have stopped, and Kemble never gone faster. The declamation of Mr. Kemble seemed to be fetched from the schools of philosophy—it was always pure, and perfectly correct. It demanded admiration, and secured it. Though a studious man, there was no discipline apparent in the art of Henderson; he moved and looked as humour or passion required, and was not so much approved as felt. The cadence of Mr. Kemble was artificial, and formed upon the principles on which the verses he spoke were constructed. Henderson cared little about the measure of the line; he would not consider the fame of the versifier while the heart was to be struck. He *lightened* upon the word on which the charm was deposited, and gave all the rest to hurry and neglect. What he once said to Pope, shewed the element of his style. It was in Othello, if I remember rightly.

" Haply for I'm *black!*"

His friend Pope having a remarkably fine sonorous voice, had given their full time to *all* the words in the line " Haply for I am black." Henderson, imitating the hurried suggestions of a tortured imagination, would have him instruct the audience as fast as he himself conceived, " Haply for I'm black." His reading of the great scenes in this noble tragedy agonized himself, and every body fortunate enough to hear him.

This great man, dressing as carelessly as did the Quins and Cibbers, quite regardless of the *costume*, and the *tailor*, and the *cephalic* artist, who makes even a *wig* speak powerfully for an actor— now gave to the few real amateurs of the art his Hamlet—his Lear—his Richard—his Sir Giles— his Macbeth—his Iago—his Falstaff; and a great variety even after these. The re-appearance of Mrs. Crawford, in Lady Randolph, on the 13th of November, afforded him an opportunity of affecting in Old Norval beyond every thing that has succeeded him. The rustic simplicity, and tearful earnestness, with which he uttered the following lines, banished in an instant all the *boards* and *lamps* of the stage.

> " As I hope
> For mercy at the judgment seat of God,
> The tender lamb that never nipt the grass,
> Is not more innocent than I of murder."

But he enters upon the most interesting narrative that perhaps was ever written—the stormy night; the shrieking spirit of the angry waters; the cry of one in jeopardy. The circling eddy below the pool; the basket whirled round and round, drawn speedily to the bank; and within it, his gentle and expressive action aiding the language, and almost painting the portrait—

" *nestled curious,* there an infant lay."

That infant the spectators knew to have been saved, they had just seen him flourishing in manly beauty ; but this was no shield against the instantaneous shriek of a mother's agonizing effort to know *all ;* the sublime " WAS HE ALIVE?" of Mrs. Crawford. It checked your breathing, perhaps pulsation; it was so bold as to be even hazardous, but too piercing not to be triumphant; sympathizing nature found itself completely captive, spell bound in the circle of these mighty magicians.

As to the subject of this play, Home saw something in Lady Barnard's *Gil Morrice,** but more,

* The locality is there—and Home had at first preserved Lady Barnard's name.

" But it was for a lady gay
That liv'd on Carron side."

We have the daring spirit of the Douglas in the noble child's message to his mother.

" And bid hir cum to Gill Morice,
Spier nae bauld baron's leave."

He perishes in consequence of the baron's jealousy, not suspecting him to be her son.

much more, in the *Merope* of Maffei, or that of
Voltaire.   To use the happy figure of the French
writer; " He was in the situation of one to whom
" an eastern king, had made a present of the
" richest stuffs of the country. But the monarch
" would no doubt permit the foreigner to *make*
" *them up* in the fashion of his own." This Home
has done, by retaining much of the pastoral simplicity and deadly feuds of Scotland. It is almost
incredible how Aaron Hill, in his Merope, has
perverted the beautiful expression of Voltaire.
But as the latter has taught us,—" Il faut toujours
" beaucoup de temps aux hommes pour leur ap-
" prendre, qu'en tout ce qui est grand, on doit
" revenir au *naturel* et au *simple*."—Lettre à M.
de Maffei.

This was a favourite theme with antiquity, and
the tender Euripides wrote a play upon it called
Cresphontes, of which only a few fragments now
exist; yet even these seem to have been remarked for their homely wisdom by the author of
Douglas. e. g.

> " The only gains which ought to be pursu'd
> By man, are those whence no repentance springs."

There is a singular mystery as to the production of this beautiful
ballad, which, at least in print, appeared but a short time before the
play of Douglas.

Again, and still more in his manner.

> " Collecting all our friends, we should bewail
> The new-born child who comes into a world
> Where mischiefs swarm around him : but bear forth
> Amidst rejoicings and auspicious songs,
> Him who is dead, and ceases from his toil."

But enough for the present of a poet, whom, as far as Douglas went, Mr. Hume, the historian, thought worthy to be named with Shakspeare and Otway.

Mrs. Siddons had now the prospect of acting in some few plays with her brother, Mr. Kemble, and the first effort to combine them was happily without offence to any other performer. The Gamester had not been acted for four years. Smith did not care for the part of Beverley ; into which, therefore, Kemble slid with every propriety: and as to Brereton and Palmer, they could not be more at home than they were in Lewson and Stukely. J. Aickin acted Jarvis delightfully, and Mrs. Brereton, · by anticipation, was the sister-in-law of Mrs. Siddons, by performing Charlotte to her Mrs. Beverley.

The passion of gaming, said the author of the Night Thoughts, needed such a caustic as the last scene of this tragedy. I know not what may in fairness be called the vices of this passion, perhaps it may easily conduct to all—but an earnest gambler could not fail to point out that Beverley is the victim rather of the rancorous hatred of a rival in love : of a schoolfellow long noted for sullen mischief, sordid and cruel, whose manhood had confirmed and extended all that was bad about him. Stukely still labours to supplant Beverley in the affections of his wife. The gambler, I believe, has but one passion.

The character now sustained by Mrs. Siddons, was one of fond suffering virtue ; she can really account herself rich while she fancies her husband's affection unabated. She, therefore, repels at once the suspicions with which Stukely would impress her, while disclaiming all design to alarm her. Her answer was beautifully pointed by the actress.

" *Mrs. Bev.* Nor have you, Sir. Who told you of suspicion ? I have a heart it cannot reach."

In the scene of Stukely's absurd attempt to excite jealousy about the *jewels*, nothing was ever better spoken than—

" Know, Sir, my injuries are my own, and do not need a champion."

But all the gradations, from strong reluctance to credit him to a compelled belief of Stukely's story about a mistress, till he unmasks, by hinting revenge. to her, and proposing himself as the means, had the most surprising effect. Her eye was always full of meaning, " but it flamed " amazement" when she uttered these lines.

" Would that these eyes had heaven's own lightning, that with a look, *thus* I might *blast thee !* O villain ! villain !"

The recovered dignity too was very striking.

" Keep thy own secret and begone."

But, perhaps, the finest *coup de théatre*, was the quick contradiction of Jarvis about the quarrel with Lewson, and the eager rush up to his breast, as if she would at once banish *him*, along with testimony so alarming.

" No; I am sure he did not.
'Tis *false*, old man; they had *no* quarrel,—there was no *cause* for quarrel."

The merits of the actress must not keep me from remarking Moore's charming observance of nature. The danger of Beverley leads to a momentary oblivion of Jarvis's important services and affectionate zeal; *old man* is the rather disparaging term, which Mrs. Beverley annexes to her contradiction.

Of equal beauty is the exquisite delicacy of this *inimitable* old man, as described by Charlotte; who, when he has hurried off a *creditor* from

Beverley's door, " begs pardon that *his friend*
" had knock'd so loud." It is not without tears,
that I notice a trait so perfectly divine. When
the stage teaches such conduct, it is one of the
best, as it is certainly the most pleasing of moral
instructors.

Notwithstanding the elegance of Moore's genius,
and the excellence of his character, he was rather
unpopular; and however ludicrous the preven-
tion* of the audience, or the alarm of the author,
Dr. J. Spence bore for the first four nights the
credit of the Gamester, which lost some of its admirers when it recovered its owner.

The scene of contest between Lewson and
Stukely, the first of the fourth act, has been attributed to Mr. Garrick, and I should think the
suggestion of it likely enough to proceed from
him. It is the scene *of* and *for* an actor; one
written in full parallel with that between Horatio
and Lothario. As the hits in a fencing match,
have been applied to the witty contests in comedy,
I may call these a resemblance to the scene between Hamlet and Laertes, where the points of
the weapons are

" Unbated and envenomed."

Aware as I am, that the Gamester was written

* I thus use the word on the *authority* of Dryden, with the
sanction of Dr. Johnson.

partly in blank verse, I confess the scene here alluded to does not seem to me to have proceeded from the *pure* taste of Moore. *Ceci sent des coulisses*—

> " And Beverley
> Shall yet be sav'd, be sav'd from thee, thou monster;
> Nor owe his rescue to his wife's dishonour."

If Roscius contributed this scene, he _was *generous* indeed, and meant only to strengthen the play; for he acted *Beverley* himself. The dialogue possesses his characteristic love of smartness.

As to the general impression of the play, if it was not originally popular, I should not, with the author's friends, attribute its cold reception to the arts of those whose *vice* it exposed; but to a kind of moral disgust to see the worthy and elevated, made the prey of heartless calculating villany; drawn into inextricable misery, and perishing by poison. As to the hero himself, few will be of Lewson's, that is the author's opinion, " save but one error and his life was lovely."— No; that one error had absorbed the man entire, and he had ruined all those who reposed in full confidence upon his honour and his love. The family mansion had dwindled into a lodging—the sister's fortune had been stolen and lost—the wife had been beggar'd, slighted, and plundered even of her ornaments—his son cheated of his

inheritance, robbed of what death even was expected to bestow. Beverley was like our savage
ancestors in Tacitus, staking at hazard till ALL
was gone, and then risking *personal* and *lasting*
slavery. "Tantâ lucrandi perdendive temeritate,
"ut cùm omnia defecerunt, extremo ac novissimo
"jactu de libertate et de corpore contendant."

DE MORIB. GERMAN. S. XXIV.

The acting of this play exhibited a perfection
in the art, which has never been exceeded. But
what must be done when the performers are gone,
who so enchanted the public?—ANSWER: "Re-
"build the Theatres."

Their Majesties, although they had again commanded the Grecian Daughter, to enjoy the
virtuous energy of the heroine as acted by Mrs.
Siddons, allowed the Gamester to run on, without
a wish to be present—the interest is of that kind
which oppresses more than it improves the heart.
It is as Cowley expresses it—

> "And on my soul hung the *dull weight*
> Of some *intolerable* fate."

A wish had been entertained to see Mr. Kemble
in some play with Mrs. Siddons; and Shakspeare's King John having been gotten up with
great attention, a royal command honoured the
first night's performance of it, on Wednesday the

10th of December. In this place I am not called upon to enter particularly into the performance of John by Mr. Kemble. It would display his *mastery* in the art, the extreme subtlety of his mind, and his power of impersonation. It is one of the characters in which he has in every spectator fairly substituted his own face and figure for the *picture sense* of King John. You think of the *Lack-land* of history and Shakspeare; but call upon the fancy for an *image*, and she immediately returns you the dark sullen brow of Kemble, his rigid features and solemn manners; walks with his gait, and murders in his voice. I do not say that the *picturesque* of an actor's person will do everything—but to be externally like your object secures a welcome at the first appearance; you have only to maintain an interest, not struggle with unwilling reception.

The character of Constance had been the *chef d'œuvre* of Mrs. Cibber, and had been acted by Mrs. Yates with what Davies thought kindred talent; but his own description of her effects shews me that Mrs. Yates could only have touched the assumed *irony* or the *majestic* sorrow of her predecessor; the piercing notes of wild maternal agony were not in the scale of her voice. Mrs. Crawford had these assuredly, and to an extent almost " too terrible to enter human hearing." Of all the performances of the great subject of these memoirs, no one was more questioned, or, in my opinion, less questionable, than this of Lady Constance. She here took ground upon the inspired realms of Shakspeare; and it might be therefore a point with the disingenuous of the critic tribe, to compliment her as far as Otway or Southerne could carry her, but " to hint a fault " and hesitate dislike," when she seized on the too brief, but striking heroines of our greatest poet.

A fashionable writer of the day, the same who had so cruelly persecuted her sister, Mrs. Twiss, ventured almost to restrict her merit to the speaking of a single *word* in the line—

"For grief is proud, and makes his owner *stout ;*"

which the reader may remember is one, but the very weakest, perhaps, of a speech, which she delivered with an energy of sorrow so mighty, as, seated but on the bare earth, rendered the splendid chair of state less venerable and majestic.

" I will instruct my sorrows to be proud;
  For grief is proud, and makes his owner stout.
  To me, and to the state of my great grief,
  Let kings assemble; for my grief's so great,
  That no supporter but the huge firm earth
  Can hold it up: here I AND SORROW SIT;
  Here is my throne, bid kings come bow to it."
            (Throws herself on the ground.)

Sure I am she had uttered nothing up to that time that possessed a tithe of the power by which these wonderful lines are sustained.

Upon the coming in of all those royal recreants by whom her cause had been abandoned, and the distinct announcement of the marriage with Blanch, what could equal her impression while exclaiming as she rises—

" A wicked day, and not a holy day !"

again :

" A WIDOW cries ; be *husband* to me, HEAVENS !"

one of the very boldest flights of him who " flew " at infinite."—After the furious demand of " WAR " —no peace ;" and the withering contempt, that clogged the very *name* of Lymoges ; who can remember her look, her action, and her tone, and not be sure that, in real life, such a Constance *prepared* the victim for the future sword of Faulconbridge ?

" He *liv'd* a COWARD in his *own esteem.*"

The only other scene, the fourth of the third act, is too well known to the readers of Shakspeare, to make it necessary that I should quote from it. Constance is too impassioned for *hope;* she sees the future in the instant : Arthur in the power of her enemy is already dead to her; and it is in *another* world that, worn down with early sorrow, she fears she shall not know him. Her prophetic soul has disposed of him in *this*. She, therefore, does not linger in expectation, but expires of frenzy, before his own rashness, rather than his uncle's violence, has ended her pretty Arthur. In the exit of Constance, the sharp shrillness of the organ itself will do something for an actress not highly intellectual:—however vehement in her exclamations, Constance has meaning in her language, this was truly given by Mrs. Siddons, and not an inarticulate *yell*, the grief of merely savage nature.

I preserve the dresses of Mrs. Siddons, where I find a note of them in my papers: in Constance she wore a *black* body and train of satin, and a petticoat of white, disposed in certainly the most tasteful forms of that day. The true actress is in every thing an artist; the genius before us dishevelled even her hair with graceful wildness.

By whatever power of *writing* adorned, the frank bravery of Faulconbridge, the quick succession of opposite tidings, and the fate of John, it was dangerous to shew such a meteor as *Constance*, and linger two acts further, after she has disappeared. Such is the inconvenience of chronicle plays; passion demands one termination and history another:—You call on individual interest as your aid and are ruined by your auxiliary. It is the Æneid after the fate of Dido.

That the theatre should teach history is little extraordinary. A most ingenious writer, William Godwin, was now publishing " Sketches of His- " tory," in six *sermons !*

But whatever might be the motive for acting John at the theatre, it was not then so popular as it was expected to be. Two scenes of Siddons, however exquisite, were not enough for those who had been accustomed to see her occupy every act, of plays more essentially female. Kemble, too, was much nearer *excellence* than he was to his subsequent *steady attraction.* At the other house, Henderson was acting Macbeth to vacancy, with the Lady Macbeth of Mrs. Bates, and Mrs. Yates and Miss Younge both in the theatre, and Mrs. Crawford only absent upon *leave.* The *Trunk-maker,* however, assured that fine actor, that in 1759 and 1760 he had sitten quite cool at the *Macbeths* of GARRICK and PRITCHARD ! " I " beg *cold* comfort," as King John exclaims.

In a former page, with the proper freedom of a critic, I have pointed out the charm of the great scene in Douglas, as it was acted by Henderson and Mrs. Crawford. Perhaps the most serious moment of the professional life of Mrs. Siddons, was that in which she resolved to contest even Lady Randolph with her rival. She wisely made her impression on the night of her benefit—it secured the greatest measure of encouragement, if any apprehension at all existed. She had many advantages in the competition, youth, beauty, a finer figure, more power of eye, a voice in its whole compass, sound, and unbreaking. Her declamation, too, was more studied, finished, and accurate. She was sure to give a better *reading* of the part; the only question was, what was to balance the *storm of passion*, by which her great rival had surprised and subdued a long succession of audiences.

I cannot but think it a peculiar happiness to Mrs. Siddons, that she seems through life so little to have imitated what other performers did in the parts she acted. I willingly believe this not to have been sufficiency, as despising others, or disdaining help; but from a settled conviction, that she could only be great by being truly original; and that she ought to deliver her *own* conceptions of character, with absolute indifference by what other artists they were either disputed or confirmed. How the fact may stand is of little moment, but I think if her first audience to Lady Randolph had been asked for an opinion upon the point, the answer would have been uniform, that no one could suppose that she had ever seen Mrs. Crawford in the character.

Before we examine her own performance, it

may be proper to inquire what support she received from the other actors on the scene with
her—and, first, the disparity was immense between Bensley, the Old Shepherd of Drury, and
Henderson, the Norval of Covent Garden. Bensley looked one part of the character truly—

"For he *had* been a soldier in his youth."

But pathos rendered his voice ragged as well as
repulsive, and he never, as to his feet, either stood
or walked with the character of age. His helpless action had a character of restrained vigour;
he implored pity in the noisy shout of defiance.
His understanding, however, was of a superior
kind, and it rendered him always respectable,
and sometimes nearly excellent.

Brereton in Douglas *was* a tragic actor; which
Lewis could never be, but by the greatest courtesy. I could have wished the *son* less confirmed
in manhood, less bulky, I mean in reference to
the person of Mrs. Siddons —but Palmer, in Glenalvon, was gigantic, and happily towered far
above him. Then he had the " ravishing stride"
of Tarquin himself, and was quite tragedian enough
for this miserable shred out of the skirts of Shakspeare's Iago. Farren at the one house, and
Wroughton at the other, were equally at home
in the " bauld baron," Lord Randolph. The

Anna, by Miss Wheeler, was rather under-cast.
She is more than the faithful attendant upon Lady
Randolph; she is neighbour to the dearest secrets
of her bosom.   Miss Kemble would have here
been exactly the point desired—looking *intelligence,* her sympathy would have strongly aided
the passion of the scene, and the congenial nature
would have justified so important a confidence.
I measure these things by . no prompter or
treasurer's standard—the salary goes with me,
and should go, for nothing; it is the demand of
the part that is to be considered, the combining
interests of the drama.

How is the *moppet* of some loose man of fashion,
whose little power is smothered in the waste fer-
tility of her personal attractions, and who therefore is all prettiness, and affectation, and constraint,—how is such a one to catch the key-note,
and continue the harmonious elocution of . a great
actress; still farther, as Shakspeare strongly expresses it, how is she to—

" Tend her in the *eyes,* and make her bends adornings ?"

But the great La Clairon shall herself teach us
the importance of a confidante.   " I remember
(she writes,) " being exceedingly unwell at a time
" when I had to act Ariane *(Ariadne);* and fear-
" ing that I should not be able to go through the

" fatigue of the character, I had caused an easy
" chair to be placed upon the stage, to sustain
" me in case I should require it. In fact, during
" the fifth act, while expressing my despair at the
" flight of Phedra and Theseus, my strength did
" fail me, and I sunk almost senseless into the
" chair. The *intelligence* of Mademoiselle Bril-
" land, who played my confidante, suggested to
" her the occupation of the scene at this moment
" by the most interesting attentions about me.
" She threw herself at my feet, took one of my
" hands, and bathed it with her tears. In the
" speech she had to deliver, her words were
" slowly articulated, and interrupted by her sobs.
" She thus gave me time to recover myself. Her
" look, her action affected me deeply; I threw
" myself into her arms, and the public, in tears,
" acknowledged this intelligence by the loudest
" applause." After this tribute of the Siddons
of the French stage to Mademoiselle Brilland,
nothing is wanting but the actual speech, broken
so judiciously by her sobs, and graced by her
expressive attentions, and that is with great certainty supplied by the page of Corneille. Thus
it stands :—

NERINE.

" Calmez-cette douleur ;—où vous emporte—t'elle ?—
Madame,—songez—vous—que tous—ces vains projets—
Par l'eclat—de vous cris—s'entendent—au palais ?"

The French critic cannot fail to see how admirably the address of the actress is seconded by the language of Corneille; and I am not at all sure that this accidental heightening of the scene should not pass into a custom, and the invention of Mademoiselle Brilland, *brille* à jamais dans la tragedie d'Ariane!

I have many reasons for wishing to press this event upon the English actress. It is true, in general, that little attention is paid to the inferior characters, and such *intelligence* might often be thrown away upon our noisy audiences; but, if the effort strike one true admirer of the stage, it will not be lost; nor will the imitator of Mademoiselle Brilland remain long in obscurity. The quickness and adroitness of the French confidante, I do not *quite* expect, however, from my fair countrywomen.

In considering the performance of Lady Randolph by Mrs. Siddons, the attention will seize upon the capital point of distinction between her and Mrs. Crawford. It has been said, that the execution of her " was he alive?" was so piercing, that it was triumphant—but was it *just* under the circumstances?—they must be accurately stated. Assassins hired by Glenalvon assail the life of Lord Randolph—he is preserved by young Norval. A pursuit directed after these ruffians, brings to the castle a stranger, who was found lurking in the wood; and who on being searched is discovered to have upon his person very costly jewels, surmounted with the crest of Douglas. Of these circumstances, Lady Randolph is accurately informed by her faithful Anna, who herself discerned the cognizance so important to her noble mistress. They enter together to the examination of the wretch in custody; and observe what passes between them, and the conviction of Lady Randolph that her son certainly perished, or the jewels could never have been in possession of any stranger.— Observe, too, the necessity of avoiding any disclosure from acute feeling.

> " *Anna.*—Summon your utmost fortitude, before
> You speak with him. Your dignity, your fame,
> Are now at stake. Think of the fatal secret,
> Which in a moment from your lips may fly.
>   *Lady Randolph.*—Thou shalt behold me with a desperate
>   heart,
> Hear how my infant perish'd."

Here are two points given of much weight in our decision. Caution as to *disclosure*, and conviction as to the child's *death*, whatever the stranger has to tell. His narrative is in every memory, I had almost said in every heart. The infant is described as found nestled curiously in a basket, which the eddy of the boiling torrent has thrown up. The question, " was he alive?" is not, therefore, to be uttered, as if the answer in the affirmative gave any hope of his *present* existence—nor does the answer, " *he was*," at all change the tendency of Lady Randolph to believe him destroyed. A breast agitated so as to shriek out Mrs. Crawford's question, ought to have been lulled by the answer she received. But is this the case with Lady Randolph?—by no means; the answer yields no relief: persisting in her notion of his fate, she now, incensed as well as afflicted, exclaims—

" Inhuman that thou art !
How could'st THOU *kill* what waves and tempests spar'd ?"

I am certain, that Mrs. Siddons thus reasoned the passage, and that it was the conviction of her mind such an explosion was unsuitable, that led her into a manner less alarming but more natural. It was, therefore, neither ambition of difference, evasion of difficulty, or fear of competition, that produced her hurried breathless mode of putting that question, on whose effect the Lady Randolph of her rival principally rested.

Often have I examined, by the only steady lights, the page of the author, and that of human nature, these *tours de force* on the French stage, as well as our own; and very rarely indeed is there *one* of which an accurate reading does not dispel the charm. In a crowded theatre, with beauty before you, and the most affecting thing in the world, a woman's voice, thrilling to your soul, the *nerve* is gained, and the judgment dethroned. When the Dumesnils and Crawfords were, therefore, said to know " the *readiest* way to " the heart," it may always be proper to inquire, whether they did not surprise that fortress into a surrender, whose garrison they had " frighted " with false fire ?" However delightful the charming agonies may be, inflicted by these enchantresses, we should yield only to *true* emotion ; and, even in ecstacy itself, be found CUM RATIONE INSANIRE.

Having thus, perhaps, disposed of the great point of comparison, I believe the effects of the minor passages were uniformly on the side of Mrs. Siddons—her narrative had more interest, her attention more intelligence, her ascendancy more awe. In the scene with Glenalvon, villany sunk under her glance, and her action added definition to a general term. " Thou art KNOWN " to me"—was the most expressive of dignified, but contemptuous menaces.

The narrative to Anna in the opening of the play, evinced the soundness of her taste. The poet never failed *her*, and she in perception was another self. She knew the magnifying power of a diminutive, as the representative of hasty joy, and used it exquisitely in the description of her union with Douglas.

" Three weeks, three *little* weeks, with wings of down"—

One of the lines of this narrative has done the most delicate service in nature ever since the play was written—

" I found myself—
As women *wish to be,* who *love* their lords."

But we can hardly, current as it is, expect to hear it again so spoken, as it mournfully lingered from the half-alarmed modesty of this finished orator.

If Doctor Johnson had intended to do justice to any writer of the north, he might have commended Home for the beautiful image which follows, so *very* Shakspearean, and yet not his.

" Can thy feeble pity
Roll back the flood of never-ebbing time ?"

He has in Othello what might have suggested it—
" his pontick sea"—

" Ne'er feels retiring ebb, but keeps due on."

But genius only can thus employ the materials of genius. Any *inspiring* subject found in Home deep pathos, and the true poetic style; but his mind was not fertile in combinations, and he seems not to have mastered any great variety of characters. I read *Agis*, and the Siege of *Aquileia* languidly, in spite of prepossession; and wished, for the fame of the modern stage, that their author had written *only* Douglas.

A few points of that *chef d'œuvre* still await us, which derived an accession to their beauties from the inimitable actress. The comparison of the fancied happy mother of Norval with herself—the discrimination between two persons, whom the audience so keenly anticipated to be one—

> " She for a living husband bore her pains,
> And *heard* him *bless her when a man was born :*"

a feminine feeling beautifully announced by the poet—

> " Whilst *I*—to a dead husband bore a son,
> And to the roaring waters gave my child."

She was sweetly interesting, too, while comparing *her boy* with *blooming Norval*.

> " Whilst thus I mus'd, a *spark from fancy* fell
> On my sad heart," &c.

This spark from fancy, (how could it fail?) kindled a flame in every maternal bosom around her. Her eye was so humid and lustrous, and her brow looked the chosen seat of fancy? She then determines to be the " artist of young Nor- " val's fortune."—I wish she had dared to break through the cross bars upon the prompter's copy, and allow Lady Randolph to utter the following beautiful simile as it came from the imagination of Home.

> " 'Tis pleasing to *admire!*—most apt was I
> To this affection in my better days !—
> Though now I seem to you *shrunk up*, retir'd
> Within the *narrow compass* of my WOE.
> Have you not sometimes seen an early flower
> Open its bud, and spread its silken leaves,
> To catch sweet airs and odours to bestow ;*
> Then, by the keen blast nipt, pull in its leaves,
> And, though still living, *die to scent and beauty ?*
> Emblem of ME; affliction, like a storm,
> Hath kill'd the *forward* blossom of my heart."

It was reserved for Home to vary at least the *application* of the famous " Ut flos in septis" of Catullus, in the *Carmen Nuptiale.*—

> "Quem mulcent auræ, firmat sol, educat imber."

Through all the Italian, and Spanish, and French poets, down to the homely version of Gay, in the Beggar's Opera, the subject compared has been the virgin preserving or losing her purity. But there is nothing, even in the poet of Verona himself, equal to this line of Home's—

> " And, though still living, die to scent and beauty."

---

* Stealing and giving odour.—SHAKSPEARE.

There is, in the fourth act of this play, some little inconsistency. Lady Randolph had written by old Norval, to the youth, her son, to meet her at midnight in privacy, to explain to him circumstances of such moment, as not to be trusted to the very *air* of Lord Randolph's residence. By accident Lord Randolph, and his kinsman Glenalvon, are summoned to meet the valiant John of Lorn, and his Lady and Norval are left together. She addresses him thus—

> " This way with me.   Under *yon* spreading beach,
> *Unseen, unheard,* by human eye or ear,
> I will amaze thee with a wondrous tale."

There is no indication of the scene changing; *yon* beech must be at some distance—a more " removed ground," suited to the disclosure; yet HERE, without retiring, she shows him the jewels—tells him who was his father: and throwing herself upon his neck, acknowledges that she is his mother.   The wondrous tale is already told; nothing remains but the recovery of his lands. For the stage arrangement no more would be necessary than thus to change the *first* line—

> " While Randolph entertains his gallant friend,—
> Unseen, unheard," &c.

In the fifth act, the meeting in the wood takes place, and at the midnight hour, as previously arranged. With respect to Mrs. Siddons, in this act, there was no question about her superiority; and her passions were displayed in the tones of harmony; her great rival seemed to me the first of a school, in latter periods much admired, which deemed discordance the natural ally of anguish, and tortured the ear to overpower the heart; forgetful of the great master's precept—

" In the very torrent, tempest and whirlwind of your passion, you must acquire and beget a temperance that may give it smoothness." ·

Mrs. Siddons, a little deferring to costume, relieved the sable body and train of Lady Randolph by a great deal of white covering upon the bosom, which took with graceful propriety the form of the *ruff*. And this was *much*, in those easy times, when nobody thought of risking the *laughable* in the CORRECT.

CHAPTER XIV.

CONSEQUENCES OF SUCH GREAT POPULARITY. — CAUTION BY
T. DAVIES. — ASSAILED ON ACCOUNT OF PRUDENT HABITS.
— ST. MARTIN'S CHURCH. — ALL ARTS OF ABUSE EXHAUSTED
AGAINST MRS. SIDDONS — SHE HAS NEVER DISGRACED HER
ADMIRERS — ACTS THE COUNTESS OF SALISBURY. — HART-
SON AND HOMER. — POINT SETTLED. — SIGISMUNDA FOL-
LOWED. — TWO STATESMEN INSTRUCT THE ACTORS OF
THOMSON'S PLAY, IN 1745 — WHO WERE *ONLY* GARRICK,
SHERIDAN, DELANE AND MRS. CIBBER! — KEMBLE AND MRS.
SIDDONS. — REMARKS UPON THE PLAY. — EPILOGUE BY
MRS. CIBBER, AS THE TRAGIC MUSE MIGHT SUGGEST TO
MRS. SIDDONS, OR SIR JOSHUA, HIS PICTURE OF THE LATTER
PAINTED IN THE YEAR 1784 — MICHAEL ANGELO. — THE
PROPHET JOEL USED AS HIS MODEL. — THAT FIGURE DE-
SCRIBED. — THE WORK OF SIR JOSHUA COMPARED. — MR.
BURKE'S ADMIRATION OF IT. — MRS. SIDDONS CLOSES HER
SECOND SEASON WITH BELVIDERA. — REPETITIONS OF THE
DIFFERENT CHARACTERS. — ATTACKS UPON HER IN THE
SUMMER. — MRS. SIDDONS AND HER SISTER. — G. STEEVENS.
— UNIFORM MIND IN ALL SHE ACTED — THAT MIND STRICTLY
HER OWN. — COMPARED WITH HER BROTHER. — AUTHOR'S
SINCERE OPINION. — MRS. SIDDONS SITTING AT THE PER-
FORMANCES OF OTHERS. — ABUSED FOR NOT BEING ABSURD.
— HER RECEPTION AT EDINBURGH — CONCLUDES WITH
MURPHY'S EUPHRASIA. — ACTING FOR THE BENEFITS OF
OTHERS. — DIGGES — BRERETON — MISS KEMBLE AT COLMAN'S,
THE GUARDIAN. — HER FRIEND STEEVENS. — MR. TWISS, AND
HIS INDEX TO SHAKSPEARE. — SEASON OF 1784-5. — KING

RETURNS.—MRS. SIDDONS PUBLICLY INSULTED.—RECORD
OF THAT AFFAIR.—MARGARET OF ANJOU.—ZARA.—CARME-
LITE.—MAID OF HONOUR.—A REMARK OF DOCTOR IRELAND
AS TO MASSINGER CONFIRMED.

AFTER all petty cavils and prejudices long ra-
dicated, the character of Lady Randolph may be
considered as sealing the reputation of Mrs. Siddons. The natural tendency of popularity so
vast and lasting might be conceived to beget a
confidence, which no previous instance had sanctioned; and notwithstanding the serious disclaimer of all pride published in the early effusion
of her gratitude,* some caution seemed to be
necessary, lest she should imagine herself to hold
by a tenure not extended to such giddy habita-
tions as the hearts of the multitude.

A very intelligent cotemporary, a member, too,

---

* "She knows the danger arising from extraordinary and
"unmerited favours, and will carefully guard against any approach
"of *pride*, too often their attendant. Happy shall she esteem
"herself, if, by the utmost assiduity, and constant exertion of her
"poor abilities, she shall be able to lessen, though hopeless ever
"to discharge, the vast debt she owes the public."

　　　　　　　　　　D. L. T., Dec. 17th, 1782.

Johnson would have said, perhaps, did say—"She has raised
herself and her family from the honours of Wolverhampton, to
those which a theatre royal can confer; she has established her
sway over the passions of all, from the sovereign to the mechanic;
she sees respect and affluence the produce of her genius, and has a
right to be proud."

of the profession, and a man of letters, thus, perhaps, *more* than cautions the delightful novelty. "Mrs. "Siddons has in Belvidera, as well as many other "parts, not only attracted the attention, but ab- "solutely *fixed* the favour of the town in her "behalf. This actress, like a resistless torrent, "has borne down all before her. Her merit, "which is certainly very extensive in tragic cha- "racters, seems to have swallowed up all remem- "brance of present and past performers; but as "I would not sacrifice the living to the dead, "neither would I break down the statues of the "honourable deceased, to place their successors "on their pedestals. The fervour of the public "is laudable; I wish it may be lasting; but I "hope without that ingratitude to their old ser- "vants, which will make their passion for Mrs. "Siddons less valuable, as it will convey a warn- "ing to her, that a new face may possibly erase "the impression which she has so anxiously "studied to form, and so happily made."

Thus did Davies temperately express himself at the very period of time which I am now pass-ing over. He adds, what I can seriously confirm, that the comedians complained that their farces did not *tell*, after the tragedy of Mrs. Siddons: but he forgot to add when such a complaint was ever made *before*. But whether Davies, from generosity or policy, hinted at equality, and pre-

sumed decline of favour, the consideration was
likely enough in prudent minds to beget great
care and economy; and purchases in the funds
were announced as disposing of the large sums
gained by her benefits.   Here at least some
gleam of comfort broke upon the discontented;
where there was the most incessant labour, there
was probably avidity of gain, possibly avarice.
It cost little to make the assertion, and she'now
began to be assailed for penurious habits, hardness of heart, and a remarkable want of charity.

> " For if a cherub in the shape of woman
> Should walk this world, yet *defamation* would,
> Like a vile cur, bark at the angel's train."

Among the lighter ornaments of detraction, one
epigram, I remember, accused her " of lingering
" behind the rest of the congregation in the gal-
" lery of Saint Martin's, to avoid a present of be-
" nevolence to the Westminster Dispensary."
With all the eagerness of general charity upon
such occasions, I do not believe, even in the *gallery* of Saint Martin's, that there could be found
so little *curiosity,* as to leave Mrs. Siddons *behind,*
in this race for the churchwarden's plate.

Another, and a subtler foe, involves her with
Mrs. Crawford, Miss Younge, and the other imperial queens of the stage, (Mrs. Abington, and one
or two more excepted) in a censure drawn down

by the most extreme hardness of heart, parsimoni-
ousness, haughtiness and inattention to the voice of
affliction, even among the fallen empresses of their
own profession. This now was really judicious,
for the whole weight of it would fall on the lady
of the party about whom the public mind was *then*
occupied. The same article took care to assert
the superior merits of Mrs. Crawford on the
stage, and represented the fame of Mrs. Siddons
as borne up only by the vapour of fashionable
folly.* The *merits* of the ACTRESS have borne her
triumphant through all changes of the moment,
though her great admirers have, to be sure, occasionally, *disgraced* themselves.

Such were the commencements of that malevo-
lence, which will be shewn hereafter to excite
clamour against her, even in the seat of her empire,
the theatre itself. Miserable as these arts are, they
claim a record; that it may be seen how keenly envy
follows great success; and that in the profession,
which gratifies self-love more quickly and forcibly than any other, all the gales are not halcyon :

* It will scarcely be believed that a cotemporary thus abused
her. " The judicious would as soon see Bensley murdering Lear,
" or kicking up the heels of Alexander the Great. Her head seems
" to dance upon wires, like that of Punch's antic queen; though a
" Gentoo might think it more resembled that of the china Mandarin
" in our drawing-rooms." Yet even this wretch admired her
beauty.

some, like a sudden frost, check all self-complacency, and others blight for a time our good will
to society, and reliance upon its justice.

The list of first-rate female characters in tragedy is not very extensive. I mean such as are
strongly discriminated by *manners*. The complaint
of Aristotle is likely to apply to the *modern* periods
of every drama. Character will not be so pronounced as that you should be able always to anticipate the decision of the speaker.* On the 6th of
March, 1784, Mrs. Siddons acted, for the first
time, Hall Hartson's Countess of Salisbury. Of
this poet, educated by the excellent Dr. Leland,
the originality has been questioned, on account of
the following very beautiful effusion—spoken by
Mrs. Siddons.

> " Never, oh, never more shall Ela run,
> With throbbing bosom, at the trumpet's sound,

---

* Dacier at least so understands the great master ; and he thus
whimsically illustrates him from Virgil. " Si Virgile ne nous avoit
" fait prévoir aucune résolution d'Enée, et que nous fussions in-
" certains, s'il obéïra aux Dieux, ou s'il leur preferera Didon, en
" ce cas il n'y auroit point de *mœurs*, quelque diligence qu' Enée fit
" pour hâter sa fuite."

If Virgil had not led us to foresee any resolution of Eneas's, but
we were doubtful whether he would obey the gods, or prefer Dido;
in that case, there would be no *manners*, whatever speed he might
make to *run away* from her.

If passages acquire even a *joke* in translation, it is something.

To unlock his helmet conquest-plum'd, to strip
The cuisses from his manly thigh, or snatch
Quick from his breast the plated armour, wont
To oppose my fond embrace.—Sweet times, farewell.
These tender offices return no more."

A friend, it seems, complimented the author
upon his very ingenious use of Homer in the preceding passage. Mr. Hartson disclaimed, as he
well might, any knowledge of the obligation;
and, like a true friend, the reminder went his
way, and asserted, that, not knowing what it contained, Mr. Hartson could not be the *author* of his
own play. The play, observe, was taken by the
pupil from Dr. Leland's romance of Longswood,
Earl of Salisbury—the doctor was in all certainty
as well acquainted with Homer, as with Demos-
thenes. But what obligation in fact has Homer
conferred upon either master or scholar?—literally in English this—

" From whom Andromache shall ne'er receive
Those glorious arms, for thou shalt ne'er return."*

Nor is Andromache even the speaker; what *is*
said, comes from Jove himself. The passage in original Homer, begins at verse 201 of the 17th book.

* —————— ὁ τοι ἔτι μαχης ἐκνοςήσαντι
Δεξεται Ἀνδρομάχη κλυτὰ τευχεα Πηλείωνθ·

ILIAD, B. 17, v. 207.

G 2

The reader sees that Hartson has given and well-given the manner of *chivalry*.   His picture is the unarming the accomplished knight, by the soft fingers of his lady, on his return from battle and victory—and it is minute enough to have gratified Don Quixote himself.

The great actress carried the Countess through three representations, and on the 24th of April acted Sigismunda, in the tragedy of Tancred and Sigismunda, being the night of her second annual benefit. This play was first performed on the 18th March, 1745. Patriotism in those days was at least as friendly to an author as poetry. The author of *Liberty* dedicated his play to Frederick, Prince of Wales, and Pitt and Lord Lyttleton interested themselves so successfully. with Garrick, that Thomson had his best services in Tancred. The two statesmen attended the rehearsals, to the *benefit*, it is said, of the piece—the actors availing themselves of the *instructions* of men so highly admired. When it is considered that the performers were Garrick, Sheridan, Delane, and Mrs. Cibber,—but we know the attention to *rank* in the play-house.

Mrs. Cibber is said to have been extremely like Mr. Garrick, below the middle stature like him, and possessing features which exhibited the true alphabet of passion. Davies says they might have been thought brother and sister—a sort of

advantage which Kemble and Siddons *fully* enjoyed, with the greatest elegance of figure.

Sigismunda opens the play, and rather awk-
wardly. The King touches it seems his last moments, and Tancred is gone out hunting. She,
therefore, till he shall return, very quietly details
to Laura all that seems to her mysterious about
his birth; her father, she adds, reared him in
Belmont's woods, with " princely accost, nay,
" with respect," language not very intelligible :
but after relating her *no* knowledge to Laura, she
suddenly recollects that the young lady probably
knows much more of him than she does, and we
have an *à propos* rather comic :—

> " Laura, perhaps your brother knows him better.
> What says Rodolpho ? does he truly credit
> The story of his birth."
>   " *Laura.*   He has sometimes,
> Like you, his doubts."

This friendly young lady, however, opening the
praises of Tancred, Sigismunda seizes the theme,
and copiously pursues a subject so inexhaustible—
when her father suddenly enters. He orders her
to retire ; but Sigismunda venturing an inquiry as
to the King, he tell her of his death, and calmly
relates the manner of it. After a second command, she leaves him to his interview with Tancred, now returned from the chace. Sigismunda
here is nothing. There is but little for her either

in the scene with Tancred; a rising alarm that his greatness may disturb their union, some common places as to the sacrifices of monarchs to the public welfare, and the first act leaves her without a point.

In the whole second act, Sigismunda only *once* appears; and that is oppressed with grief, and passing *silently* through the back scene.

The third act is opened by Sigismunda sitting in melancholy rumination; and here Mrs. Siddons found something to work upon, though I must think the language remarkably cold and weak. The *contrasted conduct* of Tancred, however well pruned, (for Thomson is redundant and heavy,) produced some effect. The entrance of Siffredi to his daughter brought out the great actress.

> " Hopes I have none !—those by this fatal day
> Are blasted all."

Where she determines upon her future conduct as to Tancred, the delicacy of her question was very finely given :—

> " What would you more, my father ?"

When the wily statesman has disclosed that *more* in the proposed union with Osmond—all the little endearing supplications, the references to her mother, which nature taught Otway, and

Thomson echoed pretty exactly, produced delightful effect, from the long sterility that preceded. Laura comes into the design of the father, inveighs against Tancred, and aids her to make herself a wretch.

On the presentation of Osmond by her father, the utmost skill faltered out:—

> " I am a DAUGHTER, Sir—and have no power
> Over my *own heart*. I die.—Support me, Laura."

The fourth act is really beautiful. The explanation of her lover—the suspicion as to her father—the determination to preserve *principle* in whatever misery—the terrible interview with Tancred—the entrance of Osmond and the result, all required only the " words that burn" to be of the very highest power; but the actress supplied all by the eloquence of *eye* and *gesture*.

Of the fifth act, the interest is in the surprise of the King by Osmond in the chamber of his wife. An author, after a death wound, may keep a heroine alive as long as his interest requires; but extreme length of conversation is, I believe, precluded by *nature*, and four long speeches no *art* ought to insist upon making, after the powerful hand of death is *felt* in the blow.

Mrs. Siddons, however, rendered the death of Sigismunda tenderly perfect; and we should have admitted her *right* to appear after it, like Mrs. Cibber, in the character of the TRAGIC MUSE.

Perhaps this circumstance, preserved in the original epilogue, might lead to the noble picture of her by Sir Joshua Reynolds, painted certainly in the present year.

Whether the suggestion came from the mind of Thomson, or one quite its equal, the President's own, I must leave unsettled; but the muse of tragedy led him to Michael Angelo, whose inspiration had executed the Sybils and Prophets in the Vatican; and he seized, as a model for his design the prophet Joel, with his two attendant figures behind the chair.

Joel is supposed to have been a contemporary of Hosea, and to have lived about eight hundred years before Christ. Michael Angelo, perhaps on no authority, has represented him as advanced in life, the hair already gone from the top of the head, but what remains of great strength and character: he slightly inclines over a scroll, which is of great width, in the form of Greek manuscripts. The greater mass is in the right hand, and the left sustains the portion which he is reading. The right foot is bare and advanced, the left retires within the folds of the garment; and an ample cloak, which covers his shoulders, falls in massy and majestic folds across the knees of the figure, which are so sundered as to allow the weight to assume the lines of grandeur. The book of Joel has but three chapters, and treats but of three subjects, the Babylonian captivity, the

descent of the holy spirit upon the apostles, and
the *last judgment*, which, it should be observed, is
the subject of the grand ceiling of the Pope's
chapel, of which the prophets are angular decorations. Such the great portions of the mighty
whole.

Sir Joshua had here a difficulty; he had to
combine portrait with mythology, the *woman* with
the MUSE. Had he intended the latter merely,
the substances of the dress would have been
more solid, and contained fewer small parts; as
he blended the characters the materials are of
modern usage, and the *forms* alone exceed the
dignity of the actress's toilet. The style of decoration chosen for the head and shoulders seems
to have been, from a variety of portraits, his OWN
decided taste, and suited to the peculiarities of
his system of colour. The figure retires a little
to the left side, the right arm depending over one
arm of the massy chair, the left raised on its
elbow, resting upon the other. The kind of expression given to the face, which is very beautiful, seems an *abstraction* of TRAGEDY; contem-
plating its essence rather than its forms, its effects
rather than its properties. Its ministers attend
behind in the Aristotelian shapes of TERROR and
PITY; the first advances, trembling with the bowl
of aconite, the second droops over the reverted
dagger. The turbid atmosphere, while it sus-

tains, accords with the figures, to which it adds its elemental strife, only less dreadful than the war of the passions.

When, in the year 1774, Sir Joshua pronóunced his sixth discourse, which treats of the use of the inventions of others; when he shewed that conceit or indifference avoiding such resources, would soon, from mere barrenness, be reduced to the poorest of all imitations; he was little aware that in ten years from that date he might have extended his arm to the magnificent portrait I have been describing; and, as his modesty would have chosen to put it, exclaimed, " See, gentlemen, behold *my* obligations to MICHAEL ANGELO." The original picture is now in the collection of Lord Grosvenor, and by his Lordship's most liberal politeness, accessible in the summer to all who wish to enjoy his collection; and you are not permitted to gratify *his* servants for the respectful attention which they are seemingly happy to shew the visitors honoured with his Lordship's card.

Mr. Desenfans had a duplicate of the picture, now in Dulwich College. As I once had frequent opportunities of inspecting the latter picture, I may as well record that it seemed to me inferior to the original in force, which will certainly surprise no artist. Sir Joshua inscribed his name and the date, 1784, on the hem of the

garment, as borne to posterity by Mrs. Siddons.
I am happy to say that the union thus given is
never likely to be sundered; for though the picture must one day perish, the engraving of Ha-
ward may be renewed for ever. The expressive
language of Mr. Burke is alone adequate to the
fame of such an artist, and I select this picture to
justify his praise. "He was the first Englishman
" who added the praise of the elegant arts to the
" other glories of his country. In taste, in grace,
" in facility, in happy invention, and in the rich-
" ness and harmony of colouring, he was equal
" to the great masters of the renowned ages. In
" portrait he went beyond them; for he commu-
" nicated to that description of the art, in which
" English artists are the most engaged, a variety,
" a fancy, and a dignity derived from the *higher*
" branches. His portraits remind the spectator
" of the invention of history, and the amenity of
" landscape. In painting portraits, he appeared
" not to be raised upon that platform, but to de-
" scend to it from a higher sphere."

Mr. Burke inspected the progress of this picture with his characteristic ardour, and with a
SIG ITUR AD ASTRA, pronounced it to be the
noblest portrait that he had ever seen of any age.
If the great actress, when it unfolded the full
magic of its perfection before her, could repress
all feeling like PRIDE, she was a model of hu-

mility as well as grandeur, which the world has seldom seen.

The second season of Mrs. Siddons closed on the 13th of May, with a sixth performance of Belvidera. She acted fifty-three times between the 8th of October and her last night, that is, allowing for the oratorios in Lent, nearly once in every three nights of the company's performance. The thermometer of attraction thus arranges the various characters she acted. Isabella, seven times; Mrs. Beverley, seven also; Belvidera and Lady Randolph alike, six repetitions; Shakspeare's Isabella and Thomson's Sigismunda, five each; Euphrasia and Constance, four; Shore and the Countess of Salisbury, three; Zara, in the Mourning Bride, two; Calista, one.

It could not be expected that an equal sum should be drawn from the public, yet the popularity of the actress continued the same through both seasons. Nor do I think, in a pecuniary point of view, that the combining her brother's excellencies in the same plays added to the receipts. Compared with her, there were many who considered him cold and artificial. During the summer recess, the war of paragraph continued in town, and means of annoyance very unexpectedly arose from a member of her own family. Miss Kemble had been retained, by the influence of her sister, in a situation of great respectability in the theatre, and 1 have shewn one effort of her powerful advocate to correct the malignant severity of public criticism. But this was not all. Mr. Steevens, whatever were his views, took great pleasure in expatiating upon this lady's acquirements, and asserted, in his tour of diurnal influence, (and he had a tongue to persuade) that diffidence alone prevented her from dividing the crown of tragedy, though in what proportions he was, perhaps, too prudent to state. It is fair to suppose that, with the friendly access he possessed, he did not refrain from making the young lady's own ear acquainted with the important discovery that her mind was " *every way* " *stronger and more cultivated than her sister's.*"— See his letter, dated 27th of July, 1784, in Mr. Hayley's posthumous Memoirs of his own life.

Perhaps some of this trash, as to the comparative strength of mind of these sisters, had no basis but the supposition that the attentions of old Mr. Sheridan were *preceptive,* and that the actual strength of mind evinced professionally by Mrs. Siddons seemed striking enough to imply a judgment superior to her own. But Mr. Sheridan has passed away, and all his lectures of elocution. She had attended to no preceptor, when Henderson pronounced her the first of actresses. She differed essentially, radically from her brother, Mr. Kemble, through life; and if

ever the efforts of mortal wore a uniform character, from the commencement of its career to
the close of it, Mrs. Siddons may truly be said—

" To be *herself* ALONE."

She knew better than any one how to indivi-
duate character, she was engrossed by it completely : her very form, expreŝsion, gesture, voice
itself seemed to be bounded by her strong conception of the part she acted. She had more
ATTENTION than I ever saw, to what was doing
and to be done. She seemed never to be thinking of an audience ; and they gratefully repaid
her by thinking, where she was, of nothing but
herself. Who was ever yet *taught* to add intensity to emotion, and communicate new dignity
to the sublimity of poetic expression ? Nor is
this the strain of required panegyric, the grace
which an author may think it discreet to bestow
upon the subject on which he works. Were Mrs.
Siddons my enemy, I should speak thus of her as
an actress ; though I might naturally regret that
the incense cast upon her altar, procured only
aversion to her admirer.

The prudence which was so strong a feature in
the character of Mr. Siddons, had been convinced
of the permanence of his wife's attraction ; and
they, consequently, had taken a house in Gower-
street, and she returned the visits of her fashion-

able friends in a carriage of her own. There was no ostentation about it. She sometimes came to the theatre to see others act, and always paid the greatest attention to the performance; but she did not, *like* some others, sit remarkably forward, and throw her whole person, I was going to say, into the lap of the audience, under the pretext of applauding strongly those whom she admired. She never applauded *at all*, and this was judicious. She was sitting with *their* judges and her's.

But indecorous as a contrary habit would have been, and dull as the poor brutes must have been who did not *feel* this, I recently turned over a long string of paragraphs, the gist of which was her penury of praise, and her cruelty in refusing the sanction of her public approbation to those whom such a testimony would have benefited. The writers forgot that her *coming* presumed some expectation of being entertained, and some little proof of being so is implied by a veteran performer's sitting out a whole play with unintermitted attention.

I shall not risk the doing injustice to persons long since departed, whose practice was said to have been different—those who can censure what is really good, are likely enough to *invent* authorities for what is bad in such cases. But if it is supposed that any of her rivals had the liberality to *praise* the talents of Mrs. Siddons, I am too well informed as to their green-room sneers and friendly predictions of returning good sense in the public, not to give such a notion the most decided negative.

That I have seen Mrs. Abington, at Colman's, applaud Miss Farren, is certain; but no two actresses in the world differed more widely from each other than these two ladies, however they may have acted the same characters; besides, from circumstances, the greater actress might be rather serving herself than the beautiful successor to her refined cast in comedy. She also demonstrated how free she was from jealousy by this attention to a rival; the impression general in the house was, that it was too strongly marked. I do not imagine that it was levelled at Mrs. Siddons, though among the writers attached to the Thalia of that period were usually found the bitterest censors of her serious sister. Something of a nature not quite theatrical might account for all this—the general reception of Mrs. Siddons in the fashionable world. The patronage of Mrs. Abington by ladies of rank was somewhat *select*.

During the summer recess, Mrs. Siddons acted at Edinburgh eleven nights. I look upon the distinction she met with in that capital as one of her chief triumphs. There was, and always will be, found there an audience never surpassed in its intelligence—high alike in taste and knowledge. The number of first-rate professors, mingling much in society, renders polished life fond of literary attainments; and the public, in its very amusements, less gross than the more mixed audiences of London. The manager had only to state to them, that his offers to the great actress had been of considerable weight, to induce them at once to agree that the admission to the pit on her nights should be five shillings. Nobody was idle enough to hint a doubt that the acting they then saw was infinitely more finished and perfect than any that they had witnessed. Her last impression was made in Euphrasia, a character of which the situations are always either brilliant or affecting. The truth is, that Murphy was by no means more indebted in tragedy to French models than he was in comedy. In the former he grounded himself upon Crebillon, Voltaire, and Belloy, and in the latter mixed together Molicre and Destouches; and in both obliged us with pieces admirably adapted to the stage. The real power of his own genius lies certainly in his farces. Yet he knew well the different characters of the two rival nations; and whatever he borrowed assumed the English dress with such perfect ease, as to pass for native with those who did not demand a scrutiny.

Dublin and Cork succeeded, and the summer yielded, naturally enough, a harvest greatly be-

yond that of the winter season, even with its two
benefits.   Such incessant fatigue, however, became at last too much for her health, and part of
her routine was given up.   It could hardly be expected in these summer excursions that she could
spare time to act for the benefits of performers,
and if she did, that she should do so unpaid
would have been a palpable injustice to her family ;
but theatrical mouths in London were soon cla-
morous with outcries against the hardness of that
heart that would not play for West Digges unless
he paid her fifty pounds, and that had so turned
against Brereton, her hero, her Jaffier, that even
money would not propitiate her; she would not
act for him at all, which blighted all his hopes,
and greatly distressed both his circumstances and
his mind.   Here, therefore, was a strong and un-
looked-for reinforcement to the clamour already
noticed; and the theatrical world suggesting to
the newspapers, a vast deal of the most positive
assertion was poured out in the daily prints, which
was canvassed in the morning at the tea-table,
and the rest of the day occupied more of the general attention than any *ex parte* statement to the
prejudice even of a gentleman ought to excite in
liberal minds.   But greatness is always in danger.

As to the performing for Mr. Digges in Dublin,
it was an affair of pure humanity.   He was of a

full habit, and in the month of July suffered a paralytic stroke, of which it was believed in town for some time that he had died; but he lingered to the end of the year 1786, and then expired at Cork. He had been near forty years upon the stage, and was greatly admired in characters of either force or feeling. Mr. Digges had not excited any great attention while acting here under Mr. Colman, and consequently it was less a personal regard to him than an envy to Mrs. Siddons that moved those who used his name against her reputation.

Brereton's case was of a different nature—he had greatly distinguished himself by acting here with her, and owed some valuable engagements to her preference. I know the deceiving nature of self-love, and how soon the auxiliary fancies that his principal could not exist without him. If a mind be quite sound, it will consider voluntary justice as a favour;* if it have a warp of vanity upon it, it will view even voluntary favour as a mere matter of justice. Now the voluntary favour intended Mr. Brereton was to take less from him than from any other performer for whom she acted. It might have been concluded that nothing was to be paid—some complaint seems to

---

* See Mr. Tooke's dedication of his great work to the University of Cambridge.

have arisen from irritated feelings, which a dispassionate consideration of all the circumstances disavowed, perhaps regretted. The effects, very disagreeable in their course, will be the very first subject noticed in the winter season of 1784-5.

In the mean time it may be agreeable to turn from the storm preparing for one sister to the more cheering prospect which just now opened to the other. Miss Kemble, as Mr. Steevens truly said, " succeeded, at Colman's theatre, beyond " the warmest expectations of her friends, in the " very delicate part of Harriet, in the Guardian." I have formerly observed, with proper feeling, upon the harshness with which her Almeria and Alicia were treated at Drury Lane Theatre, while sustaining the very terrible comparison with the powers of her greater sister on the same evenings. But it does seem to need some particular explanation, how, yielding at once the palm of tragedy to Miss Woollery, she came to accept the part of Harriet, in the Guardian, a comedy elegantly drawn by Garrick, from the delightful *Pupille,* (the Ward,) a petite piece by Mons. Fagan.

To this choice the very beautiful young actress was directed by the judgment—very probably by the passion of the celebrated commentator on Shakspeare, who, with great admiration of her accomplishments, professed now the deepest concern for her interest. Every thing here bears a relation to the hopes which he certainly entertained; and as he rehearsed with her the scenes between Heartly and Harriet, he flattered himself that the preference of the play might suggest a similar attachment of the pupil to her masterly and most insinuating instructor. Nor was the disparity greater as to the ages of the parties. Mr. Steevens was now in the forty-fourth year of his age, and possessed every advantage of mind, person, and fortune. When Hayley upon his monument inscribed these lines, those who remember the animation of his countenance, will acquit him of posthumous flattery.

> " Peace to these ashes ! once the *bright attire*
> Of Steevens, *sparkling with ætherial fire*."

A slight outline of the comedy will shew that this illustration is not fanciful. Harriet, the ward of Heartly, is presumed by him to have fixed her affections upon a coxcomb of her own age—and although the young lady exhibits many palpable indications of a much *graver* choice, the almost paternal relation in which he stands to her—his maturity, and the inbred modesty of his character, remote from every tinct of personal vanity, repel from him the conception that she can possibly bestow her preference upon himself. The exquisite address of the French author enables him to parry the very plainest declarations that she can well make, and in a scene of inimitable delicacy, she is driven to request him to write for her a letter, intended as a disclosure to *himself*. She even touches upon his *tender care of her infancy*. This, though by no means applying to the coxcomb Clackit, he considers as escaping her merely in her *confusion*, and, therefore, striking it out, closes the letter, and asks whether he shall send it? The answer is *naïve* even in English—" Yes, if you think I *ought* to send it."

Perhaps few sounds were ever more agreeable to the ear of Steevens, than those which the representative of Harriet uttered to her self-constituted guardian. But the male coquet probably never seriously sought a permanent engagement; and the prudence of the lady and her family soon broke off attentions equivocal in their object, and dangerous in their continuance. At no very distant period, she gave her hand to Mr. Twiss, a gentleman of great merit,* and her son is the pre-

---

* All Shakspeareans acknowledge themselves infinitely indebted to the persevering diligence of Mr. Twiss. He completed a task of the most irksome toil, a *verbal* index to the works of Shakspeare. Every important word being exhibited in the classical mode, with all its recurrences, it becomes absolutely certain in what *shades* of meaning the great author indulged himself. Had this work existed from the time of Rowe, the rubbish of much early *guessing* at his sense would have been happily spared the present age. All our great early writers should have this indispensable conclusion to a careful reprint of their text.

sent member in parliament for Wootton Basset.*
I recollect that Steevens, for some years, used to
support in silence the very intelligible *looks* of her
brother, Mr. Kemble. There is a head of this
lady by Sir Joshua Reynolds, an admirable likeness, which for unaffected simplicity, sweetness
and clearness of the pencil, is perhaps one of his
finest portraits. Some seasons back, it was exhibited, with a splendid selection from the works
of that great master, in the British Gallery, Pall
Mall. It was placed not far from his grand
work, Mrs. Siddons in the tragic muse; and as
much surpassed it in accurate resemblance, as it
fell below it in magnificence of design and execution. There is a fame even beyond *this* distinction, and that is the memory of an amiable
and useful life.

The appearance of Mrs. Siddons at Drury Lane
Theatre, in the winter season of 1784-5, was happily preceded by the return of Mr. King to the
exercise of his professional duties, which he was
presumed to have relinquished for a plan of retirement. Like other veteran professors, he possessed an unbounded veneration for the ornaments
of his earlier days; and as he had some little
poetical talent, he let his fancy loose among the
precious recollections of the past, and did his best
to imitate the following tender effusion, which

* January, 1826.

Garrick, with so sure a taste, made the prologue
to his, or rather Colman's, Clandestine Marriage.
Holland be it observed was the speaker.

> " Oh, let me drop one tributary tear
> On poor Jack Falstaff's grave, and Juliet's bier !
> You to their worth must testimony give;
> 'Tis in your hearts alone their fame can live.
> Still as the scenes of life will shift away,
> The strong impressions of their art decay.
> Your children cannot feel what you have known;
> They'll boast of Quins and Cibbers of their own."

The brilliant writer and unequalled actor were
now to be remembered by an old friend, if not
with equal power, by sincerity equally unquestionable, and Mr. King revived for a moment all
he could revive, the *name* of departed genius.
Nor was he a niggard as to existing excellence ;
but, with all the classical predilection of Milton,
yet afforded his generous tribute of praise

> " To what *(though rare)* of later age
> Ennobled hath the *buskin'd* stage."

The terms " living worth " used by Mr. King
were, one might think, sufficiently general to pass
unquestioned by the most attentive audience ;
but a sort of *dull demur* might be felt rather than
heard, upon this expression; and, perhaps, the
actor and his spectators understood each other
perfectly ;—the one as sounding their goodwill
afar off; and the other as shewing that, at present,

they bore no decided portion of it to the lady in whose favour the experiment was made. No man stood better, however, with the town than Mr. King—it is difficult to describe him on such occasions—his vivacity had not what might be called hilarity about it—the *smile* seemed nearly banished from his expression: his effect was almost entirely in his utterance, which possessed an articulate velocity and smartness never heard but from him; and a collected confidence in himself, that extorted an applause paid to the situation, or the sentiment, rather than the man. Weston, Edwin, or Liston were antipodes to King. Give to either of these *humourists* the *ghost* of a character, they invested its thinness in corporeal substance: or to choose another illustration, an outline of figure was all that was wanting to their art; they infused into it the richness of their own comic imagination in aid of irresistible features, and completed the work designed by another hand. But to their successors such men can leave only the *outline* they received, and the future spectators see only the *ghost* of what delighted their fathers.

To return to the immediate subject, Mrs. Siddons's re-appearance. While Mr. King thus expressed his managerial opinion of the "living "worth," which had been so rudely questioned, her husband, under whose directions she might

fairly be presumed to act, as every theatrical engagement could only be made by him or by his
power, caused the following letter to be inserted
in the principal London newspapers.

" The following is an answer to the scandalous
" stories lately circulated to the prejudice of Mrs.
" Siddons's private character.

" TO THE PRINTER.

" SIR,

" I am unused to write for public inspection,
" but I will not hesitate to state the truth; and
" I think the generous and candid will excuse
" the rest. I, therefore, declare, that Mrs. Sid-
" dons never wished, asked, nor accepted, a single
" farthing from Mr. Digges; and that, a few days
" after his benefit, that gentleman acknowledged
" his obligations to her by a very polite note,
" which Mrs. Siddons (not expecting so malig-
" nant an attack) destroyed.

" With regard to Mr. Brereton, so far from
" refusing to perform for him, she agreed to do it
" for a much smaller sum than she was to receive
" from any other comedian, though every per-
" former, for whom she played, gave her consi-
" derably less than the manager paid her nightly,
" for twenty nights together; but just as the be-
" nefits were commencing, she was taken ill, and

" confined to her bed nearly a fortnight. When
" she recovered, her strength would not permit
" her to perform immediately, more than three
" nights a week : and as the manager expected
" his engagement fulfilled, and was to leave Dub-
" lin at a particular time, she was obliged to
" forego the performing for Mr. Brereton; she,
" after that, made another attempt to serve him ;
" why it failed, Mr. Brereton can truly tell; but
" I will be bold to assert, without affording the
" smallest ground for any charge against Mrs.
" Siddons. These are solemn facts ; on which I
" leave the public to judge. Animadversions
" on her public performance, and the question-
" ing of her professional talents, I shall ever sub-
" mit to; feeling that those who so liberally
" reward her exertions, have the best right to
" judge of their degree of merit, and to praise or
" censure them, as they think proper; but all
" attacks upon her private conduct that, if un-
" noticed, would deservedly lower her in the
" estimation of the public, and render her less
" worthy of their favour and kindness, I hold
" myself bound to answer.

" W. SIDDONS.
" *Thursday, September* 30."

The date, but that might be accident, is that of
the day on which Mr. King made his compliments

to her from the stage. The line of the actor almost required explanation itself—the letter of her husband gave explanation enough as to Mr. Digges, but left much to be desired, to use a French formulary, as to Mr. Brereton. It is in truth such a one as might be expected from one unused to write for public inspection—but the importance of the occasion seemed to call for an exertion of a different character. I think it very clear that her brother, Mr. Kemble, never saw it in manuscript. It did not hold her high enough —it wanted both force and point, it was gossiping and familiar; and there was something almost ludicrous in his declarations of " *submitting* to " any animadversion on her public performance, " and the questioning of her professional talents." —Submission to an unavoidable tenure needs no declaration, and is accepted as no concession. That he holds himself bound to answer all attacks upon her *private conduct* is a position as little needed as the former; it was her *professional conduct* that was concerned in playing or not playing for two members of the profession.

That she took less from every actor for whom she played than the manager gave her for twenty nights together, and that Brereton was to be still higher favoured, or rated lower, was a miserable detail, and unfit for the public eye. The valuable consideration for valuable aid we know must

be had, but it is in all cases irksome both to give
it and receive it publicly. The lawyer's fee is left
happily with his clerk, the physician·awkwardly
waves for it as he retires, and turns away his face
as he takes it. All that could be necessary was
to give the mere fact of her illness, and the confinement which it occasioned—the rest was misfortune, for which she had many ways of compen-
sating Mr. Brereton.

But the worst symptom of the case was, the
churlishness of the letter, which Mr. Brereton was
at last induced to write:

" TO THE PRINTER OF THE PUBLIC ADVERTISER.

" *Sunday, Oct, 3, 1784.*

" SIR,

" By inserting the following (which will of
" itself prove my authority) in your paper of to-
" morrow, you will very much oblige,

" Your's, &c.

" WILLIAM SIDDONS."

" SIR,

" I am concerned to find Mrs. Siddons has
" suffered in the public opinion on my account.
" I have told you before, and I again repeat it,
" that to the friends I have seen, I have taken
" pains to exculpate her from the least unkind-

" ness to me in Dublin. I acknowledge she *did*
" agree to perform at my benefit for a less sum
" than for any other performer, but her illness
" prevented it; and that she *would* have played
" for me after *that*, had not the night been ap-
" pointed after she had played three times in the
" same week, and *that* the week after her illness—
" and I am very willing you shall publish this
" letter, if you think it will be of the least service
" to Mrs. Siddons, to whom I am proud to own
" many obligations of friendship.

" I am, Sir,

" Your very humble Servant,

" W. BRERETON.

" *To* MR. SIDDONS,
    Gower-street."

" Mr. Siddons cannot withhold his public
" thanks from Mr. Brereton, for his obliging let-
" ter, and he has no doubt but that Mr. Digges
" will in a little time furnish Mrs. Siddons with
" another written testimony, that will entirely
" confound the artful schemes of her detractors."

With all this pride of obligation, did it become
a generous man to be besieged upon such a subject? He alone could not be ignorant of the long
altercation before the public, of which he was the

cause. To explain to the friends he has *seen* was nothing—the " pains to exculpate" should have filed along with the public attacks upon her. The inference in most minds was, that he had once angrily vented his disappointment in the language of censure, and had now seen *reason* to question his discretion or his justice. Like Eolus himself he had loosed a tempest, which his desire could not still so easily as it was excited.

Mr. Siddons publicly expressed his thanks for this *obliging* letter. He might almost have exclaimed with King Lear—

> " This *tempest* will not give me leave to ponder
> On things would hurt me more."

During the very week after her illness (that illness which annulled her first attempt to serve him,) she acted three times; and Mr. Brereton's night being unaccountably fixed in the *same* week, the second attempt was as impracticable as the former. Mr. Brereton was a first-rate actor of that day, how did it happen that he allowed his night to be so predicamented? Why was it accompanied with a condition that rendered it nugatory? The youngest branch of the Daggerwood family would not permit his benefit to be fixed on the second day of Epsom races.

It has occurred to me to witness the dreadful exertion of some performers in characters of the

highest power. I have seen them stretched out
and exhausted, and needing much time to restore
their wasted strength and spirits. I, therefore, can
feel no surprise when a lady, recent from a sick
chamber, is unable to act more than three times
in one week. I continued indeed to think the
profession laborious, until a great actor of our
own times undertook to act Hamlet or Harlequin,
I forget which, possibly both, twice on the same
day, for a week, perhaps weeks together.

The letter of Mr. Brereton had certainly done
no good, it wanted warmth, there was latent bile
about it, a child might discern that the parties
were not upon the same friendly footing as they
had once been. He had formerly made sure of
being carried along with her as the favourite hero
in tragedy; but her brother was now in the
theatre, and the powerful influence of both united
to secure for Mr. Kemble every part which he
could be ambitious to play—Venice might be *preserved*, but Jaffier was lost for ever.

The reader will find yet another letter from
this gentleman; but, like the shades that were
shewn to the *eye* of Macbeth, but which " *grieved
" his heart*," the " second was like the former ;"
and by the way of explanation asserted, in *general*
terms only, what the letter which had *not* been
clearly understood exhibited even in detail.

"TO THE PRINTER OF THE PUBLIC ADVERTISER.
" SIR,

" HAVING been informed that the letter signed
" by me in the several morning papers of yester-
" day, respecting Mrs. Siddons's conduct to me
" while in Ireland, has not been so clearly under-
" stood as it was both the intention on my part,
" and justice to her that it should, I think it ne-
" cessary again to repeat, that it was in no respect
" owing to Mrs. Siddons that I had no benefit in
" Ireland ; but, on the contrary, that in the course
" of a long and dangerous illness I received proofs
" of friendship from her, which I shall ever recol-
" lect with gratitude, and avow now with sincere
" satisfaction.

" W. BRERETON.

" *October* 5, 1784."

I know nothing so severely mortifying in life as
this condition of an actor's profession, that he has
occasionally to meet an audience prepared to re-
vile or insult him, perhaps endanger his very
existence; and that the almost awful respect paid
to his genius at one time is, for something or for
nothing, thrown to the passing winds, and he is
assailed like the vilest of mankind. Something
more liberal, at all events more dignified, might
be looked for from the visitors of a theatre royal ;
but touch any of the passions strongly, and all

are MOB alike. A feeling mind cannot avoid considering the mortification which must have depressed the great mistress of our affections, as
she got into her carriage to proceed to the theatre
on the afternoon of the 5th of October. She
would be reminded, *mutatis mutandis*, of the pathetic remonstrance of Shakspeare's inimitable
Richard the Second, addressed to the *ungentle*
Northumberland :—

> " Must I do so ? and must I ravel out
> My weav'd up follies ? Gentle Northumberland,
> If thy offences were upon record,
> Would it not *shame thee*, in so FAIR A TROOP,
> To read a lecture of them."

Her choice of Mrs. Beverley for the occasion
gave her brother, Mr. Kemble, an opportunity of
leading her before the audience; so that when the
curtain rose, they advanced together. There was
an advantage even in the *simple attire* of Mrs.
Beverley; the robe and the tiara of the heroine
would have seemed braving or farcical before a
people who disdained to govern their roaring
throats, and grumbled everything but pity.

At this time, in the full vigour of youth, I
dined in the neighbourhood, and made a point of
obtaining my favourite position in the pit. I was
too near her to have any other feelings than those
of *respect* for the grave composure and unaffected

dignity of her manner, only yielding at intervals to the grateful acknowledgment of that applause which tried to drown the clamours of her enemies.

Mr. Kemble had long been *studied* in these popular exhibitions, and finding that for the present nothing was likely to be done, he wisely concluded that her *absence* was most likely to decide the house in her favour; and repeating their respects in the usual manner, he led her off the stage, and left her noisy assailants to *consider*. After some interval, the calls for her became less mixed with opposition than before, and she came again on the stage, but *alone;* and deliberately advancing to the very front, with all the self-possession of truth, and the inimitable grace which always attended her, thus addressed the audience.

" Ladies and Gentlemen,
" The kind and flattering partiality which I
" have uniformly experienced in this place, would
" make the present interruption distressing to me
" indeed, were I in the slightest degree conscious
" of having deserved your censure. I feel no such
" consciousness. The stories which have been
" circulated against me are calumnies. When
" they shall be proved to be true, my aspersers
" will be justified: but till then, my respect for

" the public leads me to be confident that I shall
" be protected from unmerited insult."

It was not very usual to hear a *lady* on such
occasions; the delicacy of the sex, while it becomes accustomed to repeat the sentiments of
others, shrinks from the seeming boldness of
publicly uttering their own. But there was a
male dignity in the understanding of Mrs. Siddons, that raised her above the helpless timidity
of other women; and it was certainly without
surprise, and evidently with profound admiration,
that they heard this NOBLE BEING assert her innocence and demand protection.

> " Intestine war no more our passions wage,
> And giddy factions *hear away* their rage."

The extensive view I am taking of the professional course of this great woman offers various
points to my selection, and we can rarely judge
with entire accuracy of the feelings of others;
but if I were to mark the moment, which I
should think she most frequently revolved, as
affording her the greatest *satisfaction*, the fortitude of this night, and its enthusiastic reception
by all who heard and saw it, seem most worthily
to claim so happy a distinction.

But the firmness that sustained her while before the audience, a little failed her when she retired to her dressing-room.. To afford the agitated nerves a short season for composure, Mr. King, the manager, now requested a few minutes indulgence; and the necessity to become somebody else, soon restored her to herself. The attack upon her was quelled by her seasonable resolution, and poor Digges soon completed the evidence of its injustice, as well as cruelty, by making his son write for him, " THAT he had paid " to Mrs. Siddons NO MONEY whatever, and had " written a letter expressing his obligation to " her; that as he understood it had been mislaid, " he with great pleasure repeated his acknow- " ledgments."

The more I reflect upon this affair, the more astonished I am that Brereton, who acted Lewson this very evening in the play, neither came voluntarily forward, nor was called for, to my remembrance, by the audience. If his letter was deemed unsatisfactory, and he knew that what he intended to amend it could not appear till the day following, when he heard a shower of revilings whistling about the head of a lady to whom he was so *proud* to profess his obligations, what so natural, so manly, or so proper, as to step forward with frankness and spirit, and assure the people, from authority that could not be questioned, " that he had never sanctioned, by a murmur, the

" calumny of which he was the subject : that no
" attempts, if such could be made, would ever
" induce him to palter in any declaration called
" for by the public : that Mrs. Siddons had done
" all, and more than he had any right to look for,
" and that this would always be his feeling with
" respect to her?"

For some time after, annoyance constantly attended her coming upon the stage. She used to
acknowledge by a *reverence* the applause by which
it was overborne, and go on steadily with the
character; but it flattened her manner for a few
evenings. Before the subject of provincial benefits is quite dropped, I confess I somewhat doubt
the propriety of an opinion formerly delivered by
me, and think more favourably of the *right* of
leading actors to the aid of such STARS as occupy
the public attention strongly. When such a prodigy for instance as Mrs. Siddons has been acting for twenty nights anywhere, what chance is
there that a profitable house can be obtained
without her? Besides, if such aid be of vital
importance to him who is assisted, it should not
be forgotten that it is *one* source of profit also to
the great actress herself. Some cases will now
and then arise, which properly claim a service
perfectly disinterested. They afford a consolation
which can never be weakened, in whatever circumstances we may be placed.

" One self-approving hour whole years outweighs
Of *stupid* STARERS, and of *loud* HUZZAS."

It was on the 3rd of November that Mrs. Siddons added to her impression the full display of regal majesty, by the performance of Margaret of Anjou, in the tragedy of the Earl of Warwick. This play was an imitation, without acknowledgment, by Dr. Thomas Franklin, of the much admired Comte de Warwick of Laharpe. The French author had the mortification to see the tender interest in his piece fritter'd away, and a figurative invasion upon his style, which he piqued himself upon keeping pure and natural. The metaphoric mode of the English play he ascribes to the English taste—that the figures are sometimes low and trivial, he properly imputes to Franklin himself.

Succeeding Mrs. Yates in the character of the Queen of our Sixth Henry, I should conceive, from the boldness of her style, that Mrs. Siddons still more resembled Dumesnil, the heroine of Laharpe, in 1763—to whom the grateful author paid an elegant tribute, which closed with these four lines :—

" Poursuis ; et regne encor sur la scène ennoblie,
Elle assure a ton nom un éclat éternel.
Il n'est rien de sublime, il n'est rien d'immortel
Que la nature et le Genie."

Mrs. Siddons had unluckily fallen upon an age too cold or weak to pay *her* such a compliment, however great were her exertions.   During the period of my personal observation, the stage has possessed nothing of an *original* or highly poetic character.   At the time I am writing, the same unacknowledged plunder of the French stage is going on, as is stigmatized above in the year 1766.   We are not in the condition of men whose ancestors are unknown—our dramatic forefathers are immortal; but their descendants die either smothered in the birth, or never attaining maturity.

The Earl of Warwick is now remembered only by school boys, for its *long sword* fencing match in the scene between Edward and Warwick, which has often alarmed the visitors of the spouting *seminaries* about town.   This is no bad specimen of that pointed, and, perhaps, gothic taste, which, however condemned as artificial, suits the temper of an English audience.   Smart altercation seems to keep the interest alive, for the tender emotions are all languid when protracted.

It is amusing to hear the young Frenchman, Laharpe, echoing the fierce spirit of the north. Scotland, somewhat elevates the tone of the Gallic muse.

" Et du haut de ses monts, contre un joug qui l'offense,
Lutte et défend encor sa fière indépendance ."

The next choice made for Mrs. Siddons, was also from the French school, the character of Zara, in the play of that name. This was the initiatory part of her tender predecessor, Mrs. Cibber; an actress with whom, if our fathers can be credited, Mrs. Siddons might be compared, at least for the early part of her course. When the enlargement of her figure, and the strength of her features disinclined her to the youthful heroine, she shewed that she could be Pritchard, as well as Cibber, and astonish the minds by her force which she had subdued by her softness.

But the effects produced on the first appearance of Hill's Zara at Drury Lane Theatre, in 1736, could not revive again. Mrs. Siddons performed Zara on two following Wednesdays, and certainly exerted herself greatly; but Voltaire, however deeply he had felt the *passion* of Shakspeare's Othello, was little disposed to borrow any of the bustle of that play; and the modern audiences at least thought Zara cold and declamatory. It may be as well to observe, too, that Milward at first, and Garrick afterwards, had made very powerful effect in the part of Lusignan:—the secret how to do so appears to have expired with them. I once saw Henderson try it, and I suppose as closely as he could bring himself to Garrick—but he was not regal, and barely venerable. He had that *within,* which could not impress his exterior.

On the 2nd of December, Cumberland's tragedy of the Carmelite, in the Lady of St. Vallori, afforded our heroine a new and even a powerful character, but not strongly diversified from some other parts, which she was in the habit of acting, and lining almost exactly with Lady Randolph in Douglas. ·Mrs. Siddons acted with great dignity and pathos, but subjected herself to the wonderful acumen of a critic, who thus expressed himself:—" She exerted herself greatly, but gave no " new specimens of her art. The most interesting " situations of the play are *similar* to those in Isa-" bella and Douglas, where she has already been " seen; and she is too *guarded* and *methodical* in " her manner of performance, to colour the same " subject in different styles."

This I consider to be the highest compliment that malice or folly ever paid, when it meant to decry. Where the same situations recur in the subject, and no discriminations of character are afforded by the author, the styles of performance CANNOT be *different,* when the original manner was drawn from actual nature; because this would be a gross error in philosophy, where the effects should be different, the causes remaining exactly the same. But nothing can be more un-

founded than the remark. The *character*, though
in its leading features, the passion of the scene
and the relations of life, going parallel with others,
is discriminated much by manners, and something
by object. She breeds up Montgomeri to *avenge*
his father—the principle of *chivalry* is strong in
this drama. It has the gloom which seems to
hover over Norman castles—their impenetrable
secrecy, their murky terrors. The Lady of St.
Vallori is also deeply coloured by the piety, or,
as I suppose I must term it, the *superstition* of her
times. You see nothing of this in *Douglas*, though
accurately it should have been there. Authors
often forget the world *before* the Reformation.
One might think they had a descendant of Knox
for the licenser of the north—so utterly divested
is Home's play of every thing *Catholic*.

I, therefore, hazard little in affirming, that so far
was either her *caution* or her *method* from imposing
sameness upon the great genius of the stage, that
the fable, and not the actress, alone recalled the
characters compared with the Lady of St. Vallori.
The catastrophes, however, essentially differ;
and in the Carmelite moral and poetical justice
are the same. The husband returns to *happiness*
—the son does *not* perish—and the hideous Hil-
debrand alone presses the green floor cloth of
dramatic expiation. But happiness and tragedy

seldom will unite, and the great efficacy of the stage is the tear for expiring virtue.

Mr. Kemble, in the early part of his life, was much devoted to the writings of that mild and moral poet, Massinger. The purity of his style, and his peculiar eloquence, seem to have first excited his attention; and for the purposes of the *lecturer*, I know no dramatic author who affords more perfect matter for selection. He considered the *Maid of Honour* to be worthy of the talents of Mrs. Siddons; and but that the interest of the piece was restricted entirely to *calculated* and *balanced* affection, and the most imperious of the passions submitted to the discipline of an affected honour, there is matter demanding such an artist; though to a mixed audience, the whole play may seem brilliant only

"With the moonshine's watery beams."

Camiola is, in the opinion of Dr. Ireland, a character of infinite value. "Everywhere she ani-
"mates us with her spirit, and instructs us with
"her sense. Yet this superiority takes nothing
"from her softer feelings. Her tears flow with a
"mingled fondness and regret; and she is swayed
"by a passion which is only quelled by her
"greater resolution."

The grossness of the author's age has tainted her reproof to Fulgentio with a little too much *muscular* preference in the person of a lover. I dare only touch upon the lighter requisites, of complexion, and so on.

> " Give me the lovely brown,
> A thick curl'd hair of the same die, broad shoulders,
> A brawny arm full of veins, a leg without
> An *artificial* calf."

She is sometimes coarse even to a proverb.

> " Rich you are,
> Devilish rich, as 'tis reported, and sure have
> The aids of Satan's little fiends to get it;
> And what is got upon his *back*, must be
> Spent you *know where ;*—the proverb's stale."

But Kemble knew well what to do with stuff like this. And the inimitable actress knew equally well how to improve and sharpen points of a finer temper. In the 4th scene in the 4th act, there were some transcendent touches of this kind. To the king, upon an unworthy accusation which had escaped him—

> " *Cam.*—With your leave, I must not *kneel*, Sir,
> When I reply to this; but thus *rise up*
> In my defence, tell you, as a man," &c.

Again at a short distance, where the thoughts approach the magnificence of Shakspeare himself.

> " But, be no more a king,
> Unless you do me right.   Burn your decrees,
> And of your laws and statutes make a fire,
> To thaw the frozen numbness of delinquents,
> If HE escape unpunish'd."

But how preserve the noble grace with which she turned upon the Duchess, her rival, who insulted her with " self-comparison ?"

> " *Aurel.*—Yes ; the OBJECT,
> Look on it better, lady, may *excuse*
> The change of his affection.
>   " *Cam.*—The object!
> IN WHAT ?—forgive me, *modesty,* if I say
> You look upon your form in the false glass
> Of flattery and self-love, and that deceives you."*

But she is too unhappy to sustain this important tone, and the following check was delivered with a *truth* that thrilled to the very soul.

---

* A young writer should be made to observe the beauty of the expression " forgive me, *modesty,*" where it occurs.   It was so at hand *to* use the term of cold respect, *Madam,* when addressing Aurelia.   She has, however, then a *higher* appeal.   The reverse of sentiment brings it out lower down, with a quiet sinking of the spirits—" No, *Madam,* I recant."

" *Cam.*—Down, proud heart !
Why do I rise up in defence of that,
Which in my cherishing of it hath undone me ?
No, Madam, I recant—you are all beauty,
Goodness, and virtue ; and poor I not worthy
As a foil to set you off.
But though to all men else I did appear
The shame and scorn of women, HE stands bound
To hold me as the masterpiece."

I must, however, bid farewell to the Maid of Honour, who certainly never had a more fascinating representative. I allow myself but one more literary illustration, excited by the following remark of Dr. Ireland. " If the reader will com- " pare the speech of Paulo with the *Penseroso,* " he cannot fail to remark a similarity in the " cadences, as well as in the measure, and the " solemnity of the thoughts." Nothing can be more ingenious than this observation. It is, however, much strengthened by finding the expression, which in Milton's Comus startled some of his commentators—" She fables not"—in this very play of the Maid of Honour, which appeared in print in 1632, and so preceded, by two years, the Mask at Ludlow castle.

" *Camiola.*—I fable not."—Act 2. Scene 2.

CHAPTER XV.

IT has been said that, since the Eumenides of
Eschylus, tragic poetry had produced nothing so

terrible and sublime as the Macbeth of Shakspeare. It may be said, with equal probability,
that, since the happy invention of man invested
dramatic fiction with seeming reality, nothing
superior, perhaps equal, to the Lady Macbeth of
Mrs. Siddons has been seen.

She had experienced much of the illiberality of
criticism, to which it seems not to have suited her
temper or taste through life to pay any court.
The distributors of daily and monthly fame had
not scrupled to assert, that the sagacious actress,
conscious of the limits of her powers, had wisely
avoided the boundless demands of Shakspeare,
and devoted herself to the tender effusions of inferior spirits. That a melodious flow of declamation was a happiness but of the ear; a majestic person and an expressive as well as beautiful
countenance, accidental advantages of nature;
BUT that the burst of passion, the bold inspiration
of positive genius superior to all precedent, and
trammel and tuition, of *these* gifts she had positively NOTHING, and was of a temperament too
cold and systematic ever to suspect even the
want of them.

To use the language of the late Dr. Parr, when
speaking of Warburton, on the 2nd of February,
1785,—" from her towering and distant heights
" she rushed down upon her prey, and disdaining
" the ostentatious prodigalities of cruelty, de-

"stroyed it at a blow." She acted Lady Macbeth on that night, and criticism, and envy, and rivalry sunk at once before her. The subject was as fortunate to her as to the GREAT POET himself, and from that hour her dominion over the passions was undisputed, her genius pronounced to be at least equal to her art, and Sir Joshua's happy thought of identifying her person with the muse of tragedy confirmed by the immutable decree of the public.

The reader or spectator of Shakspeare's *Macbeth* is not inquisitive as to his real history, and would not be a little surprised were it laid before him. The gracious Duncan, too, besieging Durham without success, is said, soon after his return, to have been slain by his *people*, thus closing a rather inglorious reign of only six years. The death, on which his *immortality* was built, is assigned by the celebrated Chronicon Elegiacum.

But astonishment will succeed surprise, for the reader is next to learn that the epithet, *gracious*, is quite as applicable to Macbeth himself as to Duncan; and the *historic doubts* as to Richard the Third may be revived, on perhaps surer ground, in relation to the actual qualities of the usurper of Scotland. "He seems," says a learned inquirer, "to have been an able and beneficent "prince. The *Chron. Eleg.* represents fertile "seasons as attendants of his reign, which Win-

" ton confirms. If a king makes fertile seasons,
" it must be by promoting agriculture, and diffus·
" ing among his people the blessings of peace.
" Had he paid more attention to his *own* interests,
" and less to those of his subjects, the crown
" might have remained in his family. But ne-
" glecting the *practice* of *war*, he fell a martyr to
" his OWN VIRTUES."*

But, if he was really guilty of the murder of
Duncan, he took at least the usual road of expiation; for he certainly made a pilgrimage to Rome
in the papacy of Leo the Ninth.

> " All his tyme was gret plenté,
> Habundande bathe on lande and se :
> He was in justice richt lauchful,
> And til his legis al awfulle.
> Quhen Pape was Leo the Nynt in Rome,
> As pilgryme to the court he come;
> And in his alms he sew silver
> Til al pur folk, that had myster.
> In al time oysit he to wyrk
> *Profetabilly* for HALY KIRK."
> WINTON, VI. 29.

It was to gratify Malcolm III. and his descendants that he was represented, like Caliban, to
be the son of a devil, and connected with witches.
Happily for us, Shakspeare, as to these often
compared tyrants, Richard and Macbeth, was

* See Mr. Pinkerton's Enquiry, Vol. 2, p. 197.

acquainted only with the histories written under the patronage of their enemies. Macbeth was supplanted at last by a foreign force, and reigned in great tranquillity seventeen years.

Particulars so curious, and so little known, I would not suppress. They suggest to my mind one important reflection. In the play of Macbeth, the hurry which *presses on* the events of his life, from his coronation to his death, allows the poet little time to dilate upon the particular disposition of such a man; yet I cannot but think that had he known of this pious excursion, he would have made fine use of it in the gloomy reveries of Macbeth; have shewn him struggling between the efficacy of religious ceremony and magical illusion, and that it would have supplied some dreadful images to the perturbed slumbers of his more fiend-like wife.

The first scene of Lady Macbeth is decisive of the whole character. She lets out in a few lines the daring steadiness of her mind, which could be disturbed by no scruple, intimidated by no danger. The occasion does not change the *nature* here, as it does in her husband. There is no struggle after any virtue to be resigned. She is as thoroughly prepared in one moment, as if visions of greatness had long informed her slumbers; and she had awaked to meditate upon every means, however dreadful, that could secure her object.

When Mrs. Siddons came on with the letter from Macbeth (the first time we saw her,) such was the impression from her form, her face, her deportment—the distinction of sex was only external—" her spirits" informed their tenement with the apathy of a demon. The commencement of this letter is left to the reader's imagination. "They met me in the day of success," shews that he had previously mentioned the witches. Her first novelty was a little suspension of the voice, " they made themselves—*air :*" that is, less astonished at it as a miracle of nature, than attentive to it as a manifestation of the reliance to be built upon their assurances. She read the whole letter with the greatest skill, and, after an instant of reflection, exclaimed—

> " Glamis thou art, and Cawdor—and SHALT BE
> What thou art *promised*."

The amazing burst of energy upon the words *shalt be*, perfectly electrified the house. The determination seemed as uncontrollable as *fate* itself. The searching analysis of Macbeth, which she makes, was full of meaning—the eye and the hand confirmed the logic. Ambition is the soul of her very phrase :—

> " Thou'dst have, *great* Glamis."

Great Glamis! this of her *husband!* metaphysical speculation, calculated estimate—as if it had re-garded Cæsar or Pompey. He is among the means before me—how is such a nature to be worked up to such *unholy* objects?

" Hie thee hither," says the impatience, which longs to begin its strife with the antagonist virtue —" Hie thee hither,

> " That I may pour MY spirits in thine *ear*,
> And chastise with the *valour* of my tongue," &c.

But a different style of beauty was called forth by the hasty entrance of a servant, to announce the coming of the King that night into the very meshes she is about to spread for his destruction. Shakspeare alone, perhaps, would have written the daring compromise of all decorum, which bursts from the exulting savage upon this intelligence :—

> "Thou'rt MAD to say it."

Aware of the inference to be drawn from an earnestness so marked, he immediately cloaks the passion with a *reason* why the intelligence could not seem true. The actress, fully understanding the process, after the violence of the exclamation, recovered herself with slight alarm, and in a *lowered* tone proposed a question suited to the new feeling :—

> " Is not thy master *with* him ? who, wer't so,
> Would have inform'd for preparation."

The murmured mysteriousness of the address to the spirits " that tend on mortal thoughts," became stronger as she proceeded :—

> " Come to my WOMAN'S BREASTS,
> And take my *milk* for GALL, you murd'ring ministers."

A beautiful thought, be it observed ; as if these sources of infant nourishment could not even *consent* to mature destruction, without some loathsome change in the very stream itself which flowed from them.

When the actress, invoking the destroying ministers, came to the passage—

> " Wherever in your sightless substances
> You wait on nature's mischief,"

the elevation of her *brows*, the full *orbs* of sight, the raised shoulders, and the hollowed hands, seemed all to endeavour to explore what yet were pronounced no possible objects of vision. Till then, I am quite sure, a figure so terrible had never bent over the pit of a theatre ; that night crowded with intelligence and beauty, in its seven front rows.

The salutation of Macbeth—the remark upon the abstraction on his countenance, which follows

her brief intimation of all that is to be done—
all claimed notice.

> " O never
> Shall sun *that* morrow see."

Macbeth himself (Smith) sunk under her at
once, and she quitted the scene with an effect
which cannot be described ; in short, the TRIUMPH
of NATURE, rightly interpreted by the greatest
writer and greatest actress that had ever laboured
for the delight and instruction of mankind.

The following scene is the beautiful reception
of Duncan at Inverness. The honoured hostess
received his Majesty with all the exterior of profound obligation. She was too *pure* an actress to
allow a glance of triumph to stray towards the
spectators.

Macbeth, conscious of his design, is even ne-
glectful of his duty as a host; he is absent from
the royal banquet, and his absence provokes inquiry. His lady, bending steadily to her purpose, is equal to all occasions, and now breaks in
upon her husband's fearful rumination. He had
determined to proceed no farther in the business,
and she has again to revive the unholy flame
which gratitude had quenched. She assails him
with sophistry, and contempt, and female resolution, seemingly superior to all manly daring. She
quotes his own bolder against his present *self*,

and urges the infamy of receding from so proud a design. Filled from the crown to the toe with direst cruelty, the horror of the following sentence seemed bearable from its fitness to such a being. But I yet wonder at the *energy* of both utterance and action with which it was accompanied :—

> " I would, while it was smiling in my face,
> Have pluck'd my nipple from his boneless gums,
> And *dash'd the brains out,* had *I so sworn* as you
> Have done to this."

There was no *qualifying* with our humanity in the tone or gesture. This really beautiful and interesting actress did not at all shrink from standing before us the true and perfect image of the greatest of all natural and moral depravations —a *fiend-like woman.*

The scene after the murder exhibits Lady Macbeth as bold in *action* as she had, during speculation, asserted herself to be. " Give ME the " daggers," excited a general start from those around me. Upon her return from the chamber of slaughter, after gilding the faces of the grooms, from the peculiar character of her lip she gave an expression of *contempt* more striking than any she had hitherto displayed.

From the third scene of the second act Lady Macbeth has long been banished ; so that we had

no opportunity of seeing how the highly-wrought
agonies of Macbeth would have stood contrasted
by the delicate affectation of his wife.   But the
natural exclamation of Macduff—

> " O Banquo ! Banquo !
> Our royal master's murder'd,"

excites one from Lady Macbeth, which I should
like, I confess, to have heard from Mrs. Siddons :—

> " Woe, alas ! what ! in OUR house ?"

" This," says Warburton, " is very fine.   Had
" she been innocent, nothing but the murder it-
" self, and not any of its aggravating circum-
" stances, would naturally have affected her.   As
" it was, her business was to appear highly dis-
" ordered at the news.   Therefore, like one who
" has her thoughts about her, she seeks for an
" aggravating circumstance that might be sup-
" posed most to affect her personally ; not con-
" sidering that by placing it there, she discovered
" rather a concern for herself than for the King.
" On the contrary, her husband, who had repented
" the act, and was now labouring under the hor-
" rors of a recent murder, in his exclamation, gives
" all the marks of sorrow for the fact itself."
The introduction of Lady Macbeth in this scene,

must depend entirely upon the *credit* which the actress has with the audience. Coarse hypocrisy excites derision. Garrick would not trust Mrs. Pritchard with either the *astonishment* or the seeming *swoon*. Macklin thought Mrs. Porter alone could have been endured by the audience. I feel equally confident with regard to Mrs. Siddons. There Lady Macbeth ought most assuredly to be. She is the last of human beings to have absented herself on such an occasion as a night alarm, because her absence could not *fairly* be accounted for in the first place, and in the second, she had fully prepared her mind to act what she thought the occasion demanded. The upper gallery should never be the guide, where a manager is himself worthy of Shakspeare. What *he* shews may always be shewn; the temperaments of *person* and *manner* are all that the manager is to take care of. Liston, in the *Fool*, certainly could not be trusted by the side of King Lear, but Farren might. The *dryness* of the one actor would add to the effect of Lear's madness; the irresistible countenance of the other would confound all sensibility in immoderate laughter.

By the second scene of the third act, we find that the possession of his object had rendered Macbeth moody and solitary. Their attention, while apart, seems to have been directed to the same object; for his Queen, on her entrance, immediately inquires whether Banquo be *gone from court?* She is ready to suggest the murder of that nobleman and his son. "In them nature's "copy's not eterne." But she soon learns the mistake of the adage "nemo *repente* fuit turpis- "simus." The first crime in Macbeth hath the *greatest* extent. He has no prelude of insect de- struction, like Domitian. For his own good "all "causes" must give way. He would not leave a virtue alive. She recommends him to be *bright* and *jovial* among his guests that night at the ban- quet. To which scene we hasten, to look at the manner of our great actress. "Mrs. Pritchard," says Davies, "shewed consummate art in endea- "vouring to hide Macbeth's frenzy from the ob- "servation of his guests, by drawing their atten- "tion to conviviality. She smiled on one, whis- "pered to another, and distantly saluted a third; "in short, she practised every possible artifice to "hide the transaction that passed between her "husband and the vision his disturbed imagina- "tion had raised. Her reproving and angry looks, "which glanced towards Macbeth, at the same "time were mixed with marks of inward vexa- "tion and uneasiness."

I should think Mr. Davies, from his minuteness of observation, must have figured there as one of the nobles, only a few covers from the royal state. But the truth is, a great deal of this is impossible—there has been *no time* for it—the lords *observe* as soon as anything occurs to excite attention, as the text shews us.

> " *Macb.*—The table's full.
> *Len.*—Here is a place reserv'd, Sir.
> *Macb.*—Where?
> *Len.*—Here, my good lord. What is't that moves your highness?
> *Macb.*—Which of you have done this?
> *Lords*—What, my good lord!"

On Rosse's calling upon them to *rise*, his highness not being well, Lady Macbeth desires them to keep their seats—explains his malady, which notice only augments; begs them to feed, and regard him not; and *then* coming down to Macbeth, endeavours to *baffle* his terrors. Davies closes the eulogium thus: " When, *at last*, as if " unable to support her feelings any longer, she " rose from her seat, and with a half-whisper of " terror, said ' are you a man?' she assumed a " look of anger, indignation, and contempt, not to " be surpassed."

This is very far from being clearly put; a half-whisper of *terror*, attended by a look of *anger*, *indignation*, and *contempt*, is a rather singular mode of encouraging *dismay*. The whisper is for concealment of what is said from others; but the words whispered are a reproach, and something *more*, incompatible with TERROR. She is so much mistress of herself, as even to assail him with ridicule. His conviction is " *proper stuff,*" the " painting of fear"—the " air-drawn dagger," " which, he *said*, led him to Duncan"—Such *flaws* and *starts*, as became only a story told by a *woman* at a *winter's fire*, under the wise authority of a *grandam*. " When *all's done*, he look'd but " on a stool." But so it is, without perfect re-collection of the scenes, praise is drawn from the imagination rather than the fact, and much is imputed which was never done by the actress; and if it had been done, would have merited no commendation.

The greater beauties of Mrs. Siddons's manner were to be found, I think, in the—

> " Think of this, good peers,
> But as a thing of CUSTOM : *'tis no other;*
> Only it spoils the *pleasure* of the time."

And the rapidly cutting down the question from Rosse—" What sights, my lord ?"

> " *Lady M.—I pray you speak not;* he grows *worse* and *worse;*
> Question enrages him : *at once* good night:
> Stand not upon the *order* of your going,
> But go at *once.*"

The address displayed here drew down a thunder of applause.

The task of Lady Macbeth is here finished; as

when the force of volition a withdrawn

the great tempter she has done her office, and her husband must now defend by military skill and bravery, the crown which his crimes have acquired and hazarded. But Shakspeare has one more terrible lesson to give; namely, to shew that, when the force of volition is withdrawn, the fancy becomes a dreadful victim to the images of past guilt: and she who waking can dispel her husband's terrors and her own, in sleep beholds her bleeding victims for ever present, and the circumstances of their fate passing continually in their original order.*

In the performance of this scene, Mrs. Siddons differed essentially from every other actress. I will explain myself. The actresses previous to herself seemed to consider such a perturbation as not possessing *full* power upon the frame; they, therefore, rather *glided* than walked; and every

---

* SCHLEGEL just touches upon this scene, with a high compliment to the poet.—" Shakspeare est peut-être le seul poëte, qui " caracterise les maladies de l'ame, la melancholie, la folie, le *som-* " *nambulisme,* avec une parfaite verité ; elle est telle, qu'un medicin " pourroit s'instruire a cette ecole."

Cours de Literat. Dram. vol. 2. p. 379.

I prefer the French translation for two reasons ; because it is that by which alone the author *consents* to be judged ; and that there is a hardness in the English translation, and, from keeping too literally to the German arrangement, an obscurity as to the meaning, which is never observable in its Gallic rival.

other action had a *feebler* character than is exhibited by one awake. Their figure, too, was kept
perpendicularly *erect*, and the eye, though open,
studiously avoided motion.

But the theory of somnambulism is somewhat
at variance with the *stage* exhibition; and if the
doctor of physic, who attends upon Lady Macbeth, had been very profound in his art, he would
have considered the *eyes being open* as the most
extraordinary part of the scene before him.   The
cases quoted in our books all state the sleep-
walker to have his eyes *closed*.   It is only when
any object of his fancy has been removed from its
expected place, that the eyes are feebly unclosed,
as if to find the position of it, and are immediately
shut, to leave the fancy to controul entirely its
own operations. It has been observed that the iris
on such occasions appears fixed, and the eye *dim*.

Mrs. Siddons seemed to conceive the fancy as
having equal power over the whole frame, and all
her actions had the wakeful vigour; she laded the
water from the imaginary ewer over her hands —
bent her body to listen to the sounds presented
by her fancy, and hurried to resume the taper
where she had left it, that she might with all
speed drag her pallid husband to their chamber.
The excellent Dugald Stewart, thinks that " in
" the *somnambuli*, the mind retains its power
" over the limbs, but possesses scarcely any over

" the body, excepting those particular members
" of it which are employed in walking."* A
larger reign must be allowed to the fancy, however, if the actions of gathering and eating grapes,
or climbing trees, or composing exercises for the
school, can be performed, " yet all this while in a
" most fast sleep."

Although the general effect of Mrs. Siddons
was what I have stated, one idle cavil crept out
against her manner in this noble scene. People
cant about originality, and yet dote upon precedent. " When she sets down the candle, who
" does not perceive she varies from her predeces-
" sors, only that her hands may be more at liberty
" to imitate the process of ablution." That her
hands are more at liberty, for *all* purposes, by
setting down the light, will be readily conceded;
but here the waking process must be followed,
and who, bearing a taper from one apartment to
another, does not set it upon a table when the
room contains one? Who about to wash the
hands retains any thing in them? The critic was
too purblind to perceive that the real trick was in
retaining the light to shew unconsciousness of
what the sleeper was doing—whereas all the
habits of life are by the somnambulist done me-
chanically.

* Elem. of the Philos. of Mind, p. 347. ed. 1802.

The quantity of white drapery in which the actress was enveloped, had a singular and striking effect—her person, more truly than that of Pierre, might be said to be " lovelily dreadful," but extremely majestic both in form and motion —it was, however, the majesty of the *tomb ;* or as Shakspeare, in a previous scene, expresses it :—

" As from your GRAVES rise up, and walk *like sprites,*
To countenance this horror."

Perhaps her friend, Sir Joshua Reynolds, might have suggested the almost *shroud-like* clothing of this important scene. I saw him on this occasion in the orchestra, with great pleasure, sitting " all " gaze, all wonder." She was in truth so strongly articulate, that I have no doubt he heard every syllable that *breath* made up, for she hardly allowed the voice any portion of its power.

There is a mezzotinto print in existence of Garrick and Mrs. Pritchard in the scene after the murder of Duncan. The ridiculous (not because inaccurate, but) because unpicturesque costume of Garrick does all that dress can do to defeat the startling terrors of his countenance; but the Queen is a kind of angry Hecate, rather than Lady Macbeth, and, however terrible was much lower in the scale of being than her sublime successor. It is difficult to imagine how such a consummate

artist as Garrick could play Gloucester, Richard
the Third, who lived in the year 1480, in what is
called a shape, and yet act Macbeth, who I think
murdered Duncan 440 years earlier, in a general's
uniform of the reign of George the Second. However the fact is unquestionable, and he so acted it
all his life.

I will not, at this distance from the performance, endeavour to describe the Macbeth of
Smith. In its outline, I suppose him to have
given what he remembered of Garrick;—he
walked the character; but, though much in
earnest, he never *looked* it. The perpetual strain
upon his features reminds me of an absurd reading in this very part; and the multitudinous
passions, in his expression of them, at the wafting
of his *hand*, became *incarnardine*, or as Murphy
would say—ONE RED. How so sensible a man,
as Smith certainly was, could endure the heavy
monotony of his tragic utterance, with all the
variety of nature by his side, would surprise, if
any self-delusion could surprise one acquainted
with human nature. A great actor, who spoke in
a key much higher than any performer existing
who speaks at all, told me once seriously, that his
voice was a *deep bass*.

With one comprehensive remark of the learned
German author whom I have already quoted, I
shall close all that Macbeth has suggested to me.

" Rien n'est comparable à la puissance de ce
" tableau pour exciter la terreur. On frissone
" en se rappelant le meurtre de Duncan, le simu-
" lacre de poignard qui voltige devant les yeux
" de Macbeth, l'apparition de Banco pendant le
" repas, l'arrivée nocturne de Lady Macbeth
" endormie. De pareilles scenes sont uniques.
" Shakspeare seul en a pu concevoir l'idée, et si
" elles se presentoient plus souvant sur la scene,
" il faudroit mettre la tête de Meduse au nombre
" des attributs de la muse tragique."

 " In the excitement to TERROR, this picture
" cannot be equalled. We shudder in recalling
" the murder of Duncan—the air-drawn dagger,
" which waves before the eyes of Macbeth—the
" appearance of Banquo at the feast the night
" progress of the sleeping Queen. Such scenes
" stand alone. Shakspeare only can imagine
" such things, and were they oftener presented
" on the stage, we must place the head of Me-
" dusa among the attributes of the tragic muse."

 Their Majesties, in conformity with the gracious
design of seeing every performance of Mrs. Siddons, commanded a repetition of Macbeth, on the
7th of the same month. Tragedy, perhaps, suffers,
as much as comedy gains, by the proximity of
royal personages. In sitting to a tragedy, they
weaken the effect by necessarily dividing the
attention of the spectators ; their silent admira-

tion inspires nothing to others ;—but, in comedy, the royal enjoyment gives a fashion to laughter; the actor does not spare his efforts in the presence of royal patrons, and I believe the late King has led some of the loudest applause that was ever heard in a theatre.

The audiences of this period were sufficiently decorous to be trusted with a scenic display of regal assassination. His Majesty's government reposed upon the revenue improvement of the GREAT MINISTER—and nothing stirred in town but the Westminster scrutiny, which in eight months absolutely struck off 105 bad votes from the poll of Mr. Fox, and 87 from that of Sir Cecil Wray. This gave a reasonable prospect, that the whole of the votes might be examined thoroughly, and decided fairly, in the *short* compass of TWO YEARS, the gentlemen of the bar receiving no unusual portion of subtlety, or its synonime, *fees.* Some little feeling for the unrepresented condition of Westminster warmed our galleries, even in the *theatre,* at this time—but a speech of Mr. Dundas, in the House of Commons, covering Mr. Pitt from a personal attack by Mr. Fox, alone merited the notice of all times.

The character of Lady Macbeth became a sort of exclusive possession to Mrs. Siddons. There was a mystery about it, which she alone seemed to have penetrated. Future, and not distant times

might supply a better Macbeth. The ingenuity of
decoration might add greater truth and reality to
the scene, and the chorusses might be rendered yet
more overpowering by singers, more exact, and a
band more numerous. All this we shall see done.
Did it shake at all the supremacy of this great
performance? By no means. Looking the other
way, did it increase the grandeur, or the terror of
her first exhibition? Not in the least. With all
great efforts of genius, it seemed disdainful alike
of help or hindrance—and every audience appeared to wonder why the tragedy proceeded further, when at the final exit of the Lady Macbeth
its very *soul* was extracted.

The policy of abstaining so long from the performance of such a character, was now apparent—for by what other poetic *wonder* could
it be followed? All other force in female character is comparative feebleness, on the English
stage. The Greek drama affords us one character,
which had Shakspeare studied it in the three great
tragedians of that people, and then, preserving
Greek manners as ably as he did Roman, written
it from his own heart and mind, might have been
worthy to succeed the greatest achievement of the
stage. The character I mean is Electra, the
daughter of Agamemnon, the sister of Orestes.

By what even Voltaire has effected, the dreadful
energies of Shakspeare may be half conceived. In

the fourth scene of the fourth act of *Oreste*, he
has something of Shakspearean vigour. The reader
will not be sorry to compare on this occasion the
dextrous Frenchman with the master-spirit of the
drama.

> " *Iphise.*—Ne vous preparez pas un nouveau repentir.
>
> [*Elle sort.*]
>
> *Electre.*—Un repentir ! qui ? Moi ! mes mains desespérées
> Dans ce grand abandon seront plus assurées.
> EUMENIDES, venez soyez ici mes dieux ;
> Vous connaissez trop bien ces détestables lieux,
> Filles de la vengeance, armez vous, armez moi,
> Venez avec la mort, qui marche avec l'effroi ;
> Que vos fers, vos flambeaux, vos glaives étincellent;
> Oreste, Agamemnon, Electre vous appellent :
> LES VOICI, je les vois, et les vois sans terreur ;
> L'aspect de mes tyrans m'inspirait plus d'horreur.
> Ah ! le barbare approche ; il vient; ses pas impies
> Sont a mes yeux vengeurs entourés des furies,
> L'enfer me le désigne, et le livre à mon bras."

I see here, however different the subject,
abundant proof to the critic of poetic feeling,
(and what is the critic without it?) that Voltaire
caught this from the dreadful invocation of Lady
Macbeth.

> " Come, you spirits
> That tend on mortal thoughts, unsex me here,
> And fill me from the crown to the toe top-full
> Of direst cruelty : make thick my blood,

Stop up th' access and passage to remorse,
That no compunctious visitings of nature
Shake my fell purpose, nor keep peace between
Th' effect and it.   Come to my woman's breasts,
And take my milk for gall, you murth'ring ministers,
Wherever in your sightless substances
You wait on nature's mischief.   Come, thick night,
And pall thee in the dunnest smoke of hell,
That my keen knife see not the wound it makes."

When I express this opinion, I am fully aware of two addresses of the *chorus* to the Eumenides, in the Choephoræ of Eschylus, and the Electra of Sophocles; of which the first is by many degrees the most sublime.

The next character acted by Mrs. Siddons, was one intended to serve her brother rather than herself. I allude to her performance of Desdemona in Othello, on the 8th of March, 1785. Mr. Kemble acting the noble Moor for the first time in town. The outrageous gallantry of French manners, had not, in the time of Shakspeare, rendered the sex more prominent in the drama than it was in real life—affectionate, modest, retiring, firm only to endure and suffer, the females of Shakspeare occupy but little space comparatively with his men. But a great critic, like Warton, might have been expected to discern the superior *delicacy* with which our great poet has invested what I even now consider to be the *loveliest* portraits of the lovely sex.

Imogen, and Juliet, and Desdemona, and Viola, and the sweet and inexperienced Miranda, are all sisters in the firm allegiance of their affections to the favoured object. But there is not one particle of the vulgar trumpery of stage heroism about them.

Brabantio, the father of Desdemona, is clearly no philosopher. He argues very perversely from his daughter's qualities. Hear him describe her.

> " A maiden never bold;
> Of spirit so still and quiet, that her motion
> Blush'd at herself."

Surely such a spirit might of all spirits be expected to devour in silence the narrative of an exalted courage—to love him for the dangers he had passed, and think a noble nature superior to all accidents of " clime, complexion, and degree." The Doge, or Duke, as he is called, seems to be worthy of his elevation—he has a learned spirit of human dealing, and is so far from thinking Othello a practiser of arts inhibited, and out of warrant, that having heard his story with the ears of gravity and age, he exclaims, with goodness equal to his sagacity—

> " I think this tale would win *my* daughter too."

When I say that such a part was little calculated to serve Mrs. Siddons, I look to the gross
estimate of the vulgar. Yet one advantage it
possessed even with *them*, it was in the fullest
contrast with the character in which she last appeared. It called upon them to observe, whether
the same great powers of art were not as faithful
expositors of all the gentle, and I will say native
properties of the sex, as of those fierce and unnatural perversions, the growth of immeasurable
ambition?

The exhibition afforded a strong proof of the
plastic power of the mind. Its operation here
absolutely seemed to *lower* the figure of the lovely
being, which had been so towering in Euphrasia,
or terrific in Lady Macbeth.

There is one thing about a character, written
by Shakspeare in his full force, greatly in
favour of its impression, I mean those stories of
gorgeous phrases, which really enrich the mouth
from which they proceed. If an actress have or
soul or sense, a tongue capable of music, or a
form susceptible of grace, what may she not effect
with passages like the following address of Desdemona to her father?

" You are the LORD OF DUTY,
I am *hitherto* your daughter."

I may observe incidentally, in support of the *legal* employment of our great poet's youth, the close of the present speech, so inimitably given by Mrs. Siddons.

> " And so much duty as my mother shew'd
> To you, preferring you before her father,
> So much ' *I challenge*' that I may profess
> Due to the Moor, my Lord."

Queen Katharine, in our author's Henry VIII. uses the same term in regard to Wolsey,

> " And make my *challenge*."

I was greatly delighted with the generous *warmth* that animated the supplication of Desdesmona to go with Othello to the wars.

> " My heart's subdu'd
> Even to the very *quality* of my lord."

Mr. WHITER might have found *here* a support to his ingenious *theory*, if it wanted one—for Desdemona touching the *military* quality of her lord, uses a metaphor drawn from his profession—

> " My downright violence and *storm* of fortunes
> May *trumpet* to the world."

I agree with that pleasing and learned writer,

that this consonance of the figure might drop *unconsciously* from the poet. Such is the sure though unfelt operation of the associating principle in our *ideas*.

The elegant deportment, cordial manners, and smothered anxiety, on the landing at Cyprus, previous to the arrival of Othello, exhibited a Desdemona, which would have enchanted Shakspeare himself, who could so beautifully *conceive* what his *own* stage most assuredly never displayed.

Through the jealous scenes of this play, I shall excuse myself from passing, by merely remarking that wherever they shew the fair victim on the stage, the skill of our perfect actress produced the most intense sympathy. She was then acting on a stage, where if her eye had ever magical power, it then displayed it. How much I regretted the barbarous mutilation of the exquisitely natural scene, which passes between her and Emilia, the third of the fourth act. The rage of the English for *action*, in its wild impatience throws away a thousand delicate and essential touches of character, which as they increase our love for the person augment our sympathy with her fate. The critic can only beg, that the play may be read in the volumes of Shakspeare, and the innocent, but melancholy effusion of Desdemona, noted among the felicities of the poet of nature. I have revisited the stage copy of this play, where it had shrunk from sight in my library—but where, curtailing fiends, is the fore-boding direction to Emilia, as to certain *sheets?*

> " If I do die before thee, prythee, shroud me
> In one of those same sheets."

The recollection of her mother's maid, poor Barbara? The song of *Willow*—

> " An old thing 'twas, but it express'd her fortune,
> And she died singing it; that song, to-night,
> Will not go from my mind," &c.

The wandering away from Barbara, to notice delicately the " proper person" of Lodovico. The return to the " silly sooth" of the willow, and as quite unavoidable, *singing* in dirge-like strains immediately before her death. The interruption to the strain—" Hark! who is it that knocks?"

> " *Emil.*—It is the wind."

Her question as to the possibility of being *false* to wedlock.—No hint of one of these things to be found in a copy of Shakspeare's Othello, as acted at a theatre royal in an age called *enlightened*, is an argument for the transfer of such an epithet

to the glorious period when such writing was felt
to be natural and interesting, and therefore suited
to the stage of our plain but intelligent ancestors.

On the last day of the month, Mr. Kemble was
permitted to play Macbeth for his own benefit.
We had now, therefore, a Glamis who could re-
spond to the alarming incentives of the lady;
and an early indication of the effect of such
intelligence was the manner of his saying at their
meeting, in reference to the going of Duncan—

" To-morrow—as he *purposes*."

Kemble appeared to shrink from the quick glance
which his sister turned upon him.—Though his
hopes had depraved his imagination, he seemed
unprepared then for the maxim " *be it thought and*
" *done*," implied in her instant determination—

" O never shall sun *that* morrow see."

Her acting throughout, on this occasion, was
of the very highest quality. And here let me
state, without undertaking absolutely to account
for it, a fact peculiar, as far as I know, to Mrs.
Siddons—I mean the very slight inequality in
her numerous performances of the same character. In her brother's acting it might be truly
observed, that very frequently he was utterly
below himself. He was cold and formal, paraded

his person and his dress, and would walk the cha
racter about, as if teaching how it should move
through the business, and logically pronounce its
sentiments. In his sister I never saw any thing
like this : it must have happened to her, as to
every other being engaged in the concerns of life,
to feel depressed by care, or absent by the rumination over probable occurrences. But on the
stage, I never felt the least indication that she
had a private existence, or could be any thing but
the assumed character. An argument, I should
think, of a very powerful imagination.

A friend of mine, to whom upon most occasions
I should gladly defer, thinks that " she was so
" various in her art, as hardly to act the same
" character *twice alike.*" I am much more inclined
to say—She was so profound in her art, that her
judgment settled *once* and *for ever* all the great
points of the character—and not changing her
view of *what* she had to convey, there was little
difference to be detected, that did not arise from
noise, among what should have been audience,
or the occasional assaults of personal indisposition. Indeed, how should the conception
remain, and the execution differ? or what is the
judgment which is in frequent mutation? FIRM-
NESS of thought is the parent of all vigorous
action and utterance.

The delicacy of Mason's Elfrida, as it had been

much admired in the closet at Buckingham
House, begot very naturally a wish to see the
great *Preceptress* represent the heroine of that
drama, upon the stage; and on the 14th of
April she acted it for the first time, by command
of their Majesties.   The *interest* of this piece is in
the resentment of a ROYAL lover, for being by a
favoured servant deceived as to the personal
graces of Elfrida, whom he makes his *own* wife,
instead of opening a way to the throne for the
ambition of her family.   The King, by a sudden,
visit, ascertains the falsehood of Athelwold in the
beauties of Elfrida; and, affecting the *generous*,
forgives the treachery of his subject, but demands
satisfaction from his rival as man to man.   In
other words securely assassinates him :—for, if
the acknowledged guilt of Athelwold " did not
" sink him,"—how was he to bend his sword
against his great master, without feeling himself
a traitor?—he, therefore, permits his Majesty's
weapon to find a ready sheath in his bosom—and
leaves his widow to the solemn devotion of
herself to the cloister.

  As the performance of a character not essentially dramatic, and written rather in imitation of
the measured splendour of the Masque at Ludlow
Castle, than the freedom and vigour of Shakspeare, could display merely the beauty and the
milder graces of the actress; as it does not stand

strongly discriminated in my memory, by more than a few speeches in a single scene. I do not in this place feel myself disposed to go further into it. The effect was heavy, for the dialogue is diffuse, and the fable thin. This may also be said of the Greek models, from which it was constructed; but as we can but ill conceive the way in which the chorusses of antiquity were rendered delightful, even when they *do* carry on the interest of the play,—so on our stages no attempt whatever can be made, but to arrange a line of vestals, or of soldiers, or of priests—all uninformed, vulgar, awkward and undisciplined; who affect no feeling while they are stationary,—file to the right or the left, as they are led by the *fugle* lady or gentleman,—endure the curses, " not loud but " deep," of the musicians in the orchestra, and only swell the score of the composer, for the most part out of harmony, and never in time.

On the same day that Mr. Mason's Elfrida received the honour of a royal command, and the impersonation of Mrs. Siddons, he was deprived, by a gentle but sudden death, of an amiable friend and very pleasing poet, in the person of Mr. William Whitehead, who, in the seventieth year of his age, expired without a groan at his residence in Charles-street, Grosvenor-square. He had on the 14th of April, 1785, sat down to table, but finding no appetite to his food, he rose, and took

his servant's arm in the way to his chamber. In
the action he died.—He had been subject to
difficulty of breathing and palpitations of the
heart—the grand organ of vitality grew powerless
in one moment, and a mild and virtuous existence closed without a struggle.

Our business with him here is as a dramatic
writer, who in one character, that of *Horatius* in
the Roman Father, supplied first to Mr. Garrick,
and then to Mr. Henderson, the means of very
powerful impression upon the stage. Mr. Mason,
in describing the modest conduct of Mr. Whitehead, and his almost actor-like love of quick
and striking effects in the scene, has given us a
valuable opinion as to Mr. Garrick himself; which
the reader will apply beyond perhaps the object
of its writer.

" Mr. Whitehead wrote with a view to sceni-
" cal effect *only;* and, indeed, if he had done
" otherwise, his then virgin muse would scarcely
" have been so favourably received as she was by
" Mr. Garrick, who, at that time, in the meridian
" of his fame as an actor, and of his power as a
" manager, was sufficiently despotic to *refuse*
" *admission* upon the stage to any performance
" in which he could not display his principal,
" and almost unrivalled merits, the expression
" of STRONG but SUDDEN effects of PASSION; for,
" conscious of his peculiar strength, he was rather

" pleased to elevate, by his *own* theatrical powers,
" feeble diction and sentiment, than to express
" that in which the poet might be naturally
" supposed to have a share in the applause.
" And so much persuaded am I of his foible in
" this point, that I believe, had Shakspeare been
" alive, and had produced his Hamlet to Mr.
" Garrick, precisely in the same circumstances
" that Mr. Whitehead did the tragedy in question,
" few *soliloquies* (which when he acted the Ham-
" let of a dead Shakspeare he was obliged to
" retain,) would have been admitted by him
" without the most *licentious pruning*. For
" though no man did more to correct the vicious
" taste of the preceding age in theatrical decla-
" mation than he did, so far, indeed, as to change
" the mode almost entirely, yet this was not his
" *principal* excellence, and he knew it; and
" therefore disliked to perform any part what-
" ever, where *expression of countenance* was not
" more necessary than recitation of sentiment."
Memoirs, p. 63. seq.

Opinionum commenta delet dies, naturæ judicia
confirmat.* Nothing can be more certain than
the judgment above cited in relation to Garrick.
The residence of Mr. Mason was so far from
town, that he probably never knew the actual

---

* Cicero de Nat. Deorum. L. 2

tradings of Garrick with the soliloquies of Hamlet. But he was borne out to the very letter of his criticism. .There is a very admirable specimen of audible thinking in the fourth scene of the fourth act of Hamlet; and very probably the passage *most essential* to the true development of Hamlet's mysterious character, is the following.

> " Now, whether it be
> Bestial oblivion, or some craven scruple,
> Of *thinking too precisely on the event*," &c.
> *   *   *   *   *
>
> " Rightly to be great,
> Is—NOT.to stir without great argument ;
> But greatly to find quarrel in a straw
> When honour's at the stake.   How stand I then,
> That have a father kill'd, a mother stain'd,
> Excitements of my reason and my blood,
> And let all sleep ?"

He then considers the imminent death of at least twenty thousand men, who for a mere trick of *fame* go to their graves as unconcernedly as they would retire to their beds ; and, for the *present*, at least, Hamlet himself determines upon vigorous action.

> " O, from this time forth,
> My thoughts be bloody, or be nothing worth !"

As, however necessary, this soliloquy still con-

tinues unknown to the common audiences, I have
been obliged to quote some part at least of so
fine a composition, which one might have thought
the most urgent actor would have found rather
spirit-stirring and effective ; but NO, Mr. Garrick
himself wrote the rhapsody which he chose to
utter, in spite of nature and Shakspeare :—

> " Awake my soul, awake !
> Wake nature, manhood, vengeance, rouse at once !
> My father's spirit calls.   The hour is come !
> From this time forth, my thoughts be bloody all.
> I'll fly my keepers.   Sweep to my revenge."

It is delightful to him who reviews the progress
of an actress, to observe the striking contrast afforded by the *female* supports of the scene.   The
theatrical LORD conceives himself paramount over
both nature and art; the justest thoughts must
give way to his personal exhibition; the finest
poetry must be measured by his organ; whether
the poet's design be understood or not is of slight
moment, where his own *display* is at stake; nay,
even the movement of a few *painted rags* must
supersede the just continuity of the action.   When
we look to his *female* PARTNER of the scene, how
different is the conduct!   Did Mrs. Porter, or
Mrs. Pritchard, or Mrs. Siddons ever re-write
the scenes of Lady Macbeth?   What did the
best of them require of a character given to their

study? " That it should be written in NATURE"
—they were then satisfied that their talent could
do the rest; and, relying upon their author, only
strove to be worthy representatives of his genius.
In some few instances, they may have done *more;*
when, like Mrs. Barry, they inspired a writer's
muse as well as his passion; and the divine Mo-
nimia and Belvidera but echoed the feelings with
which poor Otway's fancy endowed their fascinating model.

The *Rosalind* of Shakspeare's As You Like It
had been a favourite character of Mrs. Siddons
on theatres nearer to his Forest of Arden; and
for her second benefit this season, she ventured to
appear upon the London stage in a dress which
more strongly reminded the spectator of the sex
which she had laid down, than that which she had
taken up. Even this, which shewed the struggle
of modesty to save all unnecessary exposure, was
a thousand times more captivating as to female
loveliness, than the studious display of all that
must have rendered concealment impossible. At
present, the ladies on our stages take *dress* as a
matter merely indifferent, and appear, by troops,
in male attire.

The longing of every good mind must be after
the simplicity and virtue of rural, but not vulgar
scenes; elegant but unaffected, where the head
is always corrected by the heart, and the heart

itself fashioned by the surrounding beauties of nature; where the trees of the forest possess the gift of tongues, and running brooks are as volumes which murmur wisdom to the studious—

> " Vain wish ! those days were never ; airy dreams
> Sat for the picture ; and the poet's hand,
> Imparting substance to an empty shade,
> Impos'd a gay delirium for a truth."

Yet something like this, it is implied in our great poet's work, the forest magic may still yield to such as seek its shades from the avowed treachery and cruelty of the populous city. Alas! he says no more than that the persecuted VIRTUES of life, endeared by sympathy to each other, may exist in inaccessible deserts without " sin or blame," and find humanity wounded by even the necessary *sacrifice* of its *velvet friends*.

But the truth is, that Shakspeare, the interpreter of nature, corrects the poet's day-dream even while he relates it. Orlando himself, a persecuted fugitive, almost reverses the picture which the Duke had been drawing of an earthly paradise ; in which the creeping hours were *lost* as well as neglected under the shade of *melancholy* boughs ; by men who admit that they had seen *better* days, enjoyed the comforts of *worthy* hospitality, and the regulated consolations of *religion*.

Rosalind was one of the most delicate achievements of Mrs. Siddons. The common objection to her comedy, that it was only the smile of *tragedy*, made the express charm of Rosalind—her vivacity is understanding, not buoyant spirits—she closes her brilliant assaults upon others with a smothered sigh for her own condition. She often appears to my recollection addressing the successful Orlando by the beautiful discrimination of Shakspeare's feelings. "*Orlando*" had been familiar, "*young man*" now coarse :—

> " *Gentleman,*
> Wear this for me ; one out of suits with fortune ;
> That could give more, but that her hand lacks means.
> Shall we go, Coz ?"

Again :—

> " He calls us back: my pride fell with my fortunes."

And, on the discovery that modesty kept even his encouraged merit silent, the graceful farewell faintly articulated, was such a style of comedy as coùld only come from a spirit tenderly touched. The flight to the forest of Arden, which the great Shaksperean *Schlegel* seems to have taken for the *Ardennes*, extending from Thionville to the frontiers of Champagne, and in the time of the Romans a forest of immense extent, exhibits the lovely Rosalind in male attire, accompanied by her more than sister cousin Celia. Like a stricken deer, she comes into retirement to languish of a wound for which activity is the only cure; but her lover is driven to the same retreat, and as the very eloquent foreigner just named has observed, she finds that love is despotic lord of the whole forest. " He teaches his lore to the simple rustic, " as well as to the cultivated courtier;" to him whose wisdom only apprehends that " the more " one sickens, the worse at ease he is ;" and him whose very refinement leads him to render his verse continual incentives to his passion.

Rosalind is quickly aware that her preference is returned by Orlando ; and, therefore, having sought a settled low content, in a sheep-cote fenced about with olive-trees, leading to which is a rank of oziers bending over a stream that murmurs to the melancholy rustling of their branches, she soon in her disguise ventures to give her powers of wit free scope ; and, instead of feeling impatience, is disposed to await the favourable issue of those events which seem to have arranged themselves. Mrs. Siddons put so much soul into all the raillery of Ganimede, as really to cover the very boards of the stage. She seemed indeed brought up by a deep magician, and to be forest born. But the return to the habiliments of Rosalind was attended with that happy supplement to the poet's language, where the same terms are applied to different personages, and the meaning is expanded by the discrimination of look, and tone, and action—

    " To you I give myself, *for* I am YOURS."

I believe it has not been remarked with what exquisite propriety the poet has made the usurping Duke punish with the greatest severity a kindred crime committed by Oliver against *his* brother Orlando. We never approve villany, though we commit it; and always cover it with some mask, as if it originated less in our passions than in some uncontrollable necessity. Man was *made* for virtue.

A doubt has frequently arisen how far plays of a character so imaginative are suited to a theatre. Perhaps no very clear solution can be given. *As You Like It* has never been a very powerful magnet, yet it has never been without its attraction. I know not that *Rosalind* has suffered much, acted by either Mrs. Crawford, Miss Younge, or Mrs. Siddons. The roynish clown, *Touchstone*, also seemed to me perfectly suited to the manner of King. The part of *Jaques* is rather the shadow of a great humourist than " the true and perfect " image of life indeed." He is a mere indifferent spectator among the children of earth—he takes no part with or against any man—his account with the world is closed, and he is only solicitous to indulge his spleen. Of this character my friend Henderson seemed, in the poet's phrase, to have " suck'd the melancholy," and left to his successors three fine *set speeches*, to utter with good emphasis and good discretion—NO MORE.

This was a season of great exertion to our charming actress, who absolutely acted seventy-one times. The *quicksilver* in the treasury, or, without a figure, the *number* of repetitions ordered of each play, will shew their comparative attraction. But we should place in the fore-ground the novelties now introduced into her list of characters :—

Margaret of Anjou, (Earl of Warwick) -	3 times
Zara, (in Zara) - - -	2
Countess of St. Vallori, (Carmelite) -	12
Camiola, (Maid of Honour) - -	3
Lady Macbeth, (2nd of February to the 10th of May)	13
Desdemona - - -	5
Elfrida, (Mason's Elfrida) - -	2
Rosalind, (at the season's close) -	4
Characters of her former seasons.	
Mrs. Beverley - - -	5
Lady Randolph - - -	3
Isabella - - - -	3
Euphrasia - - -	4
Jane Shore - - -	2
Calista - - - -	1
Belvidera - - -	4
Zara - - - -	3
Sigismunda - - -	2
	71 times

The list which is before us claims a few remarks. Dr. Franklin, and Aaron Hill, and Mason,
and even Massinger, came and passed away like
shadows, however informed with the pathos, or
the reason, or the grandeur of the actress.

Cumberland had combined, along with Mrs.
Siddons, Smith, Palmer, and Kemble; and a
quite new tragedy, that did not look very unlike
an old one, was repeated during the season twelve
times, and gave its melancholy interest to very
respectable audiences. But it was reserved for
Shakspeare's prodigy of woman, Lady Macbeth,
to be repeated thirteen times, and become, for the
remainder of the actress's life, the most powerful
of all her attractions.

Of the early characters, the lowest in the scale
was Calista, a part of great force, and acted by
Mrs. Siddons with even transcendent effect. The
play, too, possessing one of those scenes of altercation which are the delight of our taste, and a
bier and the slain Lothario to amuse the gaping
vulgar.

CHAPTER XVI.

ABSOLUTE ATTRACTION OF MRS. SIDDONS.—NOT YET DERIV-
ING THE BEST AID FROM HER BROTHER.—THE NOTION
AS TO HIS TALENTS.—A GREAT NATIONAL THEATRE.—
PARIS.—MANAGERS.—POET REVIVES IN THE PLAYER.—
COMMON-PLACE IN THE ART.—THE ACTOR OF GENIUS A
PROFOUND OBSERVER OF LIFE.—A SINGULAR MISTAKE IN
MACBETH.—GARRICK'S LEAR BENEFITED BY AN ACCIDENT.
—EXPERIENCE ESSENTIAL.—MRS. SIDDONS A SILENT OB-
SERVER.—A WORD AS TO THE AUTHOR.—PERFECTION OF
THE COMIC THEATRE.—BUT TRAGEDY THE GREAT MAGNET
—TILL MRS. JORDAN ARRIVED TO DIVIDE THE TOWN.—
THE NATURE OF HER GENIUS.—ATTEMPT AT A GRAPHIC
DELINEATION OF HER.—PLACED FULLY HERE, BECAUSE
FIRST RATE GENIUS IS SUPERIOR TO CAUTION.—PARTISANS
OF THESE RIVAL SISTERS.—GARRICK'S SYSTEM IN THEA-
TRICALS FOLLOWED BY SHERIDAN.—THE JUBILEE.—MRS.
SIDDONS DRAWN IN IT, AS SHE HAD BEEN DRAWN BY SIR
JOSHUA.—THE STRATFORD JUBILEE.—THE RIBBON WEAVERS
OF COVENTRY.—WARBURTON, GARRICK'S POETRY.—STEE-
VENS.—SUGGESTION AS TO NEW PLACE OF THE PRESENT
WRITER.—A TASTEFUL RETIREMENT TO THE VETERANS OF
THE STAGE.—MRS. SIDDONS ACTS MRS. LOVEMORE.—OB-
JECT OF THE WAY TO KEEP HIM.—PERHAPS A RASH EX-
PERIMENT.—MONTAIGNE.—DEATH OF MR. HENDERSON.—
THE LATE KING WISHED TO SEE HIM AND MRS. SIDDONS
TOGETHER.—HER CONCERN FOR HIS LOSS.—SHE ACTS
HERMIONE.—GEORGE POWELL IN ORESTES.—HIS SUPPOSED

LETTER.—MOST AUDACIOUS PUFFING. —GREAT EFFORTS,
MONTFLEURI DIES IN THE PART.—HENRIETTE ANNE OF
ENGLAND, AND HER PASSIONS.—THE CREPE FUNEBRE OF
BOSSUET.—ADDISON.—SIR ROGER DE COVERLEY.—MRS. SID-
DONS PREFERRED BY THE AUTHOR IN THE RELATIONS OF
WIFE AND MOTHER.—DR. DELAP.—THE CAPTIVES.—MER-
CHANT OF VENICE.—MRS. SIDDONS IN OPHELIA, DESCRIBED.
—THE ART OF PLAYING IT UNFOLDED BY A PERSONAGE
UNNAMED.—SHE ACTS THE LADY IN COMUS.—MIXTURE OF
PAGAN AND FEUDAL TIMES.

THE preceding chapter will have demonstrated
the prodigious attraction of Mrs. Siddons. For
three seasons together she had delighted the town
by the repetition of a limited number of our tragedies, of which, to say the truth, she was not
only the first, but the sole moving principle. It
should also be remembered, not in the estimate of
her attraction, but her utility, that all her success
had been attended with no expence to the theatre.
Scenery, dress, decoration of every kind were
reserved for Christmas prodigalities; and the
legitimate drama in those days, it was thought,
might be kept alive by the *pathos* or the *humour*
of the performer. The comic strength of the
Drury Lane company was unquestionably at this
time as complete and perfect a force as could be
formed by skill, or kept together by kindness;
but the great receipts of the season were con

stantly numbered by the nights of Mrs. Siddons and tragedy.

When so much is thus attributed to Mrs. Siddons, it should be stated that the time was not arrived to give her the best aid of her brother, Mr. Kemble. That great actor had appeared when the fires of a proud idolatry blazed brightly upon the altars erected to the genius of Garrick; he had to make way for a style of acting essentially original, striking and learned, but bearing the marks of labour *too sensibly* in its early exertions. Smith held the first rank in the theatre, and having a host of powerful friends retained, even in tragedy, every character which he had been accustomed to play. In the lovers of tragedy Brereton, by much bustle, and a greater shew of emotion, was commonly thought no mean successor of the persuasive Barry. The very studies of Kemble were objected to him as defects, and even a scholar could assail him in diurnal trash like the following.

" As to Mr. Kemble, he has so much know-
" ledge, we are afraid to encounter him; but if
" we, in *our ignorance*, may offer him a little ad-
" vice, it would be, that he should pack up all his
" learning, his superior judgment, his punctua-
" tions, his quips, and his quiddities, his gesti-
" culations, and his graceful attitudes, and fairly

" trundle them off the boards of old Drury; and if
" he can pick up in lieu of them a little *nature,*
" we will venture to assert it will not be the
" worse for him.

" Brereton recovers his health, and will recover
" his acting; but he must not relax his attention
" against the powers that *would devour* him."

This generous *fable* was signed Esop.

The few plays of Mrs. Siddons's first season,
had now, however, sensibly abated of their attraction. Not from any doubt of their excellence,
but from their almost endless repetition. The
English are slaves only to novelty. With us
there is little of that salutary prejudice in favour
of the classics of the country; that keeps a national theatre devoted to the performance of its
chefs d'œuvres, and admits with the greatest
caution any accessions to the established reper-
tory. It is in Paris only that we find this grand
predilection encouraged in every possible way,
and the government itself supplying funds to raise,
renew, and perpetuate the literary glories of the
stage.

A commercial speculation must be profitable,
or it must close. In the hands of adventurers,
Shadwell may be of more value than Shakspeare.
It is a compliment to which ALL managers are
not entitled, that they would *prefer* the poet to

the buffoon, if the one were even as profitable as
the other. Give the usurper the ascendancy as
to attraction, and the reign of genius is at an end.
What then can bring about his restoration? Nothing but the accident of talent congenial with his
own, which must find adequate materials for the
display of its proper powers. The poet revives
in the player. I cannot talk of dividing the laurels of Shakspeare even with Garrick; they are
not to be divided; they sprung up by the side of
his cradle, and spread in endless luxuriance
around his tomb. The student of his immortal
labours knows how imperfect the greatest efforts
of the actor will always be to unfold the amazing
subtilty of his conceptions. The hurry of public
utterance, the casual interruptions among a vast
crowd of spectators, the failure of the ear itself,
all forbid even the full enjoyment of the power
which he has; shades of meaning have an exility
that baffles the nicest articulation, the finest
eye.

The bulk of mankind have neither leisure nor
faculties for very accurate study; they must be
content with the interpretations of actors, not the
most attentive readers of poetry, nor even very
minute observers of life itself; they must take
the prescriptive manner of the profession, the
habit of doing what had been done before,—the
shew of thought rather than thinking,—the mi-

micry of emotion, not very scrupulous as to its source or its effects—a *look* that merely bespeaks our sympathy, a *tone* that long experience has demonstrated to be the note of sorrow, and affecting us independent of particular ideas.

A genius in acting must, however, be a profound observer of life. He secretly revolves all the folds of his own heart—he mixes much abroad with the world of character, and all its indications are set down in his " tablets," as the materials with which he is to work. The poet's science is how man *thinks* and *feels*, in all the relative conditions of his nature:—the actor's, how he *speaks*, and *looks*, and *moves*. The INWARD and the OUTWARD man may be the best as well as briefest indications of their different provinces. When the author is himself an actor, (an immense advantage, *ceteris paribus*,) he will sometimes trace out both, and display not only what is to do, but how it is to be done.

> " *Macb.*—I have almost forgot the taste of fears:
> The time has been my *senses* would have *cool'd*
> To hear a night-shriek; and my *fell of hair*
> Would at a dismal treatise *rouse*, and *stir*
> As life were in't: I have supp'd full with horrors;
> Direness, familiar to my slaught'rous thoughts,
> *Cannot once start* me.—Wherefore was that cry?
> *Sey.*—The queen, my lord, is dead.
> *Macb.*—She *should* have dy'd *hereafter*."

If the reader ever saw any thing like this *frigid despair* upon the stage; the remembrance of original nature in the death of all her living signs; the bearing about in our anatomy this petrifaction of the *heart;* he has seen what it has not been my fortune to behold._ The actors all *mimic* the *lost* emotions, and shew Macbeth *mistaken.*

Such hints are few even among our early writers. When, therefore, the great actor has fully imbibed the poet's design, he then reverts to the stores of his own observation, and accidents in real life become lessons, which enable him to throw the truth of imitation upon the character which is under his study. Garrick's Lear is no doubt truly said to have benefited by the dreadful spectacle of a father, who let his child escape from his arms, while fondling it at an open window. He became fixed in a distraction which perpetually beheld the accident renewed, and displayed for ever the original agonies of the father. The reader will see the places in which it suggested to the greatest of actors;—the *recurrences,* so frequent in Lear, to the cruelty of his daughters.

Such studies are absolutely essential to the actor, for whom the closet alone will do little. Without this actual experience of life, he will certainly be unfaithful to the poet, and deliver his text in the usual style of meagre declamation.

Where does the painter study expression, in the *historian* or the *poet?* O, no; his eye is every where; he is the undetected spy upon his species, and watches for it unsophisticated and unprepared. Countenances are made up, manners are the children of discipline. Nature drest is art, and clumsy art, until use has polished it into a second nature;—a peasant, child, alone, playing upon a bank of flowers, may be a model of the graceful, and the expressive. Sir Joshua Reynolds used to shudder at the notion of a little Miss before her dancing-master. I have seen in Mrs. Siddons, hundreds of touches caught by herself from the real world—

> " She is a great observer, and she looks
> Quite through the deeds of men."

It is commonly deemed no slight ordeal to have her steady gaze bent upon you, as she sits, too willingly, silent a long time in society. Nor is this the result of prudence or reserve, for she has a sound understanding, and is well read,—it is choice: to *observe* is her mental discipline.

I had, I was going to say, gratified myself in this display of the stores which supply the great effects of art, when I was suddenly alarmed by the following passage, which I read in Warburton's works—it is in the admirable dedication of the

D. L. to the Free Thinkers. " Urceus, surnamed
" Codrus, being asked why he mixed so much
" buffoonery in his works, replied, that nature had
" formed mankind in such a manner, as to be most
" taken with *buffoons* and story-tellers." How
stand I then, in attempting to win a *story-telling*
age to the description of a great *intellectual* charm,
and the means by which it was accomplished ? I
must, like others, be contented with the approbation of those who *reflect;* till a glut of nonsense,
may make sober efforts like mine, to analyze our
best enjoyments, desirable even as novelty.

To proceed, I must observe, that comedy, however it had aided the general services of the theatre, could not be said, even with the help of opera,
to be fully equal to the single attraction of Mrs.
Siddons. Miss Farren was greatly admired ; but
her name put up in the most attractive comedy of
Congreve, or Cibber, or Vanburgh, or the more
modern attractions of Murphy, Sheridan, or Cumberland, could not boast of that string of exalted
visitors, who followed in the train of the serious
muse. The management of King, as it was natural it should, leant to the side of his own attraction, and very perfect indeed was comedy, as acted
by himself, and Smith, and Palmer, and Bensley,
with the *broader* forces of Parsons, Moody, Suet,
Dodd, Baddeley, and the younger Bannister—
to which may be added, the steady and unfailing

charm of Miss Pope, the delightful pupil and successor of Clive. But, however powerful this force might be together, there seemed no chance that any single name in comedy should ever, as to fashionable life, divide the town with Mrs. Siddons; when even *that* alarming trial of her stability was afforded by a young unpatronized actress in the York company. The reader sees that I can only allude to Mrs. Jordan. Certainly no lady in my time was ever so decidedly marked out for comic delight. She seemed as if expressly formed to dry up the tears which tragedy had so long excited, and balance the account between the dramatic sisters, which Garrick alone entirely succeeded to do in his own single person. For although his friend Johnson preferred his comedy, yet his Lear stood unapproached in the records of tragic excellence.

The mark of this great actress had been made upon all the little caresses of female artifice, that inspire confidence because they presume ingenuousness: all those sportive enjoyments of bounding youth, and whim and eccentricity; things that are usually done laughing, and provoke the laugh of unavoidable sympathy. Her sphere of observation had for the most part been in the country, and the *Country Girl*, therefore, became her own, in its innocence or its wantonness, its moodiness under restraint, or its elastic movement

when free. Her imagination teemed with the
notions of such a being, and the gestures with
which what she said was accompanied, spoke a
language infinitely more expressive than words—
the latter could give no more than the meaning of
her mind, the former interpreted for the whole
being. She did not rise to the point where
comedy attains the dignity of moral satire, but
humour was her own in all its boundless diversity.

She had no reserve whatever of modest shy-
ness, to prevent her from giving the fullest effect
to the flights of her fancy. She drove everything
home to the mark, and the visible enjoyment of
her own power added sensibly to its effects upon
others. Of her beautiful compact figure she had
the most captivating use; its spring, its wild activity, its quickness of turn. She made a grand
deposit of her tucker, and her bosom concealed
everything but its own charms. The redundant
curls of her hair, half shewing and half concealing the archness of her physiognomy, added to a
playfulness, which even as she advanced in life
could not seem otherwise than natural and delightful. But all this would have been inadequate
to her pre-eminence, without that bewitching
VOICE which blurted out the tones of vulgar enjoyment, or spleen, or resistance, so as to render
even coarseness pleasing, or flowed in the sprightly
measures of a joy so exhilarating as to dispel dull-

ness in an instant : she crowned all this by a
LAUGH so rich and so provoking, an expression of
face so brilliant, and that seemed never to tire
in giving pleasure, that the sight of her was a
general signal for the most unrestrained delight.

We know that all this was but the *imitation* of
a reality—her delight must have been not in the
part but its success—it could at most but amuse
her, and the twentieth repetition of the best written
character must be matter of business, and serious
business too—yet there was no languor to betray
the constraint of a prescribed task—her vivacity
always charactered as fresh sparkling truth, and
even life itself seemed hardly to be so natural as
her representations.

Nor did her powers as an actress stop here :
for though the accomplished woman of fashion
was not within her reach, and the heroine of tragedy was a mere day-dream of her youth never to
be realized, yet there was a power of tenderness
about her all but equal to her hilarity. I cannot
say that the exterior indicated much sensibility,
(I use the term in its restricted sense) ; the charm
was in an organ of amazing sweetness, which
when, as in Viola, it found a passage musically
constructed, poured it upon the ear in a strain of
singular melody. As to what may be called
the grammatical analysis of a passage, by which
the construction of it is forcibly marked, the

clauses well detached from each other, and yet
the *whole* meaning bound together—there was no
effort of the sort; the words streamed on from
the beginning to the close—it was a land " flow-
" ing with milk and honey," and neither had nor
appeared to need the cultivation of art. But delightful as her voice was in speaking, it shewed
its quality with rather increase of effect when, as
she frequently did, she introduced any ballad
story, serious or comic, to a common air, unaccom-
panied by the band. The effect of these volun-
taries cannot be described, nor did I ever hear
any thing like them. She would begin often in
one key, and end in another; but every key to
her unlocked the avenue to the heart.

I would not slightly pass over such a charmer
as Mrs. Jordan, in these Memoirs of Mrs. Siddons. I have chosen to recal the memory of the
only rival she could have in the profession, pur-
posely. That is not first-rate excellence which
needs any caution as to its display. The human
heart is so framed, that the person whose attraction approaches to our own cannot be dear to us;
and the ill-judging partisans of either lady used,
I remember, to undervalue the other. The cry
of one party was, " Where is NATURE ?" of the
other, " Surely she is VULGAR."

The answer to this sorry stuff was, that the

Jordan suited comedy

speaking of Mrs. Siddons was the proper delivery of *such* a composition as tragedy written in verse; and that Mrs. Jordan's utterance was *suited* to the level of the characters which she performed, without the slightest tinge of 'fashionable affectation. The dispute was about the *prize*, public favour, which they equally merited, though on different grounds; and the portion of the one actress, conferred rather more respect than that of the other. In the meantime, the accession of this new charm might have been thought to secure the fortune of the theatre so highly gifted; and this it unquestionably would have done under any other man than Mr. Sheridan. I am not going to add to the vast mass of his irregularities, by a childish love for his talents converted almost into a monument to his honour. One would really conceive from some late narratives, that the *first* of all merits was " the *art* of using the property of " OTHERS—a *plausibility*, that nothing could resist, " purveying for NEED that ought *never* to have " existed." When I number the persons connected with the Drury Lane property, who have been ruined by their confidence in their matchless chief; when I see the enormous treasure dissipated, no man could ever guess how, and perceive this great mistaken man himself, for the most part, living at the table of others; I have a problem before me, which all my knowledge of him cannot solve, and an indignation is excited, which all my respect for him cannot stifle.

Sheridan seemed decidedly adverse to innovation, in the management of his theatre—for the most part he followed that of Mr. Garrick, in all but the restless unappeasable solicitude, without which such a concern can never long succeed. The Jubilee was now revived, with what they at that time called splendour, and one grace it had, which no time will ever surpass—Mrs. Siddons drawn in state, as the muse of tragedy; and as well as mere mechanism and motion could compensate the want of back-ground, resembling Sir Joshua Reynolds's sublime portrait of her. But Jordan was not the comic muse of the show— but a tall lifeless woman, whose name was Cuyler, exceedingly pallid, and whose features were ridiculously small for her size. The whole of the company were employed in the long procession of Shakspeare's characters, and the London elements were more propitious than those of Stratford proved to this effort of Garrick to do honour to his great master. This incidental allusion to the Jubilee at Stratford may perhaps sanction what follows upon that much contested subject.

The more I consider the matter, the more I feel disposed to admit the propriety of that celebration of our great poet called the Stratford

Jubilee. The *time* of it was not so strictly appropriate. The year 1769, commemorated nothing that related to Shakspeare. *Five* years sooner would have been a bicentenary from his birth—*three* years earlier would have been distant a century and a half from his death. Nor was the month of this festival chosen more happily than the year. Shakspeare was born, and he died the 23rd of April. The first day of the Jubilee was the 6th of September.

But not to consider such matters " too curi-" ously," whether it originated in veneration or vanity, it is an enviable circumstance in Mr. Garrick's life, that he projected this tasteful celebration.

> " For Garrick was a worshipper himself:
> He drew the liturgy, and framed the rites
> And solemn ceremonial of the day,
> And call'd the world to worship on the banks
> Of Avon, fam'd in song. No few return'd
> Doubtless, much edified, and all refresh'd."

Two of the commentators upon Shakspeare amused themselves in trying their favourite weapon, *ridicule*, upon the importance and the poetry of Garrick at Stratford. The most trifling part of the business was that suggested by Dr. Johnson's celebrated line—

> " Each change of *many coloured* life he drew."

The ribbon-weavers of Coventry were set to work to compose a ribbon to be called the Jubilee ribbon, which should be an emblem of his genius, and reflect *all the colours* of the *rainbow;* and this manufacture being recommended by public advertisement, the eyes of the great steward were gratified by the affluence of these Jubilee favours on the persons of the beauty and fashion, which attended the celebration.

Warburton thus dispatches Garrick's Ode to Shakspeare. "Garrick's *portentous* Ode has but "one line of *truth* in it, which is where he calls "Shakspeare *the God of our idolatry:* for *sense* "I will not allow it; for that which is so highly "satirical, he makes the topic of his hero's en- "comium. The ode itself is below any of "Cibber's. Cibber's nonsense was something "like sense; but this man's sense, whenever he "deviates into it, is much more like nonsense."

Warburton was now Bishop of Gloucester. His severity as to the poetry of Garrick, because unworthy of the God of our *idolatry*, is surpassed, as it ought to be, by his reprobation of the vocal charms, at a musical festival for the benefit of the *distressed clergy* of three dioceses. I should rather have blushed at the *cause* itself, than the means of its relief.—But the passage is very characteristic.

"We, too, have had our Jubilee; but held in "the old Jewish manner, when it was a season

" for the relief of the distressed ; which was truly
" *singing to God with the voice of melody.* We, too,
" and with a vengeance, *exalted our singing voice,*
" in the language of old Hopkins, and Sternhold,
" the Cibber and the Garrick of their time, for
" ode-making. But here we forsook our Jewish
" model. You know that the *hire of a whore, and*
" *the price of a dog* were forbid to be offered up
" to the God of purity. But we presume to offer
" up to him, the *hire of two whores.* You may
" judge by what I am going to say, what it is that
" passes under the name of charity amongst us.
" We have got for the distressed clergy of the
" three dioceses, some £340. And to procure
" this, we have levied upon the country,
" £684. 6s. 10d., for their entertainment in *fid-*
" *dlers* and *singers ;* of which sum £100 is contri-
" buted by me and my coadjutor."—LETTER,
September 23, 1769.

The other commentator, STEEVENS, I believe
tried every way to annoy the actor, who had been
pronounced the best *living commentary* upon the
poet's works. But when his parody selected LE
STUE, the Duke of Newcastle's *cook,* as the subject of a rival statue and temple, he might be said
to dishonour Shakspeare rather than Garrick ; and
to prove how dangerous it is in these cases to the
satirist *himself,* to be cursed with more *malice*
than merriment.

The *Jubilee* at the Theatre Royal Drury Lane

contained that procession of the characters of Shakspeare, of which the *programme* had been composed by Garrick for a public progress through
the town of Stratford. But the torrents of rain,
that poured down on the Thursday and Friday,
rendered so much of the scale of entertainment
abortive. The three beautiful witches of the
masquerade, Lady Pembroke, Mrs. Bouverie and
Mrs. Crewe, seemed to adhere strictly to the
poet's text—

> " When shall we three meet again,
> In thunder, lightning, or in *rain ?*"

Their power was universally acknowledged.

Although I should be the last certainly to dis-
courage any attempts to honour the genius of
Shakspeare, yet I should hardly give my sanction,
humble as it is, to a barren erection, such as a
TEMPLE for instance, in the *unthinking* place of
his nativity. I would rather use his name to form
a provision, not for those who bear it; but im-
proving on the plan of his fellow comedian Alleyn,
to erect a retreat in Stratford itself, for a limited
number of worthy members of his own profession.
The edifice should be, if possible, erected on the
site of the *new place;* and I would give the tenants
of rather a tasteful retirement, the pleasure of

looking upon the statue of their great poet, placed in the centre of the quadrangle they might inhabit, or in the gardens behind it. The *theatrical funds* of London might be associated with such a design, and *elect* to its comforts, out of the candidates who should present themselves for SHAK-SPEARE COLLEGE.

The municipal controul to be in the Corporation of Stratford for the time being, to avoid the expense of a set of Masters and Fellows, utterly unnecessary to such an institution.

Such a thing as the above, however desirable, I am fully aware will never be done, because it administers only to human comfort, not to personal vanity. How happy would it make me, to be compelled to correct my estimate of my own times, by seeing such a hint adopted, and a neat and substantial building arise, in which such a man for instance as poor Wewitzer was, might find a welcome refuge for his age, and a security from the misery of *capricious* dependance.

It was on the 26th of November, that Mrs. Siddons acted the part of Mrs. Lovemore, in Murphy's very pleasing comedy, The Way to Keep Him. The bow must not always be kept at its full stretch; our great actress required some relief from the severity of her personal exertion;

beside this consideration for her health, some of her Bath admirers had a wish to widen the sphere of her town attractions, by the display of the woman rather than the actress; and as she always kindled enthusiasm in those who truly admired her, they conceived that so fine a figure and a speaker so eloquent, moving through the actions of merely polished life in our modern comedies, might bestow a rather unusual charm upon them, and contrast admirably with the sparkling captivations of Miss Farren.

I remember well the effect the two ladies seemed to have upon each other. The widow Belmour would undoubtedly have been gayer with any other Mrs. Lovemore; and the habit of tragedy is so clinging, that the neglected wife of the wanton masquerader, Lord Etheridge, wore something of the sorrows of Mrs. Beverley in her general aspect. The assumed gaiety of Mrs. Siddons was certainly not comic. There was an insurmountable bar in the way to her imitating the manners of her friendly and enchanting adviser.

The object of the Way to Keep Him, seems to be to recommend an impossibility to the practice of the wedded fair. To keep up the attractions which won the lover, in order to secure the husband. Perhaps only one of the author's maxims can be with much confidence relied upon

—namely, to preserve a studious *neatness* in the apparel of the wife. But the sphere of duties is totally changed—the accomplishments of the girl are unbecoming the wife, who is probably a mother, certainly the mistress of a household. That the husband should not seek parties abroad, his lady is, it seems, solicitously to assemble parties at home.—When the husband changes the *gratifying object*, it does not appear vastly important *where* he may find it; besides, that from minds thus facile and frivolous, it were quite unreasonable to expect conjugal happiness.

After all no general rule can embrace the variety of such cases. The new relations adopted by the parties will at last settle upon principle or convenience. The passions of both must be controlled either by reason or necessity. But the really important point is, early to regulate the objects of mutual expectation. Life has something of greater importance than either a drawing-room, a concert, a card party, or a ball. Superficial accomplishments soon lose their value in domestic estimate; and we are then compelled to seek our happiness in fidelity and permanent esteem. The great moralist read to his friend Murphy, in a few lines, a lesson of more intrinsic value than even the elegant comedy we are considering. " Marriage," says the Rambler, " is the " strictest tie of perpetual friendship. There can

" be no friendship without confidence, and no
" confidence without integrity : and he must
" expect to be wretched, who pays to beauty,
" riches, or politeness, that regard which only
" virtue and piety can claim."—RAMBLER, No. 18.
at the *close*.

I formerly expressed a doubt as to the policy of
permitting Mrs. Siddons to descend from the
higher sphere of tragedy—and I see no reason
now to change that feeling. It will be said—is
not the impression of the actor doubled by his
universality? Certainly; absolute risible comedy
opposed to tragedy from the same performer may
add to his fame, by exciting a pleasing astonishment. It was so when Garrick acted Lear, and
the Tobacconist—it was so when Henderson acted
Richard the Third, and on the next evening
Falstaff. But full and almost violent contrast may
be necessary, or the lighter effects will injure the
stronger. If the Country Girl of Mrs. Siddons
could have equalled her Isabella, I should with
some hesitation, even then, on account of her sex,
have said—" Proceed in the track left by Shak-
" speare and Garrick, and make the world of cha-
" racter your own." But as her figure and her features could not *bear* the debasement of ridiculous
exhibition, as the most that could be done for the
sister empire was to assume some *doubtful tenants*
upon the frontiers, subjects of either muse by

turns, the effect was not strong enough to render the task desirable.

The actress, whose mighty powers in tragedy were confessed in the agonies she excited in some, and the tears she drew from all,—in Mrs. Lovemore allowed her audience to retire with an expression much too cold for her fame. VERY WELL, is a poor commendation for her exertions. Were it even certainty that no one could act the character better, there would always arise a cruel question for her importance, *But what is it to do, when done best?* But deserting the Lovemores, and the Oakleys, and the Sullens, and the Stricklands, suppose that, looking to the works of the great bard, we select a character of simplicity and truth, of which the sensibility is the great charm, and there is an utter want of all those ruling actions and passions, which rouse and agitate, and thus delight the general audience. Alas, the fine essence of such characters is too *thin* for common perception, it will be caught only by a few, and waste its sweetness over the heads of coarse and negligent spectators. The reason of this has been pointed out in the language of an author, whom I should injure not to call the most enchanting of all thinkers—MONTAIGNE. " Nous " n'appercevons les graces que *poinctues, bouffies,* " et *enflées d'artifice :* celles qui coulent soubs la " naïveté et la simplicité, eschappent ayseement

" a une veue grossiere comme est la notre; elles
" ont une beauté delicate et cachee; il fault la
" veue nette, et bien purgee, pour descouvrir cette
" secrette lumiere." If rambling thus in quest
of authority, I should lead the reader to the
ESSAIS of the incomparable Michel de Montaigne,
he may accept a remark which will heighten his
satisfaction in their perusal. The admired printer
Didot has given the orthography of the author's
age. The etymologist will see how much closer
the French is brought by it to the primitive language; and the English scholar will be astonished
to find the idiom infinitely nearer to his own
tongue, than the modern French is to the modern
English—besides that Montaigne's French has a
grandeur in the choice of terms, and a numerous
flow and sweetness in his sentences, partak-
ing of the peculiar charm of the Spanish. The
grammarian will be pleased with this view of a
great master of language—but every thinker
should make De Montaigne one of the friends
whom he most visits. But let me bestow far higher
praise than this. There is no writer who does
so much justice to the virtues of the laborious pea-
santry as this accomplished scholar; and his
picture of the rustics who work upon his estate
" qui ne *s'allictent* que pour mourir"—has that in
it to make philosophy blush at a wisdom, and
patience and gentleness, beyond the reach of its

ostentatious pedantry. See his 12th chapter, 3rd book, on Physiognomy.

The stage, on the 25th of November, had a loss, which forty years have not repaired—I allude to the death of Henderson—a man of great genius, and possessing the most versatile powers that I have ever witnessed. He becomes associated with Mrs. Siddons, because in despite of positive igno- rance, or prejudice in the Drury Lane manage- ment, he immediately, on her retreat from town, pronounced her to be the first and best of actresses —to have in herself all that her predecessors possessed, and all that they wanted. I never was so happy as to see these excellent artists perform together. In town they were the ornaments of different theatres. The late King, with that pleasing warmth, which was characteristic of him, once said, that " if he were a *theatrical* monarch, " his two favourites should act upon the same " stage." Even a *hint* of this nature one might have expected, would have operated like a command ; but it was never attended to. During Hender- son's readings from Sterne, 1 personally witnessed his power over the feelings of Mrs. Siddons ; and the pathetic chapters of Shandy excited no few tears from the brightest eyes that I have ever seen. His alternations of humour and tender- ness kept her in the situation of her own Cor- delia.

" You have seen
Sunshine and rain at once ; her smiles and tears
Were *like*, a better way.   Those happy smiles
That play'd on her ripe lip, seem'd *not to know*
What guests were in her eyes, which parted thence
As pearls from diamonds drop'."

The loss of such a man, before he had reached
the fortieth year of his age, was deeply felt ; and
Mrs. Siddons, at the proper time, intimated to his
representatives, that if a benefit was intended for
his family, they would oblige her by the employment of her talents on that occasion.   On the
25th of February, 1786, she spoke a prologue,
which the pen of his friend Murphy supplied, and
shewed all " the glory of her art" in a performance
of Belvidera on the stage of Covent Garden Theatre ; at that time the more splendid house, and
capable of the greater receipt.   Mrs. Abington
added to the attraction her inimitable Lady
Racket.   The pit was let at box prices.

On the 4th of March, 1786, the Distrest Mother
was acted for Mrs. Siddons's benefit, and as
she had done in the Mourning Bride of Congreve,
she took the more vehement character, and performed Hermione.   However Phillips may rank
as a pastoral poet, I have no hesitation in placing
this translation of the Andromaque of Racine,
before any other version from either that poet or
Voltaire.   The *Spectator*, when it came out, prac-

tised the little disingenuous art of concealing
totally its French origin, and was full, as WE now
are at times, of the green-room tribute to its high
excellence.   " The player who read (we are told)
" frequently, threw down the book, till he had
" given vent to the *humanity* which rose in him at
" some irresistible touches of the imagined sor-
" row."   But the tragedians of the city must have
been rather different from their modern successors in *consequence*, however, the case might be as
to *talent*, when Steele, or Budgel, or Phillips himself, perhaps, could publish such a letter as the
following, purporting to be signed by the actor
who performed Orestes.   George Powell had
surely not acted Shakspeare, and Otway, and
Dryden, to be unmann'd by a *dilution* of French
tragedy.   Thus he is made to write, however.

    " Mr. Spectator,
    " I am appointed to act a part in the new tra-
" gedy called *The Distressed Mother :* it is the
" celebrated grief of Orestes which I am to per-
" sonate ; but I shall not act it as I ought, for I
" shall feel it *too intimately* to be *able* to utter it.
" I was last night repeating a paragraph to
" myself, which I *took* to be an impression of
" rage, and in the middle of the sentence there
" was a stroke of self-pity which quite unmanned
" me.   Be pleased, Sir, to *print* this letter, that

" when I am oppressed in this manner at such an
" interval, a certain part of the audience may not
" think *I am out;* and I hope, with this allow-
" ance, to *do it* to satisfaction.

   " I am, Sir,

     " Your most humble servant,

       " GEORGE POWELL."

The most impudent part of the business here,
is the very slender knowledge imputed to a first
rate actor; his fear that on any discovery of
emotion, an audience, who knew him, should suppose that he was *out:* and the assurance of *lowering* even the style of the real author, to support
the assumed character? and putting the actor's
name to the supplication of an undertaker, who
hopes " to *do* his work *to* satisfaction." The truth
is, that Powell was a scholar, and a very favourite
actor, until his boundless intemperance closed
the scene upon him. His friend, the Spectator,
could take any liberty with such a man. He is
represented as constantly inflaming himself with
pure brandy, and making love upon the stage
in so *spirited* a manner, as to be extremely
terrible to the ladies of the profession.

Racine's play was kept so completely out of
sight, that Powell might never have heard the
danger of giving up the full bent of the actor to
the part of Orestes—the violent exertion of its

original representative Montfleuri absolutely killed
him. The son of the poet tells us, that it was
whimsically said on this occasion :—" Tout poete
" desormais voudra avoir l'honneur de faire *crever*
" un comedien."

Henriette Anne of England, the first wife of
Monsieur, brother of Louis XIVth, was the avowed
patroness of the French tragedy, and its success
is said to have equalled even that of Corneille's
famous *Cid*, which Colley Cibber so rashly ad-
ventured to translate. The *Berenice* of Racine
sprung also from her taste, the " chroniclers of
" that time" say from her *passions*. But the *crêpe
funêbre*, with which Bossuet covered her remains,
secures her immortality, if genius be immortal.

Addison himself did not disdain to aid the
success of Phillips's tragedy. He took Sir Roger
de Coverley to see it acted, and made it the
vehicle of some elucidation of the knight's peculiar character, and some remarks upon the play
itself. An instance of each incidentally shall be
pointed out. Upon Andromache's obstinate re-
fusal of her lover, he exclaimed with a more than
ordinary vehemence, " You cannot imagine, Sir,
" what it is to have to do with a *widow*." And
upon Pyrrhus's threatening afterwards to leave her,
the knight shook his head, and muttered to himself—" Ay, do,—if you *can*." For criticism may
be taken the following—" He made, indeed, a

" little mistake as to one of the pages, whom, at
" his first entering, he took for *Astyanax* ; but he
" quickly set himself right in that particular,
" though, at the same time, he owned he should
" have been very *glad* to have *seen* the little boy,
" 'who,' says he, ' must needs be a very fine child
" by the *account* that is given of him.' "

The absence of the child of Hector from the *scene*
only, for his mother we hear visits him daily, will
be regretted by more than the worthy knight just
quoted ; and particularly by those best acquainted
with the resorts of tragic emotion. What a beautiful use is made by Southerne of the son of
Biron, in Isabella, to *check* and at length *decide*
the acceptance of Villeroy for a second husband !
Such an accession as a *visible* Astyanax, I can
have no doubt would have fixed Mrs. Siddons to
the widow of Hector, rather than the furious
daughter of Helen. She acted Hermione with
all that storm of passion, which is characteristic
of her nature and her provocations—but the rant
of heroic passion, from *her*, begot a regret that the
soft sorrows of Andromache lost so beautiful and
so dignified a representative. Shall I say that I
greatly preferred Mrs. Siddons in the relations of
wife and mother ? Her affections always seemed
to need the inspiration of some DUTY.

Dr. Delap had sufficient character as a classical
scholar to secure the attention of managers to his

dramatic efforts; though his Cambridge qualifications of D.D. and S.T.P. might seem to chal-
lenge his attention to very different objects. He
commenced his tragic career with *Hecuba,* and
being unable to find in Greek tragedy more
divisions than the prologue, episode, and exode
—the intervals being appropriated to the chorus,
he divided his English Hecuba into *three* acts—
the audience too restricted it to three nights
performance.—But his living in Sussex, does not
seem to have possessed that *speluncam tetram et
horridam* which his master Euripides found the
proper site for tragic composition.

There is a love of the *wild* and *gloomy,* which
is apt to seduce the tragic writer from human
passions, to modes of existence fantastic and impossible. Ossian for a time seemed to be considered, like Homer, an epic writer from whom
tragedy might be derived; but nothing was to be
had but a few figures not very well defined—and
an engraft of ancient barbarism upon the feelings
and sentiments of polished life. The *Captives* by
Dr. Delap displayed the well known names of
Connal and Everallin and Malvina, to enchant the
followers of Macpherson—and some passages of
no slight power, divested of the affected sub-
limities of that impostor; but though Mrs. Siddons
did her utmost in Malvina, and Kemble wore the
Scottish dress (the *only* one, by the way, that the

parsimony of that day would consent to in the tragedy); yet his play was treated as usual by the audience, and the *Captives,* like the great captive *Hecuba,* lived but three nights.

In the progress of Mrs. Siddons modern tragedy should not detain us long. The power of tragedy, I reluctantly say, had left the soil in which it once flourished most. The passions had owned the master hands which alone could wield their powers, and refused to repeat themselves at the call of the humble mimics of our own times. Our great actress aided the sickly tragedy of *Percy,* by acting the part of Elwina; but Miss Moore had not strength enough for the iron times of which this play faintly reminded us.

For the benefit of Mr. Kemble, his sister was perhaps rejoiced to repeat the character of Portia in the Merchant of Venice, which had first introduced her to a London audience. I have nothing to add to what I formerly wrote upon this occasion. The nerve of the comedy is Shylock, and King was not the Jew which Shakspeare drew; though, as to Bassanio and Portia, perhaps those characters were never acted with more beautiful effect. *Passion,* however, is wanting, and the great enchantress quits her wand, and the spells with which it could encircle her, to charm by personal graces and sensible elocution. The play has little real interest; it is a romance, and suited to the closet. It is always felt to be impossible that Shylock should succeed, though the quibble may not strike by which he is to be defeated. In every christian state, the bond would be illegal from its *tenour*. The other incident of the caskets is too absurd to exist among the blaze of moral wisdom in which our poet has displayed it. The chance that good men may have inspirations as to the future, should not subject human happiness to the decision of a lottery. There is as little doubt of Bassanio's *success* as of Shylock's *failure*. But no play more abounds in the peculiar splendour of diction by which Shakspeare sometimes delights to cover the feebleness of his fable. I ought also to notice the peculiarly musical flow of his lines in this play. Perhaps his works do not supply another instance of equal care in this particular; the absence of the stronger demands of *passion* and *humour* left him at full liberty to indulge the ear with his utmost sweetness.

The two benefit nights with which the policy of the management had clogged the engagement of Mrs. Siddons, imposed upon her the unavoidable search after novelties of attraction. On her second night this season she acted Ophelia in Hamlet, and I retain the impression which it then made upon me, but little lessened by time or maturer study of the great author. It might at first be thought, that her figure would not express the *fragility* of this lovely sacrifice to her affections—but the height was diminished by lowering the head-dress, and the *countenance* permitted not the eye to be discursive.

"Ophelia," says a writer of great genius, "is "a character almost too exquisitely touching to "be dwelt upon. O, rose of May, O flower too "soon faded! Her love, her madness, her death "are described with the truest touches of tender- "ness and pathos. It is a character which no- "body but Shakspeare could have drawn in the "way that he has done, and to the conception of "which there is not even the smallest approach, "except in some of the old romantic ballads." The same writer is disposed, however, to excuse some of the *free* language of Hamlet to this pure being, "as the license of the time." I am sorry to find it, notwithstanding "the fatness of these "pursey times," addressed to one who would hardly "unmask her beauties to the moon."— Hamlet took a libertine pleasure in wounding the *ear*, allowing him to rely, that Ophelia's blush

> "Would never *thaw* the consecrated snow
> That lies in Dian's lap."

There is a modesty that inspires decorum even to the dissolute. Full of the important business of

the play; anxious to seem idle that his object
might be concealed, he ought to have placed
some guard upon his fancy when he forces a conversation with Ophelia; Hamlet is *gross,* at least
in the original play.

Mrs. Siddons was the only great actress whom
I ever saw in Ophelia; but in confirmation of a
remark, made certainly with this instance strongly
in view, what she gave, and alone was competent
to give, was caviare to the multitude; too long
accustomed to receive a dishevelled *singer* as the
true and perfect image of Ophelia, all the fine
essence of such a being, breathing through Siddons herself, hardly moved their wonder; though
her deportment through the earlier scenes was
a model of graceful virtue, and that of her distraction was the truest delineation that was
ever made from a " ruin'd piece of nature."   But
methinks I hear some very inquisitive reader exclaim, " what! Mrs. Siddons *sing!*" No, Sir, it
was Ophelia who sang, or rather the *melancholy* of
the poet Collins.

As to the dialogue—the " thought and remem-
" brance fitted"—the document in madness—the
dreadful, " There's *rue* for you," to the Queen,
were then indeed powerfully given.   The art of
playing this scene is beautifully unfolded by a
gentleman in the original play.   Hear what the
poet of nature put into the mouth of a personage
without a name.

" She speaks much of her father ; says, she hears
There's tricks i' the world; and *hems*, and *beats her heart ;*
Spurns enviously at *straws ;* speaks things in *doubt*,
That carry but *half* sense : her speech is NOTHING,
Yet the unshaped use of it doth move
The hearers to collection ; they *aim* at it,
And botch the words up fit to their own thoughts ;
Which, as her winks, and nods, and gestures yield them,
Indeed, would make one think, there *might* be thought,
Though nothing *sure*, yet MUCH *unhappily*."

Incidentally, because the passage follows this, I would beg leave to notice symptoms of no common guilt acknowledged by the Queen of Denmark :—

" *Queen.*—To my sick soul, as sin's true nature is,
Each toy seems prologue to some great amiss ;
So full of artless jealousy is guilt,
It spills itself, in fearing to be spilt."

To the guilty mind every trifle seems pregnant with disaster. This is the nature of sin, to dread discovery from accidents unconnected with it in fact; and thus to drop indications of what it would *conceal*, by an undue alarm at any occurrences that excite much attention.

The " black and grained spots" upon her soul, which would not " leave their tinct" in the closet scene, seem to be equally visible to her fancy here and argue strongly for her participation in the *design*, at least, of the murderer. She would not, like Lady Macbeth, " bear the knife herself," but had allowed her passions to triumph over her reason and her virtue, and stooped to prey on garbage. In the elder play, the Queen disavows the murder; this declaration Shakspeare did not adopt; he, therefore, meant to load her with the full weight of the crime, from which two lines only would have relieved her. It may be observed too, that, as a righteous retribution, she at last perishes by the *leprous distilment* which her husband had prepared to destroy her son, as he had formerly destroyed his father.

To return to Mrs. Siddons, she closed the feast of this memorable day by performing the *Lady* in Milton's Comus—a character, be it observed, that I believe his own times to have not unfrequently exhibited. An estimate has been made, in which I entirely concur, that places the cultivated female of the middle of the seventeenth century greatly above her successors. For this fine picture of the sex we were indebted to the lives of the Hutchinsons.* But Milton himself has left us, in immortal verse, sketches of some ladies of his acquaintance,

* See the 13th Vol. of the Edinburgh Review, and the beautiful article upon this subject, which contains the estimate above alluded to.

by no means inferior to the heroine of his Masque. Her for instance of whom he writes :—

> " Thy care is fix'd, and zealously attends
> To fill thy odorous lamp with deeds of light,
> And hope that reaps not shame."

And that nearer object of his admiration, who visiting his slumbers—-

> " Came vested all in white pure as her mind :
> Her face was veil'd, yet to my fancied sight,
> Love, sweetness, goodness, in her person shin'd
> So clear, as in no face with more delight."

Such we may fairly presume his Dowager Countess of Derby to have been; and such the lamented Marchioness of Winchester. Ben Jonson would supply us with other instances, were they necessary upon the present occasion. HuMAN NATURE is interested, that the high souled heroine of Comus should not be a creature of the fancy merely. The Lady of Comus is a high Platonist, and the monstrous rout of Comus are received as of times purely pagan—but the close of the drama introduces us to the splendid festivity of a feudal chieftain. The heaven, that had tried the youthful progeny of this noble, is the *christian* heaven; and their *faith* had been subjected to trial equally with their truth and patience. The spirit, however, quits them at last for the gardens of *Hesperus ;* and celestial *Cupid* holds his *Psyche* entranced, until that union is permitted from which love and joy are to be born. Where, again, he plainly shadows that operation of *divine love* upon the *human soul,* from which eternal happiness was to proceed as the crown of terrestrial virtue.

But an interest such as has been shadowed out, and a sublime and eloquent woman, seen across an orchestra of fiddlers, with all the glitter of glass chandeliers, and all the vulgarity of a mixed audience as a chorus !—O, no, such things are not theatrical ; they belong to purer times, and the pastoral retreats of splendid rank and exalted virtue.

CHAPTER XVII.

THE management of Drury Lane Theatre
seemed to have no characteristic but indifference,
or sameness. Mrs. Siddons, in the season of

1786-7, repeated her former characters on her accustomed nights of acting, and on the 22nd of
November, Dodsley's Cleone was revived and repeated on the 24th; but it then sunk into its
former repose, from which the maternal agonies of
Mrs. Siddons (who must have been an eagle to a
wren compared with the original heroine,) were
not mighty enough to preserve this affecting play,
written by a most amiable and able man. I incline to think that even in this commercial land,
there is a reluctance to award the honours of letters to any of the sons of trade—however they
may have been gifted by nature, cultivated
by youthful or mature application. The book
seller might be considered an innovator among the
makers of books. The early efforts of this pleasing writer had the honour to be patronised by
Pope. Dodsley was often reminded by the
petulant professors of *polite* letters, that he had
once worn a livery in the service of the Honourable
Mrs. Lowther—but he soon exchanged it for that
of the muses, and honoured them by his offerings.
Few men have placed upon our shelves productions of greater value, than his fine collections of
old plays and modern poems, with the admirable
compendium of annual life called Dodsley's
Register. That he should have retired from
business with a handsome fortune, was to be expected from the discernment of his mind and the

prudence of his conduct.   Nor was he parsimo-
nious as to his authors.   Mr. Burke, by the con-
tract which I have seen, was to have had £600 for
" An Essay towards an Abridgment of English
History to the reign of Queen Anne."   It was
stipulated, whimsically enough, that it should be
printed in quarto, exactly like Jarvis's Don
Quixote.   Hughes, his printer, does not seem to
have composed more than forty-eight pages of
this work, of which Burke, however, wrote somewhere about two hundred and fifty of Jarvis's
pages.   I presume the appearance of Hume led
Burke to view his own composition as rather
oratory than history—it is a commentary upon
events with which the reader is presumed to be
already acquainted, and, I think, considerably resembles the Letters of Bolingbroke on History.
However superior in some respects, more gorgeous
even than St. John himself, imitation of that
noble Lord clung to him through life, though he
has spoken slightingly of him in his latter works,
and thinks his master's writings have taken no
hold upon his mind.   For this digression, leading
to such a genius as Burke, I apologize, not to the
admirers of Mrs. SIDDONS ; whom that great man
has immortalized, by naming her with GARRICK,
in his work on the French Revolution.

Our great actress presented her friends with
Cymbeline as her first benefit, on the 29th of

January, 1787. She performed Imogen in such a way as to at once satisfy the student of Shakspeare, that if ever complete justice could be done to the loveliest of his female characters, that wonder was then achieved. The bad taste of former times was accustomed to lend itself to a miserable series of keen or coarse invectives against the sex. The satirist has drest the libels in verse, and the daily delinquency of the man still dares to mutter the tuneful fragments upon the frailty of woman. But the real truth is, that absolute steadiness of affection, enduring all tests, and pardoning all neglects, and even injuries, resides *only* in woman.

The essence of the sex, the pure and perfect chrysolite, is to be found in Shakspeare's Imogen —nor is she a creature of the imagination. Neither is she the child alone of refinement. In humble life, and in the dangerous services of our army and navy, the village girl assumes the garb of the other sex, and fights and bleeds and dies beside the object of her untutored affection. Imogen, too, is the native of all climes.

In the first scene of the character Mrs. Siddons was fully aware of its almost infinite variety. Contempt for the affected courtesy of the Queen —the ardour of her affection for Posthumus—the delicacy of their interchange of tokens—the brutal rating of the King, answered quickly as in despair

—and the perfect tone of her reply to Cymbeline's exclamation—" What!—art thou mad?"

> " *Imo.*—Almost, Sir; heav'n restore me!—would I were
> A neat herd's daughter, and my Leonatus
> Our neighbour-shepherd's son!"

All these points, with the sarcasm as to Cloten exprest in language so truly feminine, opened a delineation, which continued equally true in every feature to the end.

> " I would they were in Africk both together,
> Myself by with a *needle,* that I might prick
> The goer-back!"

A scene succeeds this much too short to take deep effect upon the audience, though it is beautiful in the extreme. It is on the departure of Posthumus, and between Imogen and Pisanio—positively unrivalled in ardour and delicacy.

Few people would be at a loss to conceive how finely Mrs. Siddons would receive Jachimo, when he comes over upon his villanous enterprize—her appearance, as abating, from his poisons, somewhat of her confidence in her husband, and the amazing scorn and returning reliance, which compel him to change his calumnies into panegyric. Imogen is nothing like the cautious Macduff—she does not say—

> " Such welcome and unwelcome things, at once,
> 'Tis hard to reconcile."

She easily considers him to make *amends* for the freedom of his former speeches—her virtue has no fierceness about it, and knowing herself superior to all temptation, she is no longer indignant, when she has brought her assailant to entertain for her a suitable respect. He comes from Posthumus, and at length speaks him truly. Her heart satisfies her reason, and his villany immediately suggests to him a safer course. Iago himself is not so *pure* a rascal as Jachimo.

The scene of the trunk, in the bed-chamber of Imogen, is an admirable stage invention : the poet has used it to paint, with the richest colours, the sleeping charms of his heroine, and even by her favourite reading to infer her love of suffering virtue. " Where Philomele gave up," I presume alludes to her last feeling of the brutal violence of Tereus, who had torn out the tongue which reproached him. The beautiful Ovidianism closed her lecture—

> " Ipsa jacet, terræque tremens immurmurat atræ."

The arranging with Pisanio what relates to their journey to Milford Haven charactered a good deal like her Rosalind, and indeed the play partakes in a considerable degree of the character of As you Like It. It breathes of the country, but has the boldness of the mountaineer instead of the listless patience of the forester. The *agony* attending Pisanio's disclosure is written with a perfect luxury of power, and was acted so as to extend the captivations of the actress. The cave of Belarius, and the mingling with congenial nature, operates somewhat to banish the leading interest, yet it is recalled to us by the poet with his most consummate art, and the reference to it proceeds from the mouth of one who never heard of Posthumus, and is ignorant even of the very sex of Imogen. Hear Guiderius,—

> " I do note,
> That grief and patience rooted in HIM both,
> Mingle their spurs together."

When Imogen is supposed dead by her brothers, the poet invests her with new charms, and she seems like the progeny of beings superior to humanity.

On the incidents thus alluded to in the cave, Schlegel, the great German critic upon Shakspeare, has the following admirable observation.

" When a tragic event is one only in appear-
" ance, whether the spectator be informed of the
" fact, or it be only designed that he should
" divine it, no poet so well as Shakspeare knows
" how to soften a melancholy impression without
" quite effacing it. He gives to grief an harmo-
" nious expression, and bestows in solemnity
" what he takes away in energy."

What a comment on the exquisite *dirge* over
the entranced Imogen! I will just remark in
passing, that Mr. Collins's dirge, for the most
part, preserves the images of Shakspeare; though
the two first stanzas remind us of *village* life,
rather than that of the forest or the mountain.

The character of Imogen is here closed: the
rest is " labour which is not used for her," any
other way than as it explains the history of her
dangers, and restores her to Posthumus, for
whom she retains an affection of which the reader
inclines to think him hardly worthy.

When I assert that Mrs. Siddons was the only
perfect Imogen that I have ever seen, I am fully
aware that some representatives have more exactly answered to the fond and tender delineations of Fidele, which upon her recent loss are
made by the two princes her brothers. That the
form and style of features of Mrs. Siddons were
essentially majestic, and her expression always of
the most powerful kind; but we are to remember

that in the male attire the female figure always becomes visually deceptive; and that I am not speaking of the Mrs. Siddons of 1802; that in reality, Imogen is a character of infinite energy, and that the spectator must contribute to his own pleasure, by overlooking the operation of that time upon the actress, which has consummated her art. That when subsequently she had Charles -Kemble and Decamp for her brothers, she looked indeed the *perfect sister* of the family, and the illusion was complete.

The amateurs of transformation in those days, a little complained of the delicate style of her male attire; but it was exactly the strait, or frock-coat and trowsers of our modern beaux; and you saw, as you ought in fact to see, the attempt at the opposite sex not quite successful.

I restrict myself to the novelties of Mrs. Siddons's performance, because I made a determined point of seeing them in their succession, and never allowed any other attraction to dispute with the most refined of my amusements. She, I know, owes little to her admirer; but he has always retained a feeling of grateful respect towards the possessor of talents so distinguished; and in thus reviewing their effects, I, perhaps, render even a slight service to the admirers of the drama.

The character of the Countess in Jephson's

Count of Narbonne was acted by her on the 8th of March, 1787, for the first time in London. It was unquéstionably a melancholy picture of submissive dignity and maternal fondness—but without the invigorating passion of Lady Randolph. The flow of Jephson's versification had every grace from a speaker so accomplished, but whether from the spell of a first impression, or the almost enthusiastic quietism of Miss Younge, in this single instance, I could almost prefer that lady to her far greater rival.

On the 29th of the same month she acted on her brother's night Lady Restless, in Murphy's diverting comedy of All in the Wrong. The wild and ingenious jealousy of Sir John and Lady Restless is complexional in them both ; but the poet has contrived the matter of *recrimination* with much adroitness—the use made of Beverley and Mrs. Marmalet is entirely of the French school. When he had once accepted the whole act of Moliere's *Cocu Imaginaire,* Murphy could invent and talk what remained in the light and airy taste of our polished neighbours.* The business

---

* It suited Murphy to acknowledge, by an advertisement, some *hints* received from the *Cocu Imaginaire* of Moliere ; and the author of the Biographia Dramatica takes his word for it, and proceeds to compliment him upon his fable, and the conduct of it—his characters and so forth. The truth, however, is, that the Sganarelles are merely one step lower in life than the restless pair, and in some

teems upon the spectator, and is never of that sort which the dullest may anticipate. You know that the husband and wife will be confirmed in their error, but the trick escapes you till it is played. Beverley is the stage original, I think, of Falkland in the Rivals, and Sheridan has remembered his obligation by making that name the *assumed* one of Lydia Languish's lover, Captain Absolute.

Mrs. Siddons had as much bustle as the restless lady required, and spoke the dialogue naturally and skilfully—but the laughter excited was not of the hearty kind. How Miss Haughton played it from Murphy's instruction, I have no knowledge—but we know that Yates was his Sir John Restless, and I think there is more actual comedy in the wife than in the husband. I be-

---

parts of his dialogue Murphy even forgets that; but he translates literally *whole scenes*, distended, observe by the intrusion of additional characters. The French piece is of one act, containing twenty-four scenes or changes of some of the characters. To know the extent of Murphy's obligations, the reader should peruse the second, third, fourth, fifth and sixth of Moliere's scenes—then the eighth and ninth, and lastly the fourteenth, fifteenth, and sixteenth. He will find the " hints" full of the most ample detail: and the dialogue rather flattened, as it must be, containing no compensation for either Moliere's verse or his rhymes. I am obliged to add that the author would now be invaluable who could even *steal* us such plays as Murphy's—but the sources are exhausted, and our neighbour *all but* as poor as ourselves.

lieve a repetition of the play was not called for
on the present occasion; and whether welcome
or otherwise, the general judgment seemed to be,
that at least *modern* comedy did not come within
the range of our great tragedian. I have ventured
before to think the very attempt impolitic, as
sullying the consequence of female tragedy.
Mrs. Yates, it should be remembered, in this
comedy acted Belinda, (Beverley's Julia) not
Lady Restless; and Mrs. Yates had more of
Siddons than any previous tragedian of that
age.]

The revival of the Count of Narbonne at Drury
Lane Theatre, was the precursor of a new tragedy
by Captain Jephson, called Julia. The exertions of
Mrs. Siddons and her brother, in the former play,
had suggested to the ingenious author a second
display of her powerful talent, in which the passions should be touched in a deeper and alarming
key, and love and jealousy and hatred excite all
that was terrible in dramatic effect. Mentevole,
the part assigned to Mr. Kemble, worked out
considerably beyond the Julia in the composition
of the play, whatever might have been designed
in the sketch. It was the true Italian lover. The
incident it seems had once actually occurred in
Guernsey, for frantic passion is confined to no
one spot; the author, however, was certainly
judicious in chusing that soil for the birth of his

hero which is said to engender alike the deadliest crime and the greatest genius, and every produce is luxuriant even to rankness.

" It is the *bright* day that brings forth the ADDER."

This play is " the image of a murder" done in Genoa, where on the eve of his intended marriage, a young nobleman is found murdered. As he wore a picture of the bride, his assassin, passionately enamoured of her, brings it away with him. Finding the brother of the deceased likely, as he thinks, to become another bar to his wishes, he challenges him. The lady, to prevent the probable mischief, sends a message to him by his sister, who finds him in rapturous ecstacies over a portrait, which he lets fall. Upon taking it up she discovers it to be a miniature of Julia, superbly set in brilliants. With the true female estimate of such shining testimonials of affection, she carries it back with her, and leaves it upon her toilet. It is there, not very naturally, but very necessarily, discovered by the mother of the deceased, who knowing that her wretched son wore it when he was assassinated, infers a complicity between its present possessor and the person from whom it must have come into her hands—it is traced to Mentevole, and Julia is seen to have been entirely innocent. The assassin finishes the turbulent career of his passion, by stabbing the woman on whom he doats before he is led off to suffer for his guilt.

The exertions of Kemble were so great, as to prevent him from acting again for a considerable time; and the *motion* adjourned *sine die* here, as on a more real stage, is commonly lost. It is, perhaps, more truly tragic than any other effort of the same author. But when I read it some years since, I could not help regretting the absence of another power as essential as *terror*, without which healing spring the wounds of tragedy are too harsh and deep to be endured. Tragedy may fitly rest upon villainy in progress; for you sympathize with the sorrows of its victims as they succeed each other—but the mere *detection* of a murder seems better trusted to a court of justice than the drama.

The metaphorical language of Mentevole has been blamed by certain critics—but they should know that they have Longinus against them; who tells us that " the proper time for metaphor is " when the passions are so swelled as to hurry " on like a torrent." The figures, however, should share in the character of such turbid emotions, and be cloudy and indistinct, broken and irregular. The most perfect exemplification of this rule of the great critic may be found in the page of the greatest of poets.

> " And Pity, like a naked new-born babe,
> Striding the blast—or Heaven's cherubim, hors'd
> Upon the sightless couriers of the air,
> Shall blow the horrid deed in every eye."
>
> MACBETH.

When some blockheads once quoted this passage to Ben Jonson, as one they thought in its expression strained and unnatural, he told them " it was horrour." They gave the world one more proof how much discernment they wanted, by conceiving that great man to have *concurred* with them in the censure; whereas he vindicated his friend, and laid down the true law by which passion emits its expression, in a single word— " it is HORROUR."

Julia was even unfortunate during its preparation. Mr. Colman had written an epilogue, which Mrs. Siddons, after some deliberation, refused to speak. At this distance of time, it would be difficult to conceive what could induce her to turn round the most brilliant epilogue writer of the age, and deny to either Jephson or herself the interest which attached to any production of an author so admired and esteemed; himself, too, an admirable critic, and moreover a manager of a London Theatre.

Mr. Colman was naturally much hurt by the disrespect shewn to his muse; and he was even angry when he heard from rumour that the cause was its alleged *indecency*. For this strange notion, I can discover no ground, unless it might be thought indelicate to allude to an *Italian* lover. " Happy is the lady," says Mr. Colman, " born " in England—

" With pity who beholds poor Julia's fate,
Yet prizes, as she ought, *her* happier state ;
The charms of English worth who can discover,
And never wish for an *Italian lover*."

It had originally been designed for Miss Farren. Mrs. Siddons, however, was so important to the play, that it was deemed advisable to compliment her with the epilogue. Now all this was injudicious. Why should an actress, who *dies* during the play, be compelled to *giggle* down her own serious effects, simply to have the unnecessary plague of recovering instantly from what is supposed to be great *toil*, and even *pain*, and ask personally the reward of her exertions? Surely to convert the gloom that has been inspired into pleasant feelings, is better suited to the *natural* comedian, than the daughter of Melpomene. I do not like to see that I can be tortured at so little an expense of suffering by the actress. Illusion there must be, but it should not look like a trick; and I should hate the buffoon, who, rising from the *curse of Lear*, could run off the stage in the mimic character of *Harlequin*.

It is no mean gratification in writing the memoirs of such a genius as Mrs. Siddons, that the regard every author feels for his subject calls upon his discretion for no sacrifice of the merits of others. He can view them in their course, and speak of their excellence; he can follow them to the grave, and be the register of their fame. This reflection is suggested by the death of Mrs. Yates, which occurred on the 3rd of May, 1787.

This great performer began her town essays with the same incident as Mrs. Siddons herself. She was engaged by Mr. Garrick in one year, and discharged or permitted to retire the next, as no longer worth retaining. When upon her marriage with Yates she returned to Drury Lane Theatre, she was endured for the most part as a substitute in any indisposition of Mrs. Cibber; and, in 1759, was perhaps the most beautiful representative of Shakspeare's Cleopatra, then compressed for the stage, by his editor, Capell.

She had decided talents for comedy, and at the death of Mrs. Cibber, in 1766, was left without a rival in tragedy. It is difficult to account for her frequent retirements from the London Theatres, except that the excellence which is alike admitted by the public and the managers, may in a commercial estimate not be quite worth the emoluments, which, the rare talent considered, it may by no means be avaricious to demand.

I could obviously only see her in my youth. But it is impossible to forget the dignity of her person, the beauty of her features, and the pensive music of her declamation. She had a decided preference, it should seem, for tragedies of the descriptive kind, and gave a graceful existence to compositions of little more than tuneful feebleness. The gentler passions seemed more within her scope than the terrible. Her Andromache was distinguished by all the tenderness of soul, which our imagination bestows upon the widow of Hector. Her last performance was the Duchess of Braganza, in Jephson's play, on the 24th of May, 1785, when she acted for the benefit of Mrs. Bellamy, who had once been no mean rival even to Mrs. Cibber herself.

I should not forget the manner in which she recited Sheridan's monody on Garrick, which, however unsuited to the stage, inasmuch as it flows in a languor of melodious verse at great length—with few breaks—no bold apostrophes, and no attempts at impersonation, yet I cannot but pronounce to have charmed me beyond any thing that I had previously heard from a human voice. It taught me what it was that Henderson intended six years afterwards to combine with his own public readings. Had he lived, the design would have taken effect the year following, 1786; but the close of 1785 put an end to his efforts; and within a year and a half his beautiful associate followed him, and our hopes of amusement were doomed to a frightful disappointment; a herd of presumptuous spouting mediocrity invaded their desk; and poor READING was not permitted to die a *natural* death among us.

The English I am truly afraid are fond of the striking, the forcible, and the explosive—it is a tendency that grows upon them, and will leave in their amusements nothing but pantomime and mechanical contrivance. There have been writers among us, who once persuaded Mrs. Siddons to quit the *gentle*, and I will say the virtuous Shore, for that professing, shameless wanton, Alicia. On the 7th of May, she made the experiment, and amazed the distant gods. I cannot but be of opinion that Rowe intended in this lady to exemplify a very favourite lesson, that in woman the departure from chastity is usually the loss of every virtue. Her mind seems framed only for irregular but brilliant passion, and she attributes her particular feeling to the whole sex. Finding her dearest and most intimate friend dejected, and in tears from the consequences of her past life, she chuses as a topic of consolation, that she must *once* have been happy, when a glittering court and its amorous monarch were sighing at her feet. The presentiment of Shore looks to the result of all this mischief, and announces it as at no great distance from her. Alicia has a blessing in reserve for her unhappy friend, a female friendship superior to all the assaults of adversity. The trusting Shore confides to this remaining blessing a casket containing her jewels, and Alicia thus imprecates a curse upon her own conduct.

> " If I not hold her nearer to my soul
> Than every other joy the world can give,
> Let poverty, deformity, and shame,
> Distraction, and despair, seize me !"

The scene changes only once, Lord Hastings arrives at Shore's house from the court : not encouraged by her, he has formed designs upon her person ; and this *friend* instantly flies to ruin them both, in which her headlong passion fully succeeds. Distraction and despair, invoked on her apostacy from the faith pledged to poor Shore, are shewn to have seized upon her, but surely it is impossible she should excite the smallest sympathy from the beginning to the end. She blazes fiercely in rhymed couplets at the closes of the violent scenes in which she is engaged, and excites a senseless applause for ravings that disgrace her sex. I never heard any lady, but one of the theatre, utter a syllable upon the character of Alicia—in the theatre we endure this fiend because we admire the actress, who is her representative—but we can only think in private upon Shore.

The great actress held on this occasion opinion with Pythagoras. Her soul appeared to be as much at home in the second habitation as it had been in the first, and seemed to have lost every particle of compassion for her *former self;* in plainer language, nothing whatever of Shore appeared in Alicia. But scream for scream, and distortion for distortion, the Alicia of Mrs. Crawford was many degrees more *terrific* than that of Mrs. Siddons. The " nodding ruin" of the former was announced in the wild scream of the vulture; and of the whole rant it might be truly said—

" This NOTHING is much *more* than MATTER."

The intellectual dignity of Mrs. Siddons rendered every thing of this sort a degradation of her talents. Where in truth could she wish to reign but in the *heart* or in the *judgment?* But guilty passion is still passion; and in the scene with Hastings, she poured out her tenderness and her confession, her contrition and agony, in tones which more perhaps than half surprised our pity.

From Rowe up to Shakspeare is a distance that no geometry can compute—and yet, what should we now be willing to give to the poet who could produce such a tragedy as Jane Shore? But we are grown too familiar with our actual wealth, and accept inferior metal for the sake of variety, though we know it to be intrinsically worthless, and that it cannot last.

Another instance of the taste about the benefit nights of Mrs. Siddons is to be recorded. On the 21st of January, 1788, the tragedy of King Lear was revived, in which she herself performed Cordelia, a character of no great power; and it may, therefore, be presumed that her principal object in the choice was to shew Mr. Kemble in King Lear. The play acted was Nahum Tate's alteration, who has the fame of contriving the love intrigue between Cordelia and Edgar, without which circumstance, perhaps, the youngest daughter of Lear would hardly have been deemed of sufficient importance to call upon the talents of a great actress. But it is usually dangerous to meddle with the fable of another man's play. Alterations can seldom be so fitted, as not to leave some original provision neglected. For instance, upon the frantic desertion of Cordelia by Lear, in the original play, the King of France, feeling himself rich in the possession of her virtues, bears her away with him to that kingdom—

whence she subsequently returns with an army to punish the persecutors, and heal the maladies of her father. Tate keeps her unconnected, and in Britain through the play, that he may finally bestow her upon Edgar; without reflecting that as she had forfeited her third of the kingdom, and must be equally obnoxious with Lear himself to her dog-hearted sisters, there was for her no comfortable or splendid establishment within the verge of the court, and that she must be as certain a wanderer as her father. But in the true style of chivalrous romance, from which the means of existence are to Sancho's astonishment so constantly withdrawn,—she, in her unprotected state, attended by her confidante Aranthe, in their poor thin court covering, which scarcely keeps them warm, ventures out in the pityless storm, to find the wretched Lear; and in the fifth act she is discovered in a chamber, we must presume her own, with physicians and armed knights awaiting the result of the means used under her direction for his recovery, in defiance of the sovereign prohibition making it death to relieve him. And all this inconsistency and absurdity is brought upon us, that Cordelia, in the night and the storm, may be seized by the emissaries of Edmund, delivered by the seeming lunatic Edgar, who is caressed by her as the best and dearest of men, and in his beggar's garb receives that return of affection, which had been refused to his happier hour.

I do not mean to say that such a scene would be objectionable, if it would naturally work with the business of the play; for though it breaks in upon the filial singleness of Cordelia's mind, and the lover takes his turn to reign with the father there, yet female interest should be had for our audiences if it can be admitted without serious injury to the work. *Kent* here, when he determined himself upon his course, might have bestowed upon Cordelia the possession of his land and the use of his fortune:—but this resource should have been made known to us; which it is not in the play as acted by Mr. Kemble.

There is one part of Tate's alteration which every reader will approve: he has made the unnatural daughters profligate and oppressive sovereigns.

> " The riots of these proud imperial sisters
> Already have impos'd the galling yoke
> Of taxes, and hard impositions, on
> The drudging peasant's neck, who bellows out
> His loud complaints in vain.   Triumphant queens !
> With what *assurance* do they *tread* the crowd !"

To be sure, Edmund, although their gallant, speaks of them as if he were at least a reprover of their vices—but as every thing that Tate does

must'be more or less inconsistent, the lover not
only is disposed to second their riots, but would
reign himself precisely in the same outrageous
manner! Having immediately after this speech
received *billets doux* from the two sisters, he naturally thinks of going through the family, and vio-
lating Cordelia in the storm. But it is really
shocking to see the inventions of Shakspeare thus
placed at the mercy of Bedlam and the Mint, in
which latter asylum for indolent sottish imbecility Tate dozed away much of his existence.
The church may owe him something, for he
translated the Psalms, in conjunction with Dr.
Brady — but his *new version* of Lear should
neither be sung nor said on any stage in christen-
dom.

For the just limits of stage innovation, the
reader may consult the elder Colman's alteration
of this play for Powell. In compliance with the
general taste, he has preserved both Lear and
Cordelia, without disturbing her union with the
King of France; and has retained nothing of Tate
but the animating speech of Cordelia, which follows the mental recovery of her father, in the fifth
act. It is proper to observe, that Mrs. Siddons
gave this with a filial tenderness, an ardour and
a piety highly impressive. It closes a very pathetic scene by bringing down that vehemence of

applause, that a performer must have to keep him from being dissatisfied with his own effects, and flat in spirit from the coldness of the house.

The money receipt at the door, I mean reckoning every admission at the proper rate, was £347 10s. almost equal to the famous night of Macbeth, the greatest that Drury Lane Theatre had ever known. The presents, it is probable, declined in their amount. In the advance towards the highest fame, the growing splendour of the actress increases our respect and diminishes our zeal. Patronage is protection, and to *that* acknowledged genius becomes superior—there is an apprehension of offence, if more is tendered than the proper consideration for the box we occupy.

In another work I have noticed Mrs. Cowley's Fate of Sparta, a tragedy in which Mrs. Siddons acted the part of Chelonice. I presume every thing to have been done for it that the subject admitted—its success, for modern tragedy, was beyond the usual measure, though Mr. Kemble sunk under the part of Cleombrotus. Mrs. Cowley had supplied Mrs. Siddons with an epilogue, exactly suited to the taste of the stage professor; that is, quite personal, and seducing and ensuring the claps of the audience. For a taste, and a future model together—

" Your hands they ask—*such* thunders do not fright—
Repeat the peal once more—and then, good night."

Mr. Kemble took his annual night on the 13th of March, and as a novelty gave Katharine and Petruchio, the wrangling pair by Mrs. Siddons and himself. Perhaps it was never better acted, if you could get over the conviction that such a physiognomy as that of the actress never could belong to a termagant; and that, if the bent of mind had once been given, it would not have been possible for the teasing violent and harassing discipline of Petruchio to have tamed down such a woman to so absurd an obedience to his pleasure. Of a petulant spoiled *girl* the transformation might be credited. The incidents are farcical and the whip and the crockery make noise enough for the joke sake—but there never could be an atom of farce in the composition of Mrs. Siddons; though her name might always be useful—" set it to what point you would."

The hopes of man are subject to failure, when security is rendered the most probable. The last season and the present offer two striking examples. Capt. Jephson and his friends at the Castle had so distinguished themselves in the early support of Mr. Kemble and Mrs. Siddons, that with his great talent to bear up their exertions, Julia might have reckoned upon a triumphant and durable existence on the London stage. The illness of Mr. Kemble destroyed her.

Mr. Greatheed might have equally relied upon the success of his *Regent*. He had written a part for Mr. Kemble quite up to his wishes, and in all probability fashioned by his advice; and the heroine, Dianora, was in the hands of Mrs. Siddons, who in the outset of life had resided with the Greatheed family; whose subsequent celebrity had been welcomed by their warmest friendship, and who must have had peculiar pleasure in returning one description of protection for another. But her health unluckily failed her after the *second* night, and the run of the piece, a mighty matter, was unfortunately checked.

The interest of the Regent is of the true Spanish cast. Inflexible design, dark and deadly means, and that tyranny exercised upon the maternal bosom, which only shews that it contends in vain against the strongest principle in female nature. The husband, supposed to be murdered, survives to return at the critical moment, and redeem his wife and child from the fierce grasp of the Regent. Kemble, in the present play, looked like one of those grand and terrible beings who desolated Spanish America; a class of men to be found, I would fain hope, only under peculiar excitements in any nation.

I will not refuse myself the pleasure of noticing, that Mr. Greatheed seems to have strongly felt the characteristic fulness and power of Shakspeare's soliloquies. The following ruminations of Manuel remind the reader of his Richard, and are no feeble rivals of his nervous diction :—

" My crime is past,—and, if there shall be judgment,
Will damn me certain ;—then, be *this* my heaven.
But who, lynx-ey'd, has peer'd beyond the grave,
And view'd that phœnix immortality ?
No—all may crumble in sepulchral night,
And then have I the better of the game.
Dost thou exist, or is thy being null,
Thou whom I sent to learn these mysteries ?
If thou art blessed, I shall be a demon ;
Therefore I *hope* thine essence is no more."

When we know, too, that this was a first play, and see how at times he could attain the just medium between tumour and flatness, we may regret that he did not pursue the obvious bent of his genius, and adorn at least his own times with compositions, which at least reminded us by an emulous spirit of our former glories. He dedicated the Regent to Mrs. Siddons. Mr. Greatheed was assailed by all the outrageous and rancorous wantonness of criticism ; but he was a gentleman, and continued silent.

For her second night this season, Mrs. Siddons

took the masterwork of Dryden, *All for Love*, and performed his Cleopatra. The distinction which I should make between the queens of Shakspeare and Dryden, is that the one displays the cause, and the other the effect. Every thing is *said* by Dryden that can describe unbounded passion—that is *done* in Shakspeare which alone can keep it without diminution; his Cleopatra is a character of infinite variety.

Dryden appears to me to have exhausted himself in all the artifices of poetical embellishment. His play is luxuriant in the happiest combinations of language. Nor does he confine the charm to the highest personages. I know not that there is any thing better than the following, put into the mouth of Alexas.

> " Believe me, madam, Antony is yours,
> His heart was never lost; but started off
> To jealousy, love's last retreat and covert:
> Where it lies hid in shades, watchful in silence,
> And *listening* for the sound that *calls it back*."

One part of his subject was beyond his power. The interview, which he was tempted to write between the proud Egyptian charmer and Octavia, the sister of Cæsar, and the wife of Antony. It is inconceivably vulgar; for their passions are too vehement to allow of the temperaments of

their rank.   The best sentence of their rival malice is with Cleopatra.

" YOUR LORD, *the man* who *serves me,* is a Roman."

Octavia is once even *indecent.*   It is, I have no
doubt, the worst scene in the play, and ends its
third act.

I never found that the audience sympathized
very strongly with Cleopatra.   Antony's passion
for her is the *weakness* of a hero, and her love for
him is not the *virtue* of either her sex or condition.   She is I think barely endured, for she does
not attempt to render her error respectable by her
remorse.

Shakspeare, who better understood, or more
closely adhered to nature, has represented Cleopatra as *capricious* as alluring, and as *facile* as
fond.   She can *tease* the being whom she loves,
and *betray* the hero whom she cannot survive.
That Mrs. Siddons did every thing that could be
desired for the Cleopatra of *All for Love* is readily
granted.   She was a being for whom the world
indeed might seem " well lost."   But from the
commanding style of her features, and the dignity of her person, the notion of frailty was
visually banished—she seems always to be superior to her condition.   The daring atrocity
of crime was, however, her own.   She could

R 2

completely unsex herself as Lady Macbeth, and repel the scorns of the world in Calista; but the pageant of romance, the Cleopatra of Dryden, had nothing that suited her, and did not range among her acting parts.

Of Shakspeare's superior genius the world has heard enough, though, perhaps, hardly yet *felt* sufficiently; but of his superior *judgment* little, indeed, has been said. Dryden has gone over the famous passage of the Cydnus, and so fertile was his fancy that he has left a rival description of much beauty; but he lost the great point; that is, to shew the magic of his Egyptian by her *effects*. In Dryden, Antony himself describes this gorgeous scene to the blushing Dolabella. In Shakspeare, the whole world is gone to gaze on Cleopatra, and the master of it,

> " Enthron'd i' the market place, did sit alone,
> *Whistling to th' air*."

This is beyond all the silken streamers, and the cloth of gold—the seeming Cupids and Nereids, and the love-sick winds that wafted the imperial beauty; or rather it describes the scene more impressively than the highly apposite terms chosen by either poet. It is wiser frequently to suggest to the imagination, than to satiate it. As these passages stand in the plays, Dryden's convinces

us of the *dotage* only of Antony, Shakspeare's
of the perfect attraction of Cleopatra. In the
first, *his fondness* seems to have embellished her
voyage ; in the second, HE is rendered a nullity
by it, and, but that he is named by the poet,
would have been forgotten by us, as he was by
the people.

CHAPTER XVIII.

IMPORTANCE TO MRS. SIDDONS OF HER BROTHER'S MANAGE-
MENT.—THE AGE NOT DRAMATIC—NOVELTY HOPELESS.—
THE TASTE OF MR. KEMBLE, ITS OPERATION.—MRS. SID-
DONS HAD STILL SOME IMPORTANT TASKS IN SHAKSPEARE.—
SHERIDAN AN ASSAILANT OF TRAGEDY ITSELF.—HIS MODE
OF DECLAMATION.—WESTMINSTER HALL—PASSAGE FROM
SPENSER.—SHERIDAN'S REAL POWER IN COMEDY.—NEITHER
HE NOR KEMBLE FRIENDLY TO MODERN PRODUCTIONS FROM
DIFFERENT REASONS.—THE ROYAL INDISPOSITION, EARLY
APPARENT TO MRS. SIDDONS.—QUEEN KATHARINE IN HENRY
THE EIGHTH.—REVIEW OF MRS. SIDDONS IN THAT ADMIR-
ABLE PERFORMANCE.—DISCRIMINATION BETWEEN THE TWO
CARDINALS.—THE SCENE AT KIMBOLTON.—HER KATHARINE
EQUAL TO HER LADY MACBETH.—PALMER IN HARRY.—BENS-
LEY THE WOLSEY.—MRS. SIDDONS IN THE ROMAN MOTHER.
—SHAKSPEARE AND LA HARPE.—ANOTHER WRITER ON THE
SUBJECT.—THOMSON.—BEAUTIES OF THE ACTRESS AND THE
AUTHOR.—LAW OF LOMBARDY AND LETHE.—MARY QUEEN OF
SCOTS.—SCHILLER.—AN OPINION OF THE PRESENT WRITER.
—THE KING'S RECOVERY.—MRS. SIDDONS RECITES IN
PUBLIC, AN ODE BY MERRY, DREST AS BRITANNIA.—SHE ACTS
JULIET—THE PERFORMANCE EXAMINED.—THE TOMB SCENE.
—GARRICK'S ALTERATION SUGGESTED BY OTWAY.

IT was certainly a point of great importance to
Mrs. Siddons, that her brother, Mr. Kemble,

should at all events be the stage manager of Drury Lane Theatre, and that for reasons which equally affected her family and her fame. How her fame itself was dependant upon such an arrangement shall be shewn. Perhaps, no actress ever stood so strongly *alone* as Mrs. Siddons. The tenth, twentieth, and thirtieth repetition of many of her characters, hackneyed as they had previously been for half a century by every actress worthy of the name, had still an attraction in her powers of the most respectable and profitable kind. Some of them, it is true, became a little the worse for wear; but generally speaking, what had first charmed her audiences preserved their affection beyond the useless and hopeless trials of what novelty might produce.

The genius of the age was certainly not of a dramatic cast—it supplied nothing that could be even wished to survive beyond the ninth representation, when the poet commonly found, that two benefits might have been more profitable to him than three. But it was a somewhat rare occurrence to reach that consummate number of the muses. There was, in fact, therefore, no increase to her list of parts, and an endless sameness, it might be foreseen, would wear out alike the energy of the actress, and the attention of the town.

The retirement of Smith from the stage was followed by that of King from the management,

if management that could be called, which had
no feature of the function but its name. He describes himself as having by no *written* agreement
the power either to accept or reject any new dramatic work; to engage, encourage, or discharge
any one performer; nor to order the refitting of
a single article in a worn-out wardrobe. To our
still greater surprise, he adds, that he had not
even the *wish* to possess privileges supposed to
reside exclusively in the proprietors of the concern. How he had been tempted to lend himself, his talent, his consideration, to the servile
duties that could alone remain to his situation,
he has not explained; but he might receive
occasional promises, which were made only to
pacify and be forgotten; and indeed hope, that
the exigency of the case would at last bestow
what the most indolent love of power was so
loth to relinquish.

In such effusions of spleen, the grievance most
felt is commonly undeclared, and I cannot but
suppose the feelings of a comic actor somewhat
hurt at the ascendancy of tragedy; and his perception that the actual power of Mr. Kemble
and his sister in the theatre must render him now
an absolute cypher in the concern. The comedians who had adhered to him through life, were
withdrawing fast from his standard; and the
school of Garrick must shortly submit to other

masters than those who had presided in its various classes. He knew, I conceive, that his retirement made way for Mr. Kemble's certain appointment.

Upon the peculiar studies and accomplishments of Mr. Kemble, enough has been said in the author's Memoirs of his late friend: it is here only necessary to shew *how* they eventually aided the impression even of Mrs. Siddons herself. In his system of management, Mr. Garrick was certainly the model followed by Mr. Kemble. They both, for the same reason, built principally upon Shakspeare, and looked to his characters as the materials of which their own consequence was to be composed. The difference between these great actors was, that Garrick (as indeed he well might do,) depended *more* upon himself; and with respect to the combination of other great talents with his own, or the minor embellishments proceeding from the utmost attention to the whole cast of the play, a picturesque costume as to the dresses, and scenery of reasonable accuracy, he was careless, perhaps disdainful; or, as he had decided upon a certain scale of expence, which was not to be exceeded, he employed his scene-painters and his tailors *religiously*, upon the festivals of *Christmas* and *Easter*, and left the drama, plainly and decently got up, to the genius of the poet and the actor.

Mr. Kemble, with respect to our dramatic authors, had something of the feeling of a com
mentator; he was born for accuracy, and was
convinced that the very text spoken upon our
stages needed the most careful revision; as we
grew accustomed to our elder language by the
frequent republication of Shakspeare, the num-
berless substitutions of familiar for obsolete expressions were now to be struck out; and our
great poet, upon the stage, rendered more strictly
like his own works in the closet.   He thought, in
a word, that the stage should evince a proper
attention to the prevailing studies of the times.
If this was his opinion as to the language of our
plays, he considered the *mode* in which they were
exhibited still more open to improvement.   Too
many and too considerable demands were made
upon the imagination of the spectator, " to piece
" out with their thoughts" the imperfections of
the stage.   He saw no reason why the representation in the *seeming* magnificence of the action
should yield to the reality ; and that it should be
true, as well as splendid, was a principle of illusion which was likely by its air of learning to
recommend SHEW itself to such as affect to despise it, unless it has the *verd antique* about it accurately coloured.

. The elder notion as to acting was, that the
power of the actor, " the bright metal on a sullen

"ground" was all sufficient, and needed not the
aid of ornament : every thing subordinate, as it
could make little effect, it was policy to slur over.
Kemble, on the contrary, looking to a larger field
of exertion and more ample means, made the
whole so perfect and splendid, and interesting,
that the GREATEST talents alone could be borne
with in the *higher* characters of the drama. He
consequently established the ascendancy of himself and his sister by the very accompaniments,
that would have rendered feebler merits contemptible.

When, therefore, he had accepted the management of Drury Lane Theatre, he bent
every faculty he possessed to improve stage representation. By the good taste of his alterations of the plays themselves, the fitness of the
performers for the parts allotted to them, and
the knowledge that now regulated the dresses,
the properties, and the scenery of his revivals,
a management, that was assailed at times by
puny ridicule, and often thwarted by the treasury as to supplies, and performers from a natural
desire after eminence, became really an ERA in
the art—so excellent, as absolutely to admit of no
subsequent improvement. He felt that the style
of his own acting was gaining ground upon ancient prejudices; and he never doubted for a
moment that he should ultimately establish the

grand and poetic, the BEAU IDEAL, as the standard of art among us. To second all his designs,
he had the finest tragic actress in the world;
who began to feel that either novelty must be
provided, or a novel gloss be given to the old, or
her attraction must at length decline. Shakspeare had still some demands unsatisfied upon
her. Lady Macbeth had enchanted with spells
more potent than ever muttered over the caul-
dron of the witches; and the ROMAN MATRON
promised to add a distinctive feature to her past
achievements; while Queen Katharine tempted
her with the promise of more true majesty, mental
dignity, and persistive virtue, than were ever
combined to constitute female excellence in the
imagination of man. She had but one abate-
ment to her triumph, that it could never now be
witnessed by her admirer, Doctor Johnson.

It might be imagined, that some impediments
stood in the way of this ascendancy of the tragic
muse. With the vivacity of a comic writer, Mr.
Sheridan had done his utmost to cover the business and the manners of tragedy with ridicule,
and he had levelled his satire, not like the authors of the Rehearsal, at the tragedies then in
vogue, but at the resorts of ALL tragedy; and the
Critic seems in some few points but little to regard
the prescriptive veneration attached to the tragedies of a distant age. When, in addition to all

this, he invents the absurdity he cannot find, and ascribes his monstrous nonsense to a man of consummate ability, namely *Puff*, it is quite clear his attack is levelled rather at the composition than the writer; and that he would thus indirectly recommend that style of entertainment to which his own particular genius inclined him.

It is not my intention here to enter into an examination of Mr. Sheridan's dramatic talents. When a writer has produced plays of brilliant and lasting reputation, it would be ungenerous to assemble all the originals of his characters, and trace his situations to their source; to examine how a very common thought is rendered pungent, and the face of novelty bestowed upon a very ancient simile or sarcasm. A late publication* has shewn this surprising man, whose name among us was almost synonimous to *indolent genius*, to have been the most pertinacious and elaborate polisher of points of dialogue that probably ever existed : to have always been storing up a magazine of figure and illustration, to be used as occasion might demand ; and even to watch that occasion with solicitude, or force it by address, when the painful result of much reflection and study was to fall from him as the meteor of the

* Moore's Life of Sheridan.

moment, and dazzle his hearers by a kind of mental wonder, the quickness of whose production was only equalled by the brilliancy of its point.

If the author of the School for Scandal approached Congreve in the *stream* of wit characteristic of both, there was another excellence, one of art, in which he was quite equal to his great master; I mean the suiting the sentence exactly to the organ; and being sure of the fancy and the judgment, taking care that the rhythm should please as much almost as the reason or the wit, and the ear anticipate the triumph of the appeal to the understanding; sentences written to be *spoken*—tried upon the tuneful tongue of the writer, and thus never suffered to hang upon that of the actor. The declamation of Mr. Sheridan had always this pointed and musical character; and when he quoted the rebuke to Mammon in Spenser, during his famous speech in Westminster Hall, a kind of audible surprise was felt that he should recite poetry so finely; but the prose of his whole life was to the full as metrical as even the verse of Spenser.*

* The reader might with some reason complain, if I left him to his own search as to the passage quoted by this great orator. Indeed it was combined from two distant stanzas in the seventh canto

That Mr. Sheridan could have long continued to supply even such dialogue as distinguishes his *School for Scandal* and the first act of his *Critic*, I feel no difficulty to admit: but I am rather

of the second book of the Faery Queene. As he spoke the lines, they seemed closely connected :—

> " Mammon, said he, thy godhead's vaunt is vaine,
> And idle offers of thy golden fee ;
> To them that covet such eye-glutting gaine
> Proffer thy giftes, and fitter servaunts entertaine.
> Another bliss before mine eyes I place,
> Another happiness, another end,
> And to be lord of those that riches have,
> Then them to have my selfe, and be their servile sclave."

In this manner did he chuse to repel the assertion of Mr. Hastings's friends, that the Governor General had never been avaricious; and with all the treasures of the East at his disposal, had made no provision for himself or family, and that he was now absolutely a poor man.

It was on the present occasion that I saw the historian, Gibbon, in the manager's box. Sheridan seized the opportunity to combine the " *luminous page* of the philosopher with the *correct periods* of Tacitus;" and Mr. Gibbon on the occasion says, " nor could I hear without emotion the personal compliment which he paid me in the presence of the British nation."

. On this trial, I saw Burke sensibly touched by a compliment from the third counsel for Mr. Hastings, Mr. Dallas. The learned advocate said of the great manager, that " if he had been cast into the times of Zenobia, he would have been found, like Longinus in the train of his ungrateful mistress, less concerned at the fate which awaited him, than at the weakness by which she had sacrificed the noblest of her friends." To this, in the politest manner, Mr. Burke audibly said, " VERY WELL, indeed, Sir."

disposed to think his mind not so affluent in *cha-racter* nor so inventive of dramatic *business* as would be demanded for any long reign of a comic writer. He does not seem to have discerned much of what constitutes character—his per-sonages have commonly been seen *before*, if not drest with equal neatness or elegance. The artist I confess appears always before me. It is the attribute of genius to conceal all labour. Not to mention HIM, with whom there can be no comparison, Mr. Sheridan could not have gathered the endless train of humours, which crowded about the discernment of MOLIERE. Besides that he always reminds you of some predecessor, there is little absolute nature even in his finest scenes. More merriment has seldom been pro-duced than we find in his Rivals, but the charac-ters are violently overcharged. The vocabulary of Mrs. Malaprop is full of expressions so removed from ordinary use, that she *must* have stumbled upon more MEANING, even in the search of her terms. *Acres* is not to be credited any more than Sir Anthony Absolute—they are, however divert-ing, absurdities, beyond the latitude of nature, who yet, it must be confessed,—

" Showers with copious hand."

But whatever might have been the result of a steady application to the drama, on the part of

Mr. Sheridan, he had determined to run the greater course as a politician ; and eclipse even his celebrity as a dramatic writer, by his fame as an orator. And strange as it·may be to say it— he succeeded ;. at least thus far, that he impressed those who *heard* him in Westminster Hall, that they had then witnessed the grandest display of talent of ancient or modern times. And, perhaps, so' large an assembly as that which concurred in this opinion could not be entirely deceived. Yet I may be permitted to think that he did wisely in *authentically* trusting it only to the EAR. The ostentation and boldness of its figures,—its affectation of displaying all the knowledge that he must have painfully gathered together,—its florid style—its eternal exclamation and appeals to violated nature and morals,—ALL bore too much of the character of Irish oratory ; and would have looked in the closet, to the dispassioned reader, tumid and artificial. I heard Mr. Burke's fine summing up ; and I found there the full dignity of long treasured wisdom ; an imagination rich but not gaudy, and at times invested with an almost prophetic awfulness, as it pictured forth the effects of successful guilt. The grave and masterly figure of JUSTICE, with which he solemnly closed his appeal to the Judges of Mr. Hastings, was in my judgment infinitely beyond the more *theatrical* images of Sheridan.

The constant demands of the House of Commons upon him occupied nearly all his time; and however tempting the reputation or the profits of the stage might be to a man of genius, who had determined on political independence; however ill inclined he might be to see his theatre in possession of any other comic writer; he could hardly hope for sufficient leisure to extend very considerably his own dramatic productions. He, therefore, listened with pleasure to the scheme of management proposed to him by Mr. Kemble; who, for a different reason, and with quite another sort of taste, was little disposed to encourage the modern drama. Bestowing a care so reverential upon the elder drama, and insuring its attraction by the expense with which it was embellished, made it almost an act of *presumption*, in any writer of our own day, to offer his inventions, in the region devoted to the great masters of the art. The payments to authors, too, would be slender; who sometimes were well remunerated for a very fugitive production—while such monies expended in dress and scenery and decoration, remained permanent properties in the theatre: which it has been already stated had become rather mean in its imitations of the splendour of past times. The new manager, therefore, entered upon his task with full reliance upon his own plans; and little apprehensive, perhaps, *then*, that he should ever be thwarted in his designs, and reduced to besiege the treasury for the means of replenishing its own coffers. He started, however, with considerably more actual power than King had ever possessed; and his sister's strength might be calculated as his own.

In the early part of the summer of 1788, an event occurred of the deepest moment to the nation. I allude to the late King's alarming indisposition, of which the first symptoms indicated nothing beyond bilious fever; and accordingly Sir George Baker was inclined to keep his Majesty from the hurry to which he would be exposed by going to town, and recommended that he should remain at Kew, until the complaint was quite removed. His Majesty's physicians, however, thought it advisable to try the effect of the mineral waters at Cheltenham: the King unfortunately derived little or no benefit from the springs, and returned on the 16th of August to Windsor. Soon after this, symptoms of mental aberration appeared, which called for the solemn attention of the legislature of the country.

The reason for noticing that event in this place is, that the subject of these Memoirs became among the very earliest to perceive that the royal mind was somewhat unsettled. The attention paid by his Majesty to the great actress was not

confined to the public exhibition of her talents—
he was a professed admirer of her manners in
private life, and the royal family saw her frequently at Buckingham House and at Windsor.

His Majesty's conversation always expressed
the gracious feeling of his mind, and his wish to
promote the interests of herself and her family.
However, on one occasion, the King put into her
hands a sheet of paper, merely subscribed with
his *name*, intended, it may be presumed, to afford
the opportunity to Mrs. Siddons of pledging the
royal signature to any provision of a pecuniary
nature, which might be most agreeable to the
actress herself. This paper, with the discretion
that was suited to the circumstance itself, and
which was so characteristic of Mrs. Siddons, she,
I was assured, delivered into the hand of the
Queen; upon whom conduct so delicate and
dignified was not likely to be lost.

Mr. Kemble, I think, told me, that her Majesty
was very *pointed* in the expression of her approbation at the time; and it may be readily believed,
that no individual, among the various classes of the
King's subjects, looked with more solicitude to the
progress of his Majesty's disorder, nor more sin-
cerely rejoiced in his recovery, than the lady
whom, even in his infirmity, he had intended to
render as independent as she was meritorious.

On the 25th of November, 1788, in obedience, as we may state it, to the decision of Dr. Johnson, Mrs. Siddons acted Shakspeare's Queen Katharine in Henry the Eighth, which was carefully revived by Mr. Kemble, and became, from that night, one of the most attractive pieces that the stage has ever known. The character of Katharine is historical rather than dramatic—the poet has versified the chronicler, and has added but little, except the numbers of his art, to the *very* expressions of Henry's high-soul'd Queen. I never, on any occasion, beheld our admirable actress more impressed with the matron dignity that was expected from her, and never were the highest hopes of her friends crowned with more perfect satisfaction. Yet there is but slender scope for passion. The situation absorbs the woman. The object of Katharine is to do nothing that may compromise her *own* rights or those of her *daughter;* nothing unworthy of the exalted *stock* she came from ; or the high tone to which that birth had necessarily carried the sense of all her *duties.* Her place in council is admirably sustained ; she is the soul of moderation —her candour pierces through the sophistry of exaggeration, and she looks with the keenness of an accusing angel, into the oppressions of arrogant authority.

The first entrance of Mrs. Siddons was in the

second scene of the first act. It is the council chamber, where the King appears to have been excited by Wolsey against the Duke of Buckingham, and they are upon the point of making his accuser repeat the treasons with which he has been charged, when Sir Henry Guildford without calls, " room for the Queen"—and she enters, her page bearing a cushion before her, which having placed, she kneels to the King— and after the salutations have been exchanged, proceeds to open the gracious object on which she came, to relieve the Commons from sundry *grievous* exactions, which she in fact charges upon Wolsey. The minister avails himself of the protest against more imputation than attaches to his mere voice in the measure of a cabinet council. " I know but of a single part." The temperate dignity of the reply was enchantingly uttered :—

> " *Queen.*— No, my lord,
> You KNOW no more than others ; but you *frame*
> Things, that are known alike."

It was from that moment obvious, that she would here excel any level speaking that she had ever delivered upon the stage. The dignity of her figure, admirably dressed, the intelligence of her look, and the graceful composure of her gesture, have never been paralleled.

The first allusion to the Duke of Buckingham was the gentle concern of one who did not take accusation for conviction. When the accuser adds, to his charge of treason, one that he vowed revenge upon the *Cardinal*, Wolsey presses that point stronger than a good or a great man would have done.

> " To your high person
> His will is most malignant ; and it stretches
> Beyond YOU—to your *friends*."

It is delightful to me to recal the tone of the Queen's rebuke :—

> " *Queen*.— My learn'd lord cardinal,
> Deliver ALL with CHARITY."

As *brave* as generous, she follows this with a shuddering caution to the discarded servant, who came forward to accuse his great master.

> " Take good heed,
> You charge not in your spleen a noble person,
> And spoil your nobler soul ; I SAY—TAKE HEED."

The actress far outstript here all the majestic energy, which I have heard in the grandest court that ever assembled.* Upon Wolsey's triumph in

---

* If the reader should suspect that I *may* here refer to the manner of Lord Thurlow, at the trial of Mr. Hastings in Westminster Hall, he will do me no injustice.

the strength of the fellow's accusations, and his
retort upon the Queen's lenity—equally beautiful was the " Heaven mend all," with which she
concludes.

The scene in the second act, called her trial—a
trial of nothing but the *patience* of the Queen,
had the most intense interest—it was perfectly
delusive. The address to the King made its way
to the heart by satisfying the judgment. But
upon Wolsey's insulting her with the " *integrity*
". and *learning*" assembled to plead for her, in
the King's dominions, against his own *passions*,
—the commanding air, look, and tone, with
which she called up her enemy, excited a delightful astonishment. There is no hint in Shakspeare
of any rising of Campeïus, when she utters the
words " Lord Cardinal ;" and then the waving
him aside for the other cardinal present, Wolsey—

" To you I speak."

and I do not know whether this double action
and division of the address originated with Mrs.
Siddons or not. I incline to think it did—for
though it looked more in the *subtle* style of her
brother's understanding, than, what I will call,
the more *manly* plainness of her own, yet the
action with which it was accompanied, the sway

and balance of the figure, offered a charm to the
spectator which the pencil fortunately did not
lose; though my young friend, who painted it,
perished from neglect, when he was meditating
greater things than what I call the most effective
scene that was ever transferred from the stage
to the canvass.

> " My *drops* of TEARS
> I'll turn to *sparks* of FIRE."

Expressions as vivid as the look of the actress,
by which that change was actually produced.
The rest of this admirable scene was sustained
with such true grandeur, that upon her exit it
was in truth quite time to break up the council,
for the King and his favourite vindicated each
other with very little attention from the audience.

Although we see nothing more of Katharine,
till she is at Kimbolton, and such is the rapid
course of the action that Wolsey's disgrace,
journey and death, all occur before the fourth
act, yet the spectator is sufficiently led through
the successive events, and attends the last illness
of the Queen fully prepared for the awful close
of her sublime character. The great woman,
whose progress I trace with equal veneration and
regret, (veneration for its powerful truth, and
regret that it can be seen no more,) acted this
display of languor that never wearied, with in-

imitable majesty. I can hardly bring myself to think the Lady Macbeth a greater effort: one more perfect I am sure it was not. The imagination will naturally let itself loose to consider what Shakspeare himself would have thought of such an exhibition. Though he wrote such characters for MEN, he must think of all the peculiar graces of WOMAN; and for an elevated conception of female dignity, he had only to contemplate the " lion port and awe-commanding face" of Elizabeth, who had many of his plays acted at court. If the poet really designed to exhibit Henry the Eighth before Elizabeth, he must have greatly complimented her mind, when he trusted her with so fascinating a picture of the Queen supplanted by her own unfortunate mother. Yet the great ELIZA is said to have shewn a marked indifference to her mother's memory; and to have buried all the odious qualities of her father, and his injurious conduct to herself, under the flattering throne, which she derived from him.

" O hard condition !
Twin-born with greatness."

I cannot omit to notice the very characteristic manner, in which the *defender* of the faith and author of its *rejection* was performed by Palmer; his towering figure, fair complexion, and explosive manner, gave an absolute *fac simile* of Harry.

He had enough of tragedy about him to keep his comedy from being ludicrous :—the importance of the King, and the awe which it inspired, have occasionally suffered in other hands.

. The time of Wolsey was not yet arrived—Bensley was impressive ; but he was so decided a mannerist, that the Cardinal frequently reminded his hearers of the gallant conspirator against the state of Venice, and some violent anachronism seemed to have promoted the rebel Pierre from the *wheel* to the CROSS, which Wolsey, alas, *proudly* had borne before him.

As a matter of stage convenience Mr. Kemble joined the two characters of Cromwell and Griffith together ; but the attachment of the former to his great master, Wolsey, would keep him at a great distance from the chance of ever attending Queen Katharine ; he had his fortune to make at court, and knew well the peril of seeking those who are out of favour.

The 7th of February, 1789, exhibited Mrs. Siddons as the Roman Mother of Kemble in Coriolanus.. Volumnia was evidently a great favourite with Shakspeare—he has painted that heroic mould in a manner the most natural and masterly. To use the language of another admirable writer, she has not parted with the " remains " of that fierce spirit, which sullied with bar- " barism the lofty and romantic courtesy of an-

" cient manners." She delights to contemplate the warrior crimson'd in the blood of his enemy — sees his mailed hand wiping his bleeding brows, and thinks that stain more becoming to a man, than the golden lacker upon his trophy. She does herself full justice too. She is a daughter of the Queen of nations, and can speak thus, *truly*, to Coriolanus.

> " Thy valiantness was MINE, thou suckd'st it from me ;
> But owe thy *pride* THYSELF."

As I sat revolving the figure, the expression, and the voice of the noble representative of Volumnia; brought before my imagination again the simple resorts of head-dress, by which her beautiful and noble face was made to pass for that of the mother of Kemble without demur; when in running over, in a rather tenacious memory, the free and various dialogue in which she mingles, I had again in my ear the perfect tones of that eloquence always suited to the occasion,—I could not help a smile of either contempt or pity at the affected disdain of La Harpe, for every thing that would have rendered his Coriolan natural and interesting. To hear him quote the dictum of his oracle, Voltaire—" that Coriolanus condemned at Rome " in the first act, received by the Volscians in the " third, and besieging Rome in the fourth, consti

" tuted in fact three tragedies."—THEN, to preserve any interest at all, feeling bold enough to
venture so far from the unity of place, as to open
his own third act in the camp of the Volscians,
being careful, however, in the scenery, to shew
a miniature of Rome hanging up in the distance.
As if, when he had once led his spectators from
the place they were first shewn, he might not as
well have transferred them to Antium, better
known to an audience by Shakspeare's exclamation—" A goodly city is this Antium"—than the
minikin Rome in the distance could be from the
camp of the Volscians.

I read over his character of Veturie, the mother of Coriolan, and rejoiced that Mrs. Siddons
had been delivered from the sameness of her patriotic declamations, and the few points of stage
trickery, which are the only substitutes for the
emotions of humanity. I will turn a few of these
fine things into verse, at least as good as that they
came from.

" *Corio.*—Your Roman firmness now must comfort you.
Vetur.—I am a mother *only.*
Corio.—   Nay, not now,
Since you have lost your son.
Vetur.—   How ? I have lost him !
Corio.—So Rome decides. Is she not absolute ?
Vetur.—Can Rome efface that sacred character ?

Corio.—'Twas of a *Roman* that you were the mother;—
And I am one no longer.
Vetur.—Who ? Marcius, thou !"

The climax of all this dove-tailing absurdity is
that Veturia has been fully informed of all that
happened in the forum before the entrance of
Coriolanus; and her first speech to her son ac-
quaints him that she has heard of his banishment
—but the literary fencing match was to be played
out all the same, in this region of grandeur, and
nature, and *bon sens* and *bon gout.*

La Harpe was once accused of having trafficked
a little with Shakspeare in his own third act; but
the tutor of Alexander the Russ, rather indig-
nantly vindicated his *good sense* and *good taste* from
such an aspersion, by immediately quoting from
Plutarque, Vertot, and *Tite-Live;* from the first
of whom Shakspeare had drawn the materials,
which had been common to them both.

I have never known why our great poet changed
the name of Coriolanus's mother to that of his
wife, namely, Volumnia, instead of Veturia, her real
appellation. La Harpe informs us, that an Abbé
Abeille, in treating this subject, has knotted it all
up into five acts of amorous intrigue;. where
Coriolanus and Aufidius play. at cross purposes,
or rather *partners;* the Roman being beloved by

a certain Camilla, sister to Aufidius,—he himself being a follower of *Virgilia*, who is beloved by Coriolanus. Here we have the *name* given by Shakspeare to the *wife* of the great Patrician. Is it likely that this French BEE had been buzzing among the sweets of Shakspeare, and brought away only the name of one of his flowrets instead of the honey?

I should quote the whole of the character of Volumnia, were I to detail all the charms with which Siddons adorned her. Her playful courage with the women in the outset. The welcome of her son with the peculiar

> " *What* is't? *Coriolanus* must I call thee?"

The scene after his contest with the tribunes, and that delightful—

> " O, Sir, Sir, Sir,—
> I would have had you put you power *well on*,
> Before you had worn it out."

And the rejoinder, in the key of her son's " let " them hang"—

> " Ay, and *burn* too."

The " he must and will" go to the market place,

and the relaxing of her maternal character into familiarity—

"Pr'ythee, now, *say*, you will, and *go about it*."

and the *moodiness*, with which she seemed to value his consent at nothing, because it had been given with no greater readiness,—

"Do your will." [*Exit.*]

The remainder of Volumnia in the fifth act is highly characteristic, as Shakspeare left it. Kemble admitted some of Thomson's dialogue in the French taste ; e. g.

"Rome by thy aid is *sav'd*—but thy son *lóst*."

To which the mother replies, as the whole parterre of Paris would have done,—

"He never can be *lost*, who *saves* his country."

But the greater poet had other arts of elevating a character, than by making it the strutting declaimer of patriotic conundrums. Hear him, in the mouth of Coriolanus, unfold the great principle of filial duty, to the mother who best of all the world deserved it.

" *Col.*—My MOTHER *bows*;
As if.OLYMPUS to a *mole hill* should
In supplication nod.''

How beautiful is the subsequent retort of Volumnia upon this feeling, as if she had heard
him express it—

" There is no man in the world
More bound to his mother ; yet here he lets me prate
Like one i'the stocks.''

and what follows in a strain of *divine* simplicity
and pathos—

" When she, poor hen ! fond of no second brood,
Has cluck'd thee to the wars, and safely home.''

And equally great the reproach—

" This *fellow* had a *Volscian* to his mother ;
His wife is in *Corioli*, and his child
Like him by *chance*.''

And the determination of the Roman matron, so
suitable to her true dignity—

" I am hush'd until our city be on fire,
And then I'll speak a little.''

When an author can write in this exquisitely
natural strain, and almost forget himself and his
luxuriant art, to be the true organ only of charac-

ter, passion, and business,—he achieves the *ne ultra* of dramatic power, and holds up a mirror stained by no mist of fashion, that clearly reflects the unquestionable features of MAN. To be worthy to study such a poet is no slight commendation—to display him, as Mrs. Siddons did his Lady Macbeth, Katharine, and Volumnia, is a fame that I have *endeavoured* at least to FIX and DELINEATE.

It is sometimes rather strange in the eye of the critic, to see the possessor of the greatest talent disposed to waste it upon ungracious materials; and in reviving the dead, stumbling upon subjects who were *never* worthy of existence. For her night, the 16th of February, Mrs. Siddons put up the *Law of Lombardy*, and the farce of *Lethe*. This was what Cowper would have called

"Undesign'd severity, that glanc'd:"

for the fine lady of the farce was as much forgotten, as the princess of the tragedy. That Mrs. Clive might have exhibited Mrs. Riot, and delighted her audience, I can readily suppose; she might not only with impunity, but with something *like* the vulgar ignorance of worn-out affectations, have uttered the jargon of Mrs. Malaprop. But to hear from Mrs. Siddons of *Serbeerus* and *Plutus*, and the *internal* world—of *Goats* and

Vandils, and of the waterman *Scarroon*, and of the *quincettence* and *emptity* of a fine lady, and her *anecdote* for the vapours,—why truly one is hurt to think that such a man as Garrick should imagine he was *doing* any thing, when he wrote nonsense so detestable ; and still more so, that such a woman as Mrs. Siddons did not disdain to pollute her lips with language that disgraced her fine articulation, as much as its meaning did her understanding. If she was not *generous* enough to stay away, I suppose Mrs. Jordan might be the only person who could *smile* at such an attempt.

Lord Chalkstone and his Bowman are the first sketches of Ogleby and Canton, *made out*, as the painters say, by Colman the elder, and destined to the longest possible period of modern comedy—for *our* best are not, I think, immortal, like the comedies or tragedies of Shakspeare.

The subject of Mary Queen of Scots is so interesting in history, whatever be the opinions of the historian, that we are not surprised to see a tedious confinement, ended only by the axe, become the business of the tragic poet; and a single scene of interest not very dramatic, be yet sufficient to render five acts endurable, though they should never be popular. The Duke of Wharton left an unfinished Mary; and Mr. St. John, the brother of Lord Viscount Bolingbroke, was fortunate enough to finish a tragedy upon that subject, which was produced in March, 1789, by Mrs. Siddons; and however feeble, from the charms of the heroine and those of her representative, acted several times. The inherent difficulty of this story to an Englishman is the attention demanded by the rival Queens; and notwithstanding the solid quartos, and the crowding octavos, which encumber our shelves with her vindication, Mary of Scotland is not quite the person whom I should select to blight the fame of our glorious Elizabeth. If your pathos spring from the sufferings of the Scottish Queen, you can view in her rival little more than a vain and cruel persecutor; or a sovereign, who, however arbitrary, in this case is the dupe of her ministers, and the innocent instrument by which the ruin of her dear kinswoman is accomplished. But however congested, it will always be heavy in the performance, unless the piece be animated by scenes of that courtly Billingsgate with which Schiller has marked the interview of his Mary and Elizabeth. I still think that a poet who could read German and write English, might give a version of his play that would ·live; but then it should be no affair of patchwork, no mosaic from Banks and St. John, and scraps collected from " all simples that have virtue under " the moon;" but what the author of the Robbers and Don Carlos has done with the subject:

apologizing, in some degree, for his freedom as to the facts, and his *foreign* view of the whole business.

Our great actress has been alluded to as slightly connected with the commencement of his Majesty's indisposition. She now very willingly lent herself and her talents to the celebration of his recovery. The disappointment of opposition, so near the possession of political power, as to anticipate appointments and bestow bishopricks, was presumed to have *forgotten itself* in the general joy occasioned by the King's restoration to perfect health. The predictions as to His Majesty's displeasure at certain provisions of Mr. Pitt, were answered by the contrary expressions of entire satisfaction and augmented confidence, and the minister was *preserved* for the mighty task of resisting the revolutionary power of France. But the club at Brookes's could not submit to lag behind in the festivities of the metropolis; and they gave a promenade, with a concert and recitation, supper and ball, and so on, to the ladies, in the Opera House, fitted up superbly for the occasion. Mrs. Siddons, I think idly, condescended to be drest as Britannia, and recited an ode written in the gossamer style of Della Crusca MERRY, with all the *fiction* at least of the truest poetry; for he was a furious zealot for liberty, and was at length hurried on to be the *eulogist* at least of actions, which will render in future times the veracity of the historian suspected. That decided cant, which by its vehement longings for the preservation of freedom, implies that it is considered to be in danger, was not spared. We had, in compliment, to his Majesty's recovery, " Long may he rule a *willing* land;" followed immediately by the check to inconsiderate loyalty—

> " But, oh! for ever may that land be free!"

Yet occasionally the poet wandered into *thinner* air, than the atmosphere of politics ;—and having sounded the inspiring union of George and Liberty! he immediately invokes the fairies.

> " Fairy people! ye who dwell
> In fragrant evening's vapoury cell,
> To the clear MOON oft repair."

They who have beheld the graceful form of Mrs. Siddons, and heard the solemn and melodious dignity of her declamation, may fancy the effect of such fine writing from her mouth; and imagine the astonishment of the spectators, when having finished the ode, she sat down in the exact attitude of Britannia as impressed upon our copper coin.

With the policy which the best taste is pardonable for exercising as to a benefit night, Mrs. Siddons repeated this ode on the 11th of May, at Drury Lane Theatre, after acting Juliet, which, I think, never became one of her current parts. The passion of Romeo and Juliet is entirely without dignity: it springs up like the mushroom in a night, and its flavour is earthy. To speak without a figure there is no *mind* in it; family interests it opposes, and the first glance on both sides renders it irresistible. It is adorned by all the magic of Shakspeare's fancy, and the play is consequently the text-book of our English lovers before the years of discretion. It is afterwards, I believe, deemed childish, and the actual age of the lovely Italian is thought the best justification of her vehemence and folly. There is, therefore, much to be *visually* surmounted, before the sage and sober character of the Siddonian countenance can be received as the expression of enthusiastic and unreflecting passion; or rather the face indicated more mind than is found in the character of Juliet.

But the art of the great actress made a powerful struggle against her natural strength; and so much of seeming artlessness was assumed, and so delightfully was the language modulated, that at times the ascendancy of the mother and the nurse did not seem preposterous and incredible.

The acting play has carefully expunged the traces of Romeo's previous passion for Rosaline;* so that the lovers seem predestined to complete each other's misery, and exist only for that love which destroys them. The German taste has found a vast deal of mysticism in the devotion of our lovers; and much of the " unintelligible " world" is, no doubt, faithfully described by those bulky " couriers of the air." Our duller imaginations see nothing but a disastrous and juvenile passion, an attraction of the exterior alone; where *beauty* being found, the higher requisites are overlooked, or rather presumed to be the necessary inhabitants of a graceful structure.

Mrs. Siddons was now in the " mid season of " this mortal life," and therefore numbered twenty years more than the fond enthusiast of Verona. Her beauty was of that kind, to which time adds

---

* In Shakspeare, Rosaline was to be a guest at Capulet's feast, and it was precisely to work at least a *comparative* cure of his passion for her, that his friend, Benvolio, would have him go thither. Romeo is too confident of his steadiness, and perishes by the bright ordeal he provokes. Yet Rosaline is not named by them at the banquet, and the first glance at Juliet dispels a passion, esteemed by him who entertains it incapable of change.

> " When the devout religion of mine eye
> Maintains such falsehood, then turn tears to fires !"

As Rosaline had never heard even of his passion, the punishment of his facility is rather severe.

strength, without much diminishing sweetness. Her art had more impressed her features than her age. The agonizing calls upon their expression had compelled the muscles into powerful action; and however they might be composed under the controul of the great magician, yet the countenance was *too strong* for Juliet. The eye, however, perfectly answered the mind; and what is or can be so essential to an actress as this visual eloquence?

Had Mr. Garrick, as her first appearance in London, brought her out in Juliet, the winning gentleness of her first scenes, contrasting with the ardent affection and speaking terrors of the latter, must have established her at once; but he chose to retain her as of counsel in the matter of Shylock *versus* Antonio, and exhibited as an eloquent pleader what should have been the undisguised organ of the most intense feelings of her sex.

When such an actor as Mr. Garrick had determined upon acting Romeo himself, it would follow as a branch of his own success to render the performance of Juliet as perfect as the most scrupulous attention to his fair partner could make it. The reciprocation of looks, the combinations of attitude, the meaning of every line, the quality of every sound, were to be in the most exact unison, or one of the characters must suffer from the other. It was not likely, therefore, that he should leave any very striking novelties to even the genius of Mrs. Siddons. I think upon the whole that she stood pretty much upon the former level of Juliet, except that, in the balcony, there was more perfect utterance; by which I mean that the sense came *fuller* upon the ear; and in the humouring of the nurse, there was something of a more genuine *playfulness* than I had heard before; as in the alarming scene of lonely midnight meditation, the tragic force of the great heroine rendered all competition hopeless.

There is something in the scene of Juliet's grave greatly at variance with the text, and with propriety itself. We have a churchyard, and in it the monument of the Capulets. " Why I de- " scend into this bed of death," is the expression of Romeo, who yet does not descend at all. He is furnished with a wrenching iron, which would enable him, by a proper application of his force, to remove the covering of the vault, and thus put it in his power to descend into the spacious receptacle.

> " Where for these many hundred years, the bones
> Of all the buried [Capulets] are pack'd."

But our stage Romeo batters a couple of doors fiercely with the crow in his grasp, which very naturally fly open *outwards;* and there, in all her supposed " maiden strewments," lies Juliet, above

ground, ingeniously obvious to the audience.
Surely all this is grossly absurd, and a more
creditable piece of machinery should now triumph
over the early poverty of scenical arrangement.
It would clearly be better if Romeo descended
into the monument and bore Juliet in his arms to
revisit the glimpses of the moon; a far more
natural arrangement, and in which Herculean
labour he might receive invisible assistance from
an ascending trap within the monument. However, the *start* when she is discovered is a fine
thing; the *whirling* of the iron crow is another
fine thing; and to hear the *clapping* from the gallery, at such a moment, must greatly delight the
actor and actress, who are disposed in *attitudes* so
strikingly picturesque.

I know the change made in the very action
itself, and certainly do not regret that Juliet
wakes before Romeo expires; because it affords
a scene of exquisite emotion: but it should be
consistently arranged. Romeo bears her from
the tomb, and yet two speeches afterwards she is
in the vault of death, which the mere churchyard
cannot be called. The dreadful *mining company*
of undertakers must settle this uncommon disin-
terment. I profess my inability. When I said
that the scene now given is one of great emotion,
I must not be supposed to mean more than that
the incident itself is deeply affecting. It is very

meanly written, when compared with the language of Shakspeare. The first hint of Juliet's waking before Romeo expires is from Otway, who has transformed our poet's lovers into Marcius and Lavinia; but he could lend little to the scene before us. Strange as it may sound, even Otway here has no *passion*—it is the strain of puerility. The modern scene consists,.therefore, of odds and ends, the " perfume and suppliance " of an actor's memory," not the genuine language of the situation and the passion. Snatches of the Mourning Bride may be perceived. Besides the miserable cant of—

" 'Twixt death and love I'm torn, I am distracted :"

and the infantine allusion—

" Fathers have flinty hearts, no tears can *melt* 'em :
Nature pleads in vain : children must be wretched."

As to the exclamations of Juliet, I will not.be so rude as to question their propriety. But thus it is, if any improvement of Shakspeare's interest is suggested, the frigid common-place in which it *must* be written, or *is* written, would lead us almost to the belief that the poet had breathed one common curse against the disturbers of ANY of his *remains*. See the lines over his grave at Stratford.

CHAPTER XIX.

MRS. SIDDONS QUITS LONDON FOR A SEASON.—HER OLD
CHARACTERS.—MRS. SIDDONS ACTS AT THE OPERA HOUSE.
THE EFFECT OF A LARGER STAGE UPON HER STYLE.—
HER APPLICATION TO STATUARY, ITS TENDENCY.—MORE
STRICTLY CLASSICAL IN HER DECORATIONS AND GENERAL
DEPORTMENT.—HOW FAR STAGE ILLUSION SHOULD BE
CARRIED.—MANY DIFFICULTIES OF SCENERY QUITE INSUR-
MOUNTABLE. — GLARING OFFENCE AGAINST DECORUM. —
30TH OF JANUARY, 1792, CYMON AND THE DEVIL TO
PAY.—THE PROBABLE EFFECT IN PARIS.—MRS. SIDDONS
PERFORMS QUEEN ELIZABETH IN RICHARD THE THIRD.—
RECITES COLLINS'S ODE ON THE PASSIONS.—HER PIC-
TURESQUE IMPERSONATION.—THE JEALOUS WIFE.—HOW
MRS. SIDDONS ACTED MRS. OAKLEY.—ARIADNE ACTED BY
MRS. SIDDONS.—THE YOUNGER CORNEILLE AND MURPHY.
—THE FRENCH HEROINE, LA CHAMPMELEE.—MURPHY'S
SISTERS ACTED ONLY SIX TIMES.—TAPESTRY PROUD OF
THIS SUBJECT.—SUBLIME PASSAGE IN THE MAID'S TRA-
GEDY.—MRS. SIDDONS OPENS THE NEW THEATRE IN DRURY
LANE ON THE 21ST OF APRIL, 1794.—KEMBLE THEN FIRST
OMITTED THE GHOST OF BANQUO.—ITS PROPRIETY DE-
NIED.—OPIE OF THAT OPINION.—IMPROVEMENTS OF THE
NEW STAGE.—VIEWS AS TO THE PROPERTY.—MR. CHARLES
KEMBLE.—HIS CHARACTER AS AN ACTOR.—EMILIA GA-
LOTTI.—THE WRITER'S IDEAS AS TO SPECTACLE CORRO-
BORATED BY MR. BURKE.—KEMBLE THROWS UP THE MA-
NAGEMENT.—EDWARD AND ELEONORA.—MISS FARREN RE-
TIRES, AND IS PUBLICLY COMPLIMENTED BY MRS. SIDDONS.

IT was natural to expect that the management of

Mr. Kemble would have greatly strengthened the stage consequence of Mrs. Siddons; but certainly the reverse was the fact, and the second season of it saw her leave London for a tour both friendly and professional. If I have leave to blame in such a matter, I rather incline to think my late friend somewhat disposed, at that time, to build too strongly on his own resources; or at least to have been too attentive to the idle clamour relative to the family interests; and, therefore, disposed to allow his sister to demonstrate her value by her absence. I may have neglected to note down some still better reasons alleged at the time, but it was in truth a bold step to permit any one season to be divested of its greatest ornament; and I am apt to suspect some slight misunderstanding to have been at the bottom of her temporary secession. She was happily secure in the actual transcendency of her talent; and as one prodigy was dramatically sufficient for those times, she ran no risk whatever in the experiment. On the score of novelty she lost nothing; tragic composition was at a very low ebb among us; and, indeed, since then, the only high tides we have experienced have been forced by the heavy swells of the *German* ocean.

I have not continued a comparative estimate of the attraction of Mrs. Siddons in her old characters—but for many years Isabella, the first she

acted of her brilliant period, continued to be most
frequently repeated; and I must so far think the
preference a just one, that I am quite sure I saw
it myself oftener than any of the powerful list,
those of Shakspeare only excepted, in which the
attraction was not entirely her own.   Nor did she
experience the slightest failure of patronage; on
her own night, in the season of 1790-1, she had
£412 in the house to the Gamester.   That house
it will be remembered was Garrick's, and this was
the year of its condemnation.   We shall next
survey Mrs. Siddons acting upon a larger stage,
and attend to the alteration in some degree of her
style of action, which moving in a greater space,
certainly became more grand and imposing.

In the year 1792 this experiment of her powers
upon a stage constructed for Italian Opera and
Ballet was made, and succeeded almost beyond
expectation.   That the spectators in the front of
the house lost much of her expression I know,
though I seldom sat there; for the passage between the orchestra and the pit had a very comfortable seat for about thirty amateurs of the art,
and with a little activity and address, it was
never very difficult to obtain a place there.   And
from this situation in all her towering majesty of
person, and in the maturity of her excellence, I
received impressions, which I could never consent to lose, and which have certainly not been

endangered by any effects from succeeding performers.

But I have hinted at some change of style, the
result of the new sphere of exertion. There is
nothing in Italian Opera that requires very extraordinary width of stage. It must, therefore,
have been suggested by a numerous Corps de
Ballet, which covers the whole proscenium. The
side scenes are at a great distance from the front
of the stage. In the Italian Opera, after the
singer male or female has finished the usual
colloquy with the prompter behind the central
hood which conceals his occiput, though not his
tongue, from the visitors, the usual mode is to turn
short round, and, presenting the back view to their
admirers, with the arms raised, somewhat in the
figure of a candlestick with two branches, to walk
away rather rapidly, without the smallest grace,
and if any applause should pursue their march,
or has attended their music, to make a bow or
curtesy at the wing, and hurry off to the fire-side.
But either the entrance or exit of English tragedy
is a matter that must be somewhat closer in its
bearing upon the business of the scene.

So few English performers are ever perfectly
at their *ease* upon the stage, that the springing off
with a glance at the pit, if it were not thought
energetic, would be chosen from nervous impatience at supporting the gaze of thousands,

while the performer merely walks away. All the
rhymed couplets, to carry them off with effect,
attest the misery of departure ; and the speaking
a few words as entering, also shew the desire to
come into as speedy a commerce with the audience as can possibly be achieved.

The amazing self-possession of Mrs. Siddons
rendered distance only the means of displaying
a system of graceful and considerate dignity, or
weighty and lingering affliction, as the case might
demand. In the hurry of distraction, she could
stop, and in some frenzied attitude speak wonders
to the eye, till a second rush forward brought her
to the proper ground on which her utterance
might be trusted. I will not be so ungallant as
to ascribe the composure of this grand woman to
any vain complacency in her majestic form. By
thinking so, I should ill repay that artist-like admiration with which I always beheld it. No: I
believe she thought at such moments only of the
character, and the support it demanded from her
of every kind. When Mrs. Siddons quitted her
dressing-room, I believe she left there the last
thought about herself. Never did I see her eye
wander from the business of the scene—no recog-
nizance of the most noble of her friends exchanged
the character for the individual. In this duty her
brother would frequently fail ; and he seemed to
take a delight in shewing how absolute a mastery

he possessed—that he could make a *sign* and sometimes *speak* to a friend near him, and yet seem to carry on the action and the look of the character. I never saw this in his sister—no, not for a moment. It was this devotion to what she was about, that left so little *inequality* in her numerous repetitions of the same part. Kemble, to use the extravagant opposition of one of Dr. Young's figures, in acting was a " worm or a God." He walked or dosed through the character; or sublimed it with energy and grace. Constitutional infirmity, cough, and the opium he used to quiet it, are to account for this—we had often to regret it. But I never saw an *indifferent* performance from Siddons; though I may have witnessed a cold or a noisy audience. The uniform temperance of female life had its share in the conservation of this fullness of power—but no domestic life is without its own cares, vexations, or sorrows; and the admirable art by which their effects were suspended for the duties of profession, shews a mental firmness of the highest value.

Conspiring with the larger stage to produce some change in her *style*, was her delight in statuary, which directed her attention to the antique, and made a remarkable impression upon her, as to simplicity of attire and severity of attitude. The actress had formerly complied with fashion, and deemed the prevalent becoming; she now

saw that tragedy was debased by the flutter of
light materials, and that the head, and all its
powerful action from the shoulder, should never
be encumbered by the monstrous inventions of
the hair-dresser and the milliner. She was now,
therefore, prepared to introduce a mode of stage
decoration, and of deportment, parting from one
common principle, itself originating with a people
qualified to legislate even in taste itself. What,
however, began in good sense, deciding among
the forms of grace and beauty, was, by political
mania in the rival nation, carried into the excess
of shameless indecency. France soon sent us
over her amazons to burlesque all classical
costume, and her models were received among us
with unaffected disgust. What Mrs. Siddons
had chosen remains in a great degree the standard
of female costume to the present hour; and any
little excesses by degrees dropt off, and left our
ladies the heirs of her taste and its inseparable
modesty. I have said that her deportment now
varied considerably; and I have no doubt of the
fact. In a small space the turns are quick and
short. Where the area is considerable the step
is wider, the figure more erect, and the whole
progress more grand and powerful, the action is
more from the shoulder; and we now first began
to hear of the perfect form of Mrs. Siddons's arm.
Her walk has never been attempted by any other

actress; and in deliberate dignity was as much *alone*, as the expression of her countenance.

In point of scenery little could be done at the Opera-house for the accommodation of the English drama; and the small flats of Drury Lane were lost under a roof so towering. But neither tragedy nor comedy ever seemed with me to derive a benefit proportioned to the pains that have been taken in the scenic department of our stages. When the scenes are first drawn on, or the roller descends, the work exhibited is considered a few moments as a work of art—the persons who move before it then engross the attention,—at their exit it is raised or drawn off, and is speedily forgotten, or seen with indifference the second time. If the perspective, as to the actor standing in front of the scene, was so accurate that the whole effect should be delusive, and the impression be of actual sky, and land, and building, (though an objection will always remain to the abrupt junction of the borders with the tops of the scenes—the wings, and the scoring line where the flats meet each other—the grooves in which they move, the boarded stage and other difficulties hitherto insurmountable,) I could understand the object of those who expend so much money on their elaboration—but I confess I am of opinion, that they should never do more than suggest to the imagination; and that it would not be desirable that the spectator should lose his senses to the point of forgetting that he is in a regular theatre, and enjoying a work of art invented for his amusement and his instruction by a poet, and acted by another artist of corresponding talent called a player. All beyond this is the dream of ignorance and inexperience.

I have already hinted at my impression that the powers of the truly great comedian, using the term to express an actor of either species of the drama, are superior to all this aid ; his commerce is with the judgment and the passions—it is vitality operating upon kindred life, man awaking the sympathies of man. When we have such a being as Mrs. Siddons before us in Lady Macbeth, what signifies the order or disorder of the picture of a castle behind her, or whether the shadows lie upwards or downwards on the mouldings of a midnight apartment ? It is to the terror of her eye, it is to the vehement and commanding sweep of her action—it is to the perfection of her voice that I am a captive, and I must pity the man who, not being the painter of the canvas, is at leisure to inquire how it is executed.

The historian of the stage is but seldom called to notice any glaring offence against public decorum. Managers sympathise for the most part with the public feeling, and are always alive to their own interest. I leave the following *mistake* upon record. The second or Legislative Assembly of France, in the month of December, 1791, had determined upon war with the military powers on the continent. " Louis the Sixteenth was " affirmed to be at the head of an Austrian com- " mittee in the Tuileries. A hundred thousand " Frenchmen brave and well armed—

     ' Longing wait the signal to attack.'

" The *English government* can only strike at a dis- " tance, while the *people* of England will offer up " prayers for the success, which they know will " one day be *their own.*"

  In the face of this wicked libel, read with whatever feelings, in all the coffee-houses and most of the respectable dwellings in London, a day recurs which reminds all but savages of the grand rebellion in this country, and the mock trial of its sovereign, and his public execution on the 30th of January. A venerable custom, of long standing, had kept this day as one of fast and humiliation. If our church contained within its priesthood any peculiar powers of oratory, that theme was treated by them before our two houses of parliament, and the public demonstration of concern for the errors of the last century almost guaranteed the land from any renewal of such horrors here, or the slightest countenance to their recurrence elsewhere.

The Theatre Royal of Drury Lane, boasting occasionally the presence of his Majesty and his august family within its walls, on the 30th of January, 1792, selected for the amusements of the evening the buffooneries of *Cymon*, with the farce of the *Devil to Pay*. Could any conduct be more likely to continue the miserable dupes of Paris in the opinion which I have just quoted? Could they fail to hurry forward the steps on their side the water which led to a similar catastrophe, to be treated by themselves with even superior scorn, contempt, or derision? See, they would say, how a theatre, under the direction of the accomplished Sheridan, the friend of man, respects the feelings of loyalty still lingering in a few of the privileged orders. The proceeding is of no more moment in England now than it was in 1649, when the friends of equality, who signed the sentence for Charles's execution, were so sportive as to *ink* each other's fingers, by drawing through them that pen which decreed the sovereignty of the people.

Mrs. Siddons opened her season of 1792 with Isabella, and on the 7th of February acted what is called Queen Elizabeth, in Richard the Third. A character helpless, facile, and lachrymose, a victim and a plaything to the active villany of the tyrant. In Mrs. Siddons's situation, she should have refused the part. Had I been in her brother's, I would not have asked her to perform it. I fancy he caught at the strength which her name would give to the play-bill, without reflecting that her attraction was weakened by applying her talent to matter unworthy of it. When a really great actress is in a theatre, her name should be the signal of delight. Even novelties should be sparingly graced by her performances, and they should possess unquestioned merit. If the art of the actress could produce great effects with slender materials, she should not be permitted to bear down true taste and judgment; the lips of Mrs. Siddons should be devoted to the purest strains of dramatic poesy.

On the 26th of March, after her sublime impersonation of Queen Katharine in Henry the Eighth, she indulged her friends with a recitation of Collins's Ode on the Passions. This was a composition for music, and it could not well have better than the voice of Mrs. Siddons. She was in truth the organ of passion; but the poet here describes the passion by its sympathies with particular scenes in nature, and its characteristic expression when fully displayed. The human form, under its influence, is given as the symbol of the passion. The actress who described the character, lent in a great degree her countenance and her gesture as aids to the beautiful imagery of the poet. This is unavoidable in all stage recitation, and criticism must not proudly reject the *living* commentary upon language, however forcible.

The pictures of Hope, Revenge, Melancholy, Cheerfulness and Joy, admit easily of this impersonation—they are drawn at length, and are extremely vivid. *Fear* is very slightly touched indeed, compared with the *Ode* on the subject by the same lovely Poet. *Pity* might easily be improved by some delightful illustrations from the author's Ode to a kindred being, *Mercy*. Such for instance as the following:—

> " When he, whom even our joys provoke,
> The fiend of nature join'd his yoke,
> And rush'd in wrath to make our isle his prey;
> Thy form, from out thy sweet abode,
> O'ertook him on his blasted road,
> And stop'd his wheels and look'd his rage away."

Jealousy is only described by its vacillation; and *Love* is wantoning in her beauty, with zone unbound and tresses floating in the dance of Joy, instead of exerting her mighty influence over the *mind*, swelling it to rapture and delighting even by its agonies.

On the 28th of April, Mrs. Siddons performed the Jealous Wife—a character, for whatever reason, devoted to comedy; though I have often tried to conceive a *tragic* exhibition of female jealousy, that should produce a character for the actress equal in its effects to the *noble Moor*. But, alas! invent what you might of interest or delusive appearance, the mind of Shakspeare would be still required, to fill up the outline with natural thought and its expression.

> " Such bliss to ONE alone
> Of all the sons of SOUL was known."

I look, however, upon Mr. Colman's *Jealous Wife* to be a *chef d'œuvre* of comedy, and though unsupported by wit, to have a power of truth and neatness, which he never afterwards fully equalled. Mrs. Oakley is an object of sincere pity. She never loses the respect of those who witness the self-tormentress. Murphy, after his French model, ran his Lady Restless down into farce. To this level it always hurt me to see Mrs. Siddons descend.

The original cast of the Jealous Wife, I mean as to its principal parts, it may be proper to notice upon the present occasion. Garrick himself kindly acted Mr. Oakley, though not of that importance to *himself* which might have been wished. Yates, an admirable actor, performed the Major; King, Sir Harry Beagle; and the accomplished O'Brien, Lord Trinket. Mrs. Pritchard, the Jealous Wife;—and *the* Clive that *insousciante* profligate woman of *bon ton*, transferred from

Fielding, and by her " new possessor" called Lady Freelove.

Kemble was the Oakley of the revival, and Palmer, who had been the original Charles, was become by time a very whimsical Major, and really enjoyed the extreme indulgence of his brother. Mrs. Pritchard was before my time. She was, it seems, one of those prodigies, whom the stage inspires with elegance, taste, and correctness, which she never had, or affected to despise, in private life—a dangerous trick, if it be one, or a miraculous change without an adequate cause.   Faulty pronunciation has adhered in my own time to many performers of both sexes and of great excellence—and the knowledge has exceeded the practice.   But vulgarity in utterance is itself a debasing thing, and is but indifferently palliated by either the toilet or the dancing master.

I have never been strongly tempted by the comedy of either Mrs. Siddons or her late brother —but her Mrs. Oakley was certainly the perfect representation of a sensible but jealous woman. She seemed to *plunge* into her mistakes with great ease and nature; and the scene of simulation in the second act, where she enters with good humour into the feelings of her husband for Charles, in order to extract from him all that he knows relative to the object of her jealousy—the returning fiend,

and the exclamation " Amazing!" which lets him
see that he has been only feeding the flame,
while he thought he was quenching the fire—all
was as perfect, I think, as her tragedy itself. The
comic scene, where Mrs. Oakley falls into practised fits, as a mode alarming humanity, if love
should be tired out, I hope is a libel upon the
ladies.   However I perfectly approve of the
remedy, if you are sure of the distemper.   But
nothing gave me higher gratification than to
observe in that most expressive of faces the
dawning of conviction that she had been imposing
upon herself, and the growing effects of irresistible evidence reducing her to shame for her
violence, and apprehension that she may have
trifled with love till it is lost.   What security
Oakley has against the return of a malady seemingly constitutional, the spectator may fancy for
himself—but I believe the only *moral* Proteus is
the last act of a comedy.

Colman's friend Lloyd wrote an excellent prologue
to this play, the last couplet of which he remembered when he introduced his most entertaining
son to the public as an author in the year 1784.

> " Do justice on him ! as on fools before—
> And give to *blockheads* past one *blockhead* more."

When Mr. Colman, after the prefatory IF,
directed the audience to damn him for " a *chip* of

" the *old* BLOCK"—he in fact invited them to applaud a son *worthy* of the author of the Jealous Wife, the Clandestine Marriage, and the English Terence. To think of such men is the charm of existence, and the consolation of old age.

That very clever artist, for his invention was nothing, Murphy, in the summer of 1783, had been so much struck by the talents of Mrs. Siddons, that he resolved to write a tragedy expressly for her. The subject appears to have been suggested to him by Madame de Sevigné's mention of the success of La Champmêlée in the younger Corneille's *Ariane*, performed in the beginning of the year 1672.

After a careful perusal of the French and English Ariadnes, I have not a moment's hesitation in preferring Corneille to Murphy. The latter has made more bustle without more actual business, and in his attempt to raise the diction, which Voltaire found often prosaic, he has robbed it of that truth of sentiment and almost colloquial expression, by which, spoken as naturally as written, La Champmêlée was enabled to " interest " every heart, and leave every eye dissolved in " tears."

But by raising the diction, Voltaire did not mean cramming it with figures, and talking

" In a high strutting style of the stars,
 The eagle of Jove, and the chariot of Mars."

When in Murphy's second act the back scene opens and soft music is heard, (the *minuet* in Ariadne) when Ariadne advances with a train of virgins, like Elfrida in Caractacus, and speaks her very language; when she pours out a most unnatural rhapsody upon the *sun* coming to quell the *howling blast,* and the *circling hours* with *blessings on their wings,* and *bright hope* and *rose-lip'd health,* and pure *delight* and *love* and *joy,* nothing is gained by such trash to the author, and the *actress* is destroyed by it. But hear the candid confession of Voltaire as to Corneille's language. " Ce sont là," (the 3rd scene of his fifth act) " de ces vers que la situation seule rend excel- " lens ; les moindres ornemens les affaibliraient ; " c'est un très grand merite : tant il est vrai que " le naturel est toujours ce qui plait le plus." And in another place of four lines, spoken by Ariane relative to her sister Phedra. " See," says he, " how in these four lines every thing is " natural and easy, no unnecessary word, nor any " one out of its proper place."

It should, in passing, be observed, to the credit of the French actress, that though Racine was her lover, yet in the case of the Corneilles she never sacrificed her professional duty to her personal attachments. She rendered the Ariane exquisitively touching and tenderly triumphant, though every thing besides in the play was mean

and worthless, and almost risible. The King of
Naxos is an amorous cypher, Theseus and Pirithous creeping scoundrels, and Phedra a perfi-
dious and unnatural sister; all of whom might
with true poetical justice be turned loose in the
Cretan labyrinth, without the clue to guide them
from the tyranny of Minos.

Murphy has left Phedra as bad as he found
her. Pirithous he has made at least a gentleman,
and so far improved the play; but the *poinard*,
that wretched executioner of all English tragedies, should have been spared, upon the precedent supplied by Corneille. My old friend
did not bring out his play in 1784, highly as he
thought of Mrs. Siddons, " because," as he says,
" a play that might linger *nine* nights upon the
" stage was not the object of the author's ambi-
" tion;" he, therefore, kept his piece by him
NINE years, and in 1793 it was acted *six* times,
and no more. But it must not be concealed,
our mixed English audiences have very few favourites among the personages of antiquity, and
the few they have hold rather by prescription
than fondness. The Roman part of them make
their fortune among us by high and swelling sentiments of liberty, or a grand and ostentatious
courage. Theseus and Ariadne might linger formerly upon our tapestry—their last retreat. The

skill of the artists may be questionable as to either design or execution—but that our poets could at least furnish splendid hints of this very subject we may know by that exquisite instruction to the needle given by Aspatia in the Maid's Tragedy.

" Suppose I stand upon the sea-beech now,
Mine arms thus, and mine hair blown by the wind,
Wild as the desert ; and let all about me
Tell that I am forsaken.   Make me look
Like Sorrow's monument ! and the trees about me
Let them be dry and leafless ; let the rocks
Groan with continual surges ; and, behind me,
Make all a desolation."

This and every collateral aid Mrs. Siddons availed herself of, in the conception of Ariadne ; but the truth is, the scenes were repetitions of each other ; and the heroine could only rave of the perfidy of Theseus ; and either he, or Pirithous, or her sister, could do no more than incessantly remind her that, since his affections had another object, she could not do better than change *also*, and marry the doating King of Naxos.   Incidents so meagre, worn to the very bone through five long acts, even Mrs. Siddons could not render interesting ; passages there were occasionally of great force—but the tears did not

flow, as they did at the simpler style of Corneille ;
and all the turgid efforts of the English poet only
battered the ear, and left the heart in a state of
repose unnatural to the subject.

Thus (a hard fate) the novelties of her own day
did nothing for the fame of the actress.

Mrs. Siddons, on the 21st of April, 1794, had
the satisfaction of opening with her Lady Macbeth, the new ,Theatre of Drury Lane, erected
by Mr. Holland, and in my opinion the most
chaste and beautiful structure that ever bore the
name. It was on this occasion that Mr. Kemble,
on the authority of the poet Lloyd, permitted
himself, against the declared intention of Shakspeare, to banish the ghost of Banquo. If there
resulted from the language no sort of ambiguity
—if Macbeth *named* Banquo when he started at
vacancy; despising all the philosophy of such
disorders, I should prefer being *visibly* made
acquainted with the object of his terrors to all
that speech could do for the patron of this extensive imagination.

It is thus that Lloyd expresses himself in the
actor—

> " Why need the ghost usurp the monarch's place,
> To frighten children with his *mealy face ?*
> The King *alone* should form the phantom there,
> And talk and tremble at the empty chair."

I have nothing whatever to combat where it is ludicrously done. If we are to have Banquo close to the eye, drest like Guy Faux himself, and becoming a chair no better, the matter is soon determined; but it might unquestionably be rendered both picturesque and terrible. In a former work I have reasoned upon the stage direction, still remaining in the *only* copy of Macbeth, and no doubt proceeding from the pen of Shakspeare himself. But the subject has all along been argued, as if the appearance of Banquo was only a visual *sign* to the spectators of the object of Macbeth's imagination. This is no true account of the matter. Macbeth's mind is not in a situation to shape ideal terrors; the destruction of his enemy, the grown serpent, had such charms for him as to render him ten times himself; and the worm that fled annoys him only with the prospect of venom to be bred at a future time. He is so much at his ease as even to *finesse* upon the subject, and express an anxious wish for the presence of Banquo at the banquet, to which he was invited, and which he would have graced but for the treacherous assassination, which cut him off in sight of the illuminated hall of festivity. At this moment, to confound his hypocrisy and torture his guilt, the spirit of his murdered friend, availing himself of the power to become visible to ONE* only of a mixed assembly, arrayed in all his terrors ascends the royal seat, the *living* presentment of that body which with twenty trenched gashes about it, safely, as Macbeth supposes, bides in a neighbouring ditch. It is thus that the ghost of Denmark chuses to revisit his son in the closet of the queen, visible and audible to HIM alone ; his wretched mother seeing nothing of that " gracious figure," nor hearing one syllable even of the tender admonition to Hamlet in her own favour.

> " Taint not thy mind, nor let thy soul contrive
> Against thy MOTHER aught. Leave her to Heaven."

I have known few sounder thinkers than my late friend Opie, and he was highly indignant at the innovation in question. In the kindred art Sir Joshua Reynolds had been arraigned for introducing the " busy meddling fiend," behind the pillow of his dying Cardinal. Mr. Opie went a little out of his way, to have the pleasure of noticing the effect of similar criticism applied to the designs of Shakspeare. I take the liberty of quoting his own expression, which was always masterly.

* Let us take our *faith* in this matter from Prospero himself.

> " Be subject to no sight but thine and mine:
> Invisible to every eye-ball else."
>   TEMPEST.

" I know of no one who has availed himself of
" poetic licence with more address than Sir
" Joshua Reynolds, in his celebrated picture of
" the death of Cardinal Beaufort, painted for the
" Shakspeare Gallery. The varied beauties of
" this work might well employ a great part of a
" lecture; but, at present, I shall pass them over,
" and attend only to what relates immediately to
" the question before us, the effect of the vision-
" ary devil, couched close, and listening eagerly
" behind the pillow of the dying wretch: which
" not only invigorates and clothes the subject in
" its appropriate interest and terror, but imme-
" diately clears up all ambiguity, by informing
" us that those are not bodily sufferings which
" we behold so forcibly delineated, that they are
" not merely the pangs of death which make him
" grin, but that his agony proceeds from those
" daggers of the mind, the overwhelming horrors
" of a guilty and an awakened conscience. This
" was the point on which rested the whole moral
" effect of the piece; it was absolutely necessary
" to be understood, and could by no other means
" have been so strongly and perspicuously ex-
" pressed." He then, in his forcible manner,
ridicules the objectors to this mode of treating
the subject, and proceeds thus.

" Of the same class were those who of late
" endeavoured to rob the play of Macbeth, of

" the resurrection of Banquo's *ghost* to fill the
" chair of the murderer. Happily, however, for
" the true lovers of Shakspeare, the genuine feel-
" ings of the public have decided against this
" most barbarous mutilation."

That Shakspeare believed such an appearance
possible, there can be little question. He knew
the distinction between " he *thinks* he sees him,"
and he " *knows* he sees him"—between " thick
" coming fancies," and preternatural *realities*, and
such is either the truth of tradition upon this subject, or the tendency of our common nature to
credit such an occurrence, that let the sturdiest of
the sect, the best satisfied that " nothing but *sub-*
" *stance* can be an object of *vision*," consider the
subject *alone*, in profound *silence*, and at the *midnight hour*, and if he makes a faithful report of his
condition, his startled senses will confess the in-
vincible superstition of his feelings, if he will not
allow the term to be fairly applicable to his understanding.

In point of size and even splendour, the *Apollo*
Drury did not equal the Opera House, a structure intended more particularly for the display of
beauty in higher life, and the best part of whose
exhibition is certainly before the curtain. But it
was admirably adapted to all the purposes of
playing, and could even conveniently admit within
its walls a nightly receipt of £700. Nor did it

look deserted on a *thin* night. So judiciously was its front decorated that the visitors saw well, and were well seen, and as to numbers, the house appeared respectable when the attraction fell off.

As to the general perfection of the stage of this theatre, nothing had ever among us, in thought, approached it. Every thing that machinery could accomplish was put within the grasp of the proprietors; the scenery rose from below the stage or descended thither, and was in itself vast and beautiful; and a wardrobe was absolutely necessary of more than common or o'er dyed materials, not to disgrace this palace of eastern magnificence. One might have been tempted to fancy that the eloquent prosecutor of Mr. Hastings had raised his triumphant theatre out of the divided spoils of the Governor General of India.

Mrs. Siddons on this first appearance in the new theatre would have been more than human, if she had not exulted. It was unquestionably the finest in Europe; and the conduct of it, and its main support, certainly in her own family. As to the property itself, I am very sure that they grasped it in imagination. So devoted to politics as Mr. Sheridan seemed, it might look more than a remote probability that he would one day take office with his party; and that a theatre and its concerns must be resigned to the more urgent claims of official dignity and business. At such a

time a sale might take place upon liberal and
easy terms, and the influence of Mr. Sheridan
upon the fashionable world continue a marked
preference to a theatre, of which he had been the
proprietor and was still the guardian. On this
night of opening, the Kemble family took a new
hold upon the theatre and the town, by producing
Mr. Charles Kemble, then a youth of eighteen, in
the character of Malcolm. His excellent brother
was in this, and every other part of his conduct to
him, judicious as well as kind. In my life of Mr.
Kemble, I have recorded his private opinion of the
powers he discovered; and he snatched him from
envy, as well as intoxicating vanity, by allotting
to him a range of pleasing but not important
characters, from which he was to lift himself by
his talents, rather than succeed to better as a
birth-right.

As it can form no part of my plan, however
I may respect him, to pursue him step by step to
his present confirmed rank in the profession, I
may be indulged in a summary, but I hope a
distinct, sketch of this most elegant actor; in
which I shall not disguise his difficulties, because
they must be weighed in order fully to appreciate
his merits. The first and most important was,
that he had to make himself a name in the art,
not against, but in conjunction with the splendid
talents of his brother, in the maturity of his powers,.

whether of nature or study; and constantly to sustain a comparison, which was likely to be made by every body but himself. In his countenance he perhaps more resembled Mrs. Siddons than Mr. Kemble. He had an expression of intelligent innocence, that peculiarly fitted him for the youthful heroes of the drama, and which in advanced life is so characteristic of his look, that it has retained him in the performance of parts, which otherwise he might be said to have outgrown. He never had the slightest appearance of imitating his brother, and from the first of him always struck me to act from his own perceptions. Deeply retired in himself, confident in his twofold strength of person and industry, there was a calm complacency about Mr. Kemble that kept him always upon his centre in a sort of regardless majesty—he calculated every thing, and prophesied his effects. Charles was ardent and anxious to obtain applause—he sometimes became too boisterous in his action and too noisy in his speech—his voice was frequently not under government, and pained the ear. If he had thought less of his audience, he would not to be sure have pleased them more, but served them better.

But let us look at him, now that experience has given him more confidence, and circumstances extended his range. We shall find that his pre-

dominant excellence is in comedy; and that in a
long list of tragic characters there is nothing else
near him. He is our Benedick, our Prince Hal,
(aye, and a Hal who can act Falstaff too;) our
Petruchio, our Leon, and our Orlando. He is our
Charles Surface, our young Marlow, our Lovemore, our Mirabel, our Don Felix, our Captain
Absolute, and our Colonel Feignwell. It is now
I believe clear that his Hamlet never ought
to have yielded, unless to his brother's. His
Romeo, his Antony, his Macduff, his Edgar,
his Cassio—his Jaffier, his Carlos, his Stukely,
and many others, are as near perfection as *any
thing* in our own times, and better acted by him
than by any other living performer.

The German Theatre now began to excite our
attention, and Lessing supplied our adapters with a
tragedy called Emilia Galotti. Mrs. Siddons acted
a Countess Orsina. " Rape and murder are not
" simple means," we are informed by our virtuous
friend Glenalvon—but they are called into full
exercise in this modernization of the old story of
Appius and Virginia. I know not why it had so
short an existence among us: the interest was
what is called powerful.

Mr. Cumberland wrote them a prologue, in
which Mr. Whitfield admired exceedingly the
beauty of the theatre, which he contrasted with
the " straw-built" temple (nay only *thatched* with

straw) " that held the Drama's *God*." Now, however, he proceeds, should the " eventful " time" inspire any second Shakspeare, the future Agincourt will have a nobler field than the Globe Theatre was on the banks of Thames. Our great poet has told us, with his accustomed point, that all appliances, and means to boot, will not so insure slumber, as the distressful labours of humble life.—The penury of the early stage obliged the poet to paint for the ear—and the description which set the fancy clearly to work, produced a far more splendid series of scenes than even our Loutherbourgs or Stanfields ever executed. But it is certain in the long run of what is called, and justly, improvement, the principal will be lost among his accessories—you will build upon the machinist and the painter, and you will have palaces worthy of heroes just as the race becomes extinct.

But hear the greatest of all authorities in matters of taste, which I find in letters upon a seemingly different subject, written at this very time.

" The dresses, the scenes, the decorations of " every kind, I am told, are in a new style of " splendour and magnificence ; whether to the " *advantage* of our dramatic taste upon the whole, " I very much doubt. It is a SHEW, and a SPEC-" TACLE ; not a play, that is exhibited. This is

" undoubtedly in the genuine manner of the
" Augustan age, but in a manner which was
" censured by one of the best poets and critics of
" that, or any age." BURKE's works, vol. IV.
p. 600. 4to. edition.

> " Migravit ab aure voluptas
> Omnis ad incertos oculos, et gaudia vana :
> Quatuor aut plures aulæa premuntur in horas ;
> Dum fugiunt equitum turmæ, peditumque catervæ."

Mr. Colman, the younger, in a very *serious*
epilogue, drew the attention of the public to the
anarchy of political speculation and the murders
of philosophy. This Mrs. Siddons must have had
great pleasure in speaking, from the eulogy which
it contained upon the virtues of our own sovereign.
The play needed such a corrective, for its interest proceeded from the *tyrannous* use of POWER.
We had just experienced, by the treatment of the
Royal Family of France, that power may change
hands without correcting its excesses. Emilia
Galotti lived but three nights.

On the 15th of November, Whitehead's Roman
Father was revived, that Mr. Kemble and Mrs.
Siddons might perform the Publius and Horatia
— but I do not think that this brutal instance of
Roman patriotism added much to the fame of
either of our accomplished tragedians.

I have stated, at no very great distance from

this place, the expectations that were reasonably
entertained of the triumph of the new theatre,
under the management of Mr. Kemble, and the
hopes which it was natural would be formed by
himself and his family. But improvidence was
working at the heart of the concern, to destroy all
the advantages adhering actually to that theatre,
and annoyances of so serious a kind, stood in such
a formidable array before Mr. Kemble, that he
determined to throw up the management; and
Mr. Wroughton, in September 1796, was announced to carry on the new system, or *no* system,
of that immense concern.

To Mrs. Siddons I do not imagine the change
was of any considerable moment. Talent like
hers was sure of engagement, though *payment*
might continue to be attended with difficulties.
She might even still more strictly require that
performance on the side of the manager, which
her brother no doubt often persuaded her to pass
over; and resort at last steadily to the good old
adage of Swiss reciprocity—*Point d'argent, point
de Suisse.* Wroughton, I know, had grown mature
in the Covent Garden prejudice against Kemble's
management—and was decidedly of opinion that
more money would be brought by modern
comedy, than by ancient tragedy, attended with
the vast expence incident to its revival. There
could be no doubt that Mrs. Jordan would think

so too; and her influence in the theatre was, from a variety of causes, now become very considerable.

Upon the difficulty sometimes to *find* in the treasury, the cash that had been taken at the door of the theatre, volumes might be published. Sometimes in the absence of every thing like money, the mighty master himself would try the witchcraft of his wit upon Lady Macbeth ; bring her in triumph along with him to the theatre, and pledge all he had, his *honour*, that she should be paid, if she would but perform. Yes, I hold Sheridan to have been the most irresistible of mortals.

Among the attempts to give something like novelty to Mrs. Siddons, Thomson's Edward and Eleonora, was tried for a night on the 22nd of October, 1796. But the period for such imitations of the Greek stage was long gone by; though the sacrifice of Alcestis really ennobled the wife of Edward. Thomson began life as a true poet, looking at nature with an adoration of her grand features, and a fond affection for even the minutest parts of her endless economy. He was all eye and ear; and out of the library of Shakspeare, and Spenser, and Milton, he had collected a store of bold and nervous language, which expressed much, and hinted more ; it conveyed, with an air of much *originality*, all that he saw, and how he saw it. As he went forward in life, he became connected with men who had never seen a mountain, or, to speak without a figure, critics founded upon French models. He, at their suggestion, *polished* the rough seasons of his native country— wrote interminable travels in blank verse—and tragedies on the plan of Racine. But " nature " will break out," and our poet in his latest efforts evinced the possession of the most enchanting simplicity. The first canto of the Castle of Indolence, shewed how long he had lingered in the " delightful land of Faery ;" that he had perfectly learned her Spenserian tongue, which he spoke with all the grace and fluency of a native.

While Mrs. Siddons might be said thus to struggle to keep up with her own the fame of English tragedy, the other muse was about to suffer a loss, which THIRTY years have scarcely shewn a tendency to replace. I mean the elevation of Miss Farren to a coronet, by her marriage with the Earl of Derby, in the year 1797. Perhaps, I do not refer effects to causes inadequate to their production, when I say that this theatrical demise absolutely produced the degeneracy of comedy into farce. The *lady* of our Congreves lost that court-like refinement in manners, that polished propriety in speech—the coarser parts in comedy were forced forward without a balance, without contrast—cultivated life, on the stage, became insipid as soon as its representative was without the necessary charms. This, with the natural tendency of revolutionary feelings to degrade every thing, produced the absolute fall of genteel comedy, which had been long in a state of decline, and broad laughter reigned triumphant in the unbounded hilarity of Mrs. Jordan.

Many an elegant trifle, I well know, has proceeded from the muse of Lord Derby; but when that accomplished nobleman, VATIBUS ADDERE CALCAR, spurred his Pegasus into the compliment which it contained in that remarkable line, " Perhaps a FARREN may return no more," I could have wished the provinces of poet and prophet had at least for once been disunited.

It well became such a woman as Mrs. Siddons to notice this loss with a kind wish for the future happiness of her amiable sister of the scene. Accordingly, after a most affecting performance by Kemble and herself of Lillo's soul-harrowing Fatal Curiosity, to which the Deuce is in Him was the farce, she thus noticed, that her friend on that day became Lady Derby.

" Our comic muse, too, lighter topics lending,
Proves that in *marriage* was her natural ending;
Whilst grateful for those smiles which made us gay,
Each kindest wish awaits her *wedding-day*.
And sure, such *talents, honours,* shar'd between 'em,
If 'tis not happy, why—the *Deuce is in 'em*."

How all this was instilled into either Gods or men, history is silent. The newspapers in the morning might do something; but some of my *understanding friends* said it meant a dull compliment to Miss Farren, and a pointed attack upon Mrs. Jordan.

" Why what a world is this, when what is *comely*
Envenoms HER that bears it."

CHAPTER XX.

KOTZEBUE ADDS TWO CHARACTERS TO THE LIST OF MRS. SID-
DONS.—DANGER OF THE SENTIMENTAL DRAMA.—SCHLEGEL
ILLUSTRATES ITS MORALS.—THE FREEDOM OF OUR EARLY
STAGE INNOCENT COMPARATIVELY.—THE AUTHOR'S OPI-
NION OF MRS. HALLER AS ACTED BY MRS. SIDDONS.—THE
COLLOQUIAL STYLE — RIDICULED BY MR. CANNING. —
ELVIRA.—PIZARRO.—SHERIDAN'S CONDUCT. — SUCCESS OF
THE PLAY.—OTHER SERIOUS PLAYS FORMERLY PASSED OVER.
—BOADEN—PYE—MISS BAILLIE.—KEMBLE RESUMES THE
MANAGEMENT.—MRS. SIDDONS WISHES FOR RETIREMENT.—
HER DOMESTIC LOSSES.—THE AUTHOR'S TRIBUTE OF ADMIRA-
TION AND REGRET.—EXTRACTS FROM LETTERS ALLUSIVE
TO THOSE SEVERE LOSSES.—MR. SIDDONS—HIS CHARACTER.
—RETIRES TO BATH.—MR. KEMBLE'S PURCHASE INTO
COVENT GARDEN THEATRE.—HIS INTEREST DECIDES HIS
SISTER.—THE DUBLIN ANNOYANCE.—MRS. SIDDONS'S LET-
TER TO JONES.—THE LATE MR. HARRIS FULLY AWARE OF
MRS. SIDDONS'S VALUE—PERHAPS NOT SO ALIVE TO MR.
KEMBLE'S.—HIS PUNCTUALITY IN BUSINESS.—DECORATIONS
OF THE HOUSE.—THE KEMBLES IN THEIR NEW HOME.—
TRIUMPHANT PROSPECT.—DRURY LANE.—CARAVAN.—CIN-
DERELLA.—SOLDIER'S DAUGHTER.—MASTER BETTY.—SALA-
THIEL PAVY.—FASHIONABLE ABSURDITY.—MRS. SIDDONS
DISDAINED TO COMPLY WITH IT.—HAMLET.—SHAKSPEARE.

IT was reserved for Kotzebue, through the medium of translation, to add two characters to the

list of those performed by Mrs. Siddons. The
first of these was Mrs. Haller in the Stranger, or
Misanthropy and Repentance, which was acted
the 24th of March, 1798, at Drury Lane Theatre.
I shall not repeat myself in expressing here the
opinion formerly given of the character of Mrs.
Haller. I do not deny the interest which it excited, for I admit it to have been powerful in the
extreme; but I have always thought the sympathy of my fair countrywomen in this case dangerous to their best interests. The *Stranger* himself is, perhaps, the *noblest ruin* that has hitherto
marked the moral desolation of our own domestic
manners.

Looking to dramatic effect, the Misanthropy
towers much above the Repentance. Mrs. Haller seeking friendship, and requiring protection, is
obliged to external conformity—if she feel the remorse of guilt, and would covet the deepest shades
of mysterious retirement as an indulgence, she is
afraid that singularity would draw attention, and
that she can only escape detection by every-day
conduct. Suffering much herself, and meriting
to suffer, she accepts the consolation of mitigating
the sufferings of others; her virtue has been " sul-
" lied, not absorpt," and she would fain possess
the esteem of those around her, though she has
lost her own.

Mrs. Siddons acted this character with that

subdued power which it required. The taste of
Kotzebue did not lead him, like that of Schiller, to
poetical elevation of his dialogue. He seems at
times to think the stage and society identical;
and his conversation scenes have a flatness and
even vulgarity about them which is not to our
taste. But there is an interest of the *heart* making its destined progress through all his plays,
and the tears of his audiences are under the most
absolute controul. This, according to Schlegel,
is the decided course of the sentimental dra-
matist. " The general lesson which he gives, is
" that sensibility should obtain pardon for all its
" eccentricities and faults; and that we should
" drop our rigorous principles, when the virtues
" are under our judgment. Behold how amiable
" is the youthful avowal of foibles, how sublime
" the dominion of the passions? What more is
" necessary, than that the author should provide
" in the close some benevolent patron, or forgiv-
" ing dupe, who, scattering either wealth or
" pardon with unwithdrawing hand, shall put the
" seal of oblivion upon the simulated errors of the
" stage; and, as to society, display the triumph-
" ant justification of actual depravity, and the
" glowing incentive to timid and now not shame-
" less passion."

We were alarmed at the freedom of our early
writers, and the Bowdlers were set to purify

their scenes from all loose or equivocal language ; but what are *double entendres* to that seduction which shocks by no external sign, but insinuates itself into the bosom entirely without defence, and in the disguise of that sensibility which is the chief grace of woman ?

I freely confess with respect to the Stranger, that however I rejoiced in the display of my friend, Kemble, I never could, without strong reluctance, submit to see the character of Mrs. Haller represented by his sister. Her countenance, her noble figure, her chaste and dignified manners, were so utterly at variance with the wretched disclosure she had to make, that no knowledge that it was pure, or rather impure, fiction, could reconcile me to this " *forcible* feeble ;" that which was true of the character, was so evidently false and impossible of its grand and beautiful representative.

Such a play as the *Stranger* would lead one almost to wish, that the term comedy retained among ourselves the meaning that it bore in France, during the dramatic reigns of Corneille and Racine, when they called the Cid, and Cinna, and Andromaque, and Bajazet *comedies*. Our division of the genus into its species, leaves us without a term to describe this familiar copy of arm-in-arm lounging, superintendance of the household, colloquies with the Butler, diving after his little Excellency, confessions of adultery, and meetings of the parties, in order to separate for ever, which conclude by embracing to part no more. It, perhaps, classes best with sentimental comedy. It has not the elevation of tragedy, and never borrows its tone of language ; or keeps the most affecting scenes from puerility and the mawkish softness of the nursery. It has characters below the level of the serious muse, but they are not comic.

The domestic manners, which we are so compelled to notice in these German plays, may among that people have a favourable effect, and aid the stage illusion. The immortal ridicule of our MINISTER for these and other *foreign affairs*, will best exhibit the vice of such composition.

The second character which Kotzebue supplied was even more dissolute than the first, but a woman of stronger mould. The aspiration of her mind is to be the companion of valour, and her fancy bestows upon mere courage the better feelings of magnanimity and compassion. Detecting that her hero is devoid of humanity, she hates with all the ardour of her former affection ; and loses *herself* the very virtue whose absence, in the Peruvian conqueror, endangers his life. She is at anybody's service who will but destroy him. The reader sees that I allude to Elvira in the tragedy of Pizarro, a play got up by Sheridan himself, and into whose scenes he had infused some of the brilliant figures which he had composed for the impeachment of Warren Hastings.

It is not unlikely that from any *other hand,* (as we used to write) Mrs. Siddons might have scrupled to accept a character so profligate and desperate; but Mr. Sheridan was not a man to be refused, and besides the threatening popularity of any work, to which he lent his name, made it policy in a great actress not to condemn herself to her drawing-room for the rest of the season. There can be no doubt that Sheridan saw clearly enough the bad taste of such a camp follower as Elvira; and he might also think that Mrs. Siddons would disdain to stifle her proper feelings, and render this Spanish JUDITH any jot more respectable than her whole class has ever been. However, from the natural desire to stand favourably with the audience, she mounted this lady of adventure into a *heroine,* and her performance was triumphantly shouted, by crowded audiences, as long as she continued to act the part.

But, as my friend Stuart told me, he had an opportunity of witnessing Sheridan's dread, lest Mrs. Siddons should not "*fall in*" with his notion of the character of Elvira. However, without seeking, perhaps in vain, what that notion might exactly *be,* when he found that she had made her

hold upon the house, and that, except the heroic
Rolla, nothing stood more prominent than this
brave, but rather *unsafe chere amie* of Pizarro: he
could then persuade himself that she *had* " fallen
" into" HIS notion of the character, or, in surer
language, rendered it not only bearable but successful. Upon the getting up of Pizarro, Sheridan practised all the artifices of the coy or
indolent author—

" That would be wooed, and not unsought be won."

He made his actors wait for the conclusion of
their parts, and gave them, at the last moment,
that which I have no sort of doubt he had long
meditated and laboriously written. But he knew
well the region of a play-house, where either there
is no wonder, or all is wonder. Actors believe
miracles against the evidence of their senses, and
credit the elaboration of painful thought in the
shape of *impromptu.* Sheridan would not have
trusted his *late* importations among performers
slow of study; the hurry, the anxiety, the alarm,
the hope of his agents were favourable to his
play: the *zeal* excited was like the enthusiasm
of a crusade, it carried them through every thing
dangerous in triumph.

Sheridan had no opinion of Mrs. Jordan's
tragedy; but there was one charm in her name
and another in her voice, and these recommended

her to the beloved *Cora;* though, to use his own
words, "he knew that she could not speak a line
"of it." Mr. Sheridan had a very powerful
voice, but he declaimed very much in the style
of Mr. Kemble, and was attentive to the music
of the sentences which he uttered. He knew all
the value of that great actor, and therefore worked
up the Rolla of Kotzebue, till it read more like
the Charles de Moor of Schiller's Robbers, from
whom indeed he borrowed that patriotic harangue
which applied so admirably to our political circumstances in the year 1799.

Mrs. Siddons, perhaps for the only time in her
life, acted on thirty-one successive nights of performance. But when the terrific length of the
play was somewhat abridged, and it became
smooth from repetition, there might have been
even pleasure in the constancy of applause; and,
from the full houses, a reasonable prospect of a
treasury on the Saturday morning. It is but fair
to presume that Mr. Kemble's desertion of the
management contributed to this quite unparalleled
exertion in Sheridan—preparing the Stranger and
Pizarro for his stage; but he was totally exhausted by so much industry; and, from either
Wroughton, or James Aickin, nothing beyond the
mere stage management was to be expected.

I have omitted a few pieces of the serious kind,
in which Mrs. Siddons acted at Drury Lane

Theatre, in order to bring together the two German plays, which alone still live upon our stage, and of which alone Mr. Sheridan was the avowed reformer or adapter, for he translated neither of them. I, therefore, here notice, in the first place, a play of my own, called Aurelio and Miranda, produced on the 29th of December, 1798. It was remarkable for the utter failure of the fourth and fifth acts—the three first being rather powerful in the interest. With the experience of twenty years more, since the subject first struck me, I wonder how I could consent to the feeble arrangement of the plot, which is its vital defect. The passion of love to be treated in the dress of a monastic order, is a frightful anomaly. Mrs. Siddons, to appearance, was a young monk, passionately enamoured of the superior, Aurelio. The whole piece partook strongly indeed of the nature of the Spanish romantic drama, and was drawn from the impure source of the novel entitled the Monk, by Mr. Lewis. This was the only occasion on which I was ever honoured with the professional *aid* of Mrs. Siddons.

From Mr. Pye, the learned translator of Aristotle, the rival of Twining, a poet of some experience, it was reasonable to hope for a successful tragedy from English history; but his *Adelaide* was powerful only in scenes; and I despair now of any modern muse strong enough to assume the *stage histories*, of which Shakspeare has left us so many models, that tempt by the great abundance of their business, and become abortive from the feeble delineations of character, or the little nature in the dialogue.

In Miss Baillie's tragedy of De Montfort, Mrs. Siddons did her utmost with the Countess Jane. But the basis of the tragedy was the passion of *hatred,* and the incidents were all gloomy, and dark, and deadly. On the stage, I believe, no spectator wished it a longer life, and it is to the last degree mortifying to have to exhibit so many proofs, that the talent of dramatic writing in its noblest branch was in fact dead among us; and the powers of our transcendent actress were, like the mighty arms of some paladine in romance, entirely unsuited to the feeble children, who, to their mere confusion, were tempted to employ them. As some compensation for the failure of modern tragedies, Mr. Kemble returned to the management in the season of 1800-1, and ancient tragedy returned with him.

It was now understood among theatrical people, that Mr. Kemble's resumption of the management was a step taken towards a purchase into the property, and Mr. Siddons was not disinclined to embark a considerable sum with my late friend in the concern; but I believe, he considered the only absolute security to be Mr. Sheridan's retirement altogether, and the great orator held at this time a language highly flattering to such a hope.

But this arrangement, however desirable, upon a strict inquiry was found to be impracticable; and, after a great deal of trouble and much uneasiness, the business ended by the secession of the great tragedians to the other theatre, and the purchase of Mr. Kemble into Covent Garden; the consequences of which unfortunate step are still pressing, and must long press upon all the parties.

Although principally, no doubt, occupied by the *professional* exertions of Mrs. Siddons, I cannot pass over in silence that series of domestic sorrows, which must have weighed heavily indeed upon her mind, and contributed, with an almost satiety of public applause, to cloud her progress with melancholy, and make her court a scene of repose and abstraction, however unfriendly to the business of life, indeed to life itself.

Yet Mrs. Siddons was too well read, not at all times to remember the consolatory lines of Young, who well understood the nature of man.

> " His *grief* is but his DIGNITY disguis'd,
> And *discontent* is IMMORTALITY !"

On the 6th of October, 1798, her second daughter, Maria, sunk into the grave, at Bristol, of that flattering, but usually hopeless malady, a decline. She was in truth one of the loveliest beings that I have ever known. I can hardly bring myself to allow so much; but she was, perhaps, more beautiful even than her mother; or rather what the latter would have been, if with every indulgence in her early years, she had possessed full leisure to cultivate her taste, and exercise her fancy, without any of those prodigious exertions, which give at last an appearance of strength and energy, not usually characteristic of the English female. The *gain* is on the side of grandeur; the *loss* of winning gentleness and almost angelic softness. To confirm this notion, a very early picture of Mrs. Siddons resembles this lamented and excellent young lady. There was at one time an expectation, that she would have been permitted to give her hand in marriage to the present accomplished President of the Royal Academy. But I hasten from the subject.

When those from whom we derive our being resign their *own*, full of years and attended by the general regret of society, the pangs of nature may be soothed by reason, corrected by piety, or extenuated by time. Mrs. Siddons had, however, to lament the loss of her father in a very inverted succession; for he died, about four years after her daughter, on the 6th of December, 1802; but the interval was brief indeed, when she was again alarmed by the account of the dangerous state of her eldest daughter, who followed her sister pre-

maturely on the 24th of March, 1803. So rapid
was the progress of her malady, that she died
before her mother's return from Ireland, where
the interests of the family had required her
exertions. Mrs. Siddons seems to have been long
alarmingly depressed at this second string's being
severed from the maternal bosom. The sublime
and pathetic Young has given, in his Narcissa,
what I know to be a just portrait of the person
and the loss.

> " Song, beauty, youth, love, virtue, joy, this group
> Of bright ideas, flowers of paradise,
> As yet unforfeit! in one blaze we bind,
> Kneel, and present it to the skies ; as all
> We guess of heav'n: And *these* were all her own."

But we are not left to *imagine* the sorrows of
her parent, since, no matter for the motive which
gave a private correspondence to the world, we
have them expressed in her own language, to one
whom she long presumed to be her friend. I
shall select a few sentences from the letters of
Mrs. Siddons about this time; because we are too
apt to consider those, who delight us upon the
stage, as persons upon whom private life hardly
can be allowed to attach; and who are to be
occupied, alas! solely with the agonies of OTHERS.
The tyranny of our amusements, the luxury of
our taste for simulated sorrows, hardly allows

the actual tears for her *own* to dry upon the cheek of the actress. In the theatre, too, property suffers; engagements must be fulfilled; and the true mourner must hasten to be a counterfeit. The actor shares in the common sufferings of his kind, without the sacred indulgence of his grief, which decency commands in every other condition. But let us hear Mrs. Siddons herself.

" The testimony of the wisdom of all ages, from " the foundation of the world to this day, is child- " ishness and folly, if happiness be anything more " than a *name;* and I am assured our own ex- " perience will not enable us to refute the opinion: " no, no, it is the inhabitant of a better world. " Content, the offspring of moderation, is all we " ought to aspire to *here*, and moderation will be " our best and surest guide, to that happiness to " which she will most assuredly conduct us. If " Mr. —— thinks himself unfortunate, let him " look on *me*, and be silent. The inscrutable " ways of Providence! Two lovely creatures *gone;* " and another is just arrived from school, with all " the dazzling, frightful sort of beauty, that irra- " diated the countenance of Maria, and makes " me shudder when I look at her. I feel myself, " like poor Niobe, grasping to her bosom the last " and youngest of her children; and like her look " every moment for the vengeful arrow of de- " struction."

The passage thus alluded to by Mrs. Siddons, is in the 6th Book of the Metamorphoses.

> " Ultima restabat; quam toto corpore mater
> Totâ veste tegens, unam, minimamque relinque,
> De multis minimam posco, clamavit et unam."
>
> V. 298.

But the sequel was in mercy averted.

> " Dumque rogat, pro quâ rogat, occidit."

My fair readers must not be disappointed as to an English version of the passage, which is neither feebly nor inelegantly rendered by Croxall.

> " The last with eager care the mother veil'd,
> Behind her spreading mantle close conceal'd,
> And with her body guarded, as a shield.
> Only for THIS, this *youngest*, I implore,
> Grant me this one request, I ask no more;
> O grant me this! she passionately cries:
> But, while she speaks, the destin'd virgin dies."

The relations of life are seldom changed without some injury to domestic peace. The ascendancy of the husband is justified by the duties which are assigned him, and it is his pride to be the support of his family. The merits of Mr. Siddons as an actor, had been at length so obscured by the talents of his wife, that it did not consist with the interests of the family to allow him to continue on the stage. At one time he purchased into Sadler's Wells, and the concern was for some seasons successful; but the profits at length declined, and I believe, when he quitted it, on the whole it had been rather injurious to his fortune. This fate attended another speculation from which he had promised himself great advantages, and the greatest of all in the having an object to pursue with the hope of benefiting his family. Though he might properly have considered himself as most honourably occupied in being the best of managers of that fortune which now poured in upon them, he yet felt himself to be placed below the just point of ambition, and became somewhat impatient of what the historians call the crown matrimonial. I know that he used to consider himself on some occasions neglected, and that he was deemed of slight importance, compared with the object of universal attention, his own wife. Something of this necessarily adhered to their positions in the world; more however, in the apprehension of hardly a blameable self-esteem. This unhappily produced, in a most honourable and high-spirited man, some inequalities of *temper*, which occasionally seemed harsh to a woman conscious of the most unremitting diligence in her exertions, and often endangering her health, to secure, along with fame to herself, the present and future comforts of her family. Some expressions of her *irritation* upon such annoyances have been *printed* by the person to whom I have before alluded; and, at length, Mr. Siddons, after suitable arrangements as to the property, retired to Bath. But he retained at all times the sincerest regard for his incomparable lady, and proved it by the last solemn act of existence.

I have alluded to the tendency of her mind to retirement; and like most great geniuses she was at all times disposed to covet the real or seeming quiet of a country life. But her brother had now embarked himself in the *property* of Covent Garden Theatre, and her presence there was vitally important to him. She expresses her resolution to prolong the struggle of thirty years in consequence; and there is interest of no common order in this devotion of herself to her brother's views in life, when her own are closed.

We can recur on this subject also to her own expressions.

" Alas! my dear friend, what have I *here?* Yet " here, even here, I could be content to linger " still in peace and calmness. Content is all I " wish. But I must again enter into the bustle " of the world. For though fame and fortune " have given me all I wish, yet, while my pre- " sence and my exertions here may be useful to " others, I do not think myself at liberty to give " myself up to my own selfish gratifications."—

Again, and more pointedly.—" I shall leave this
" place (Banisters) on the 4th of next month
" (September 1803,) and will write again, as
" soon as I can, after I get to town : I shall
" have a great deal of business upon my hands,
" and upon my head and heart many imperious
" claims. I find it is utter folly in me to think
" that I am ever to live one day for *myself*, while
" these various claims, dear and tender as they
" must always be, exist; nothing but my BRO-
" THER could have induced me to appear again
" in public, but HIS interest and honour must
" always be most dear to ME."

In order to combine the severe losses of a
domestic nature, I have delayed to notice a disagreeable occurrence which attended her tour to
the sister kingdom at the close of 1802. Perhaps
no actress was ever more persecuted by *cabal*
than Mrs. Siddons. The reader has not forgotten
the old attacks on the subject of her acting or
not acting for Digges and Brereton. He may,
with myself, have had opportunities of knowing
the warm and active benevolence of the Irish
character. To insinuate, therefore, that an object
of their highest admiration is *cold* in the cause of
charity, is with that nation sufficient to excite a
feeling, which is too impatient for explanation,
and often injurious even from its virtue. The
Dublin Lying-in Hospital is one of those insti-

tutions not so endowed as to be above the aid of
a performance at the theatre; and it was asserted,
on no foundation in the world, that Mrs. Siddons
had positively *refused* to act for the tenderest of
all claims that can be submitted to her sex. This
charge had been got up with great knowledge of
effect, and had been for some months ripening
into mature mischief. At length the trustees of
the institution thought proper to give a public contradiction to this aspersion upon the actress—
they said "That Mrs. Siddons had most certainly
"never *refused* to act for them, and indeed had
"never been requested to do so." The fact
turned out to be, that it had been proposed she
should play a night for some one public charity,
the choice for *which* to be, properly, at the option
of Lady Hardwicke. Why the manager, who
had himself proposed the matter to her, had
allowed it to drop, was best known to himself—
he had to give his theatre for a night, and Mrs.
Siddons had consented to act, that is to fill it, if
he did. She saw the point quite in its true light,
and though she had many objections to the conduct of the manager, addressed a letter to him,
tending to put her character and conduct right
with the public. She was never fond of such
personal explanations in print, but the occasion
seemed to demand a vindication of her outraged

humanity, and her letter to Mr. Jones does honour to her understanding and her heart.

(Copy.)

" SIR,

" I take the liberty of addressing you on a
" subject which has caused me much uneasiness.
" Public censure is, under any circumstances,
" well calculated to wound our feelings, but it is
" peculiarly distressing when it is heightened by
" injustice. That reports, most injurious to me,
" have been circulated, can no longer be doubted,
" when I assure you that I understand it is gene-
" rally believed that I refused to play for the
" Lying-in Hospital. On this subject you will,
" I am sure, be as anxious to do me justice, as I
" am solicitous to vindicate myself in the eyes of
" the public. I, therefore, beg leave to bring
" to your recollection, that you did me the
" honour of calling on me, at my house in Park-
" street, last summer, when it was liberally pro-
" posed on your part, as it was most cheerfully
" accepted on mine, that I should perform for
" some charity. You also recollect that it was
" considered by us both, as a compliment justly
" due to Lady Hardwicke, that she should have
" the *choice* of the particular charity, for which I

" was to perform ; and you thought it likely that
" her Excellency would give her preference to
" the Lying-in Hospital. You also, Sir, must
" remember, that I was not only willing, but
" desirous, of exerting myself for the benefit of so
" laudable an institution.

" Why so amiable a purpose was not imme-
" diately promoted, I cannot even guess; but
" sure I am, that its postponement cannot be at-
" tributed to any backwardness on my part. The
" same motives which actuated me *then*, are no
" less powerful *now;* and it will give me infinite
" pleasure, if, by the exertion of any powers I
" possess, I can be able to promote an important
" object of public utility.

" And now, Sir, if I may be permitted to speak
" of myself as a private individual; I have only to
" regret the sad necessity imposed upon me, of
" vindicating my character from the imputation of
" a failing as unamiable, as, I trust, it is foreign
" to my nature. I regret that I should be con-
" strained, from unfortunate circumstances, to
" endeavour to rescue myself from an obloquy,
" which I hope I have never incurred by my
" conduct. I regret that the country in which
" I am obliged to do so should be Ireland.

" I have the honour to be, Sir,
" Your obedient servant,
(Signed) " S. SIDDONS.
" To Frederic Edward Jones, Esq."

Although Mrs. Siddons had thus devoted herself to promote her brother's interest, and transferred her attraction, which continued scarcely abated, from Drury Lane Theatre to Covent Garden, it was without any junction as to the property; the sixth purchased by Mr. Kemble was exclusively his own; and he paid down £10,000, in part of the £23,000 its estimated value, leaving his accumulating profits in Mr Harris's hands to liquidate the remainder. But though she chose to be there merely as an actress upon a salary, the alteration as to the house was productive of many comforts. Inviolable respect she was sure of every where, and her brother was the stage manager also at Drury Lane Theatre during the greater period of her connexion with that house. I never could perceive that she was more attended to by him than any other lady would have been holding the same rank. He sometimes entreated the treasurer would let her have some part of her long arrears: but such offices he was disposed to render other persons equally, performers and authors. The superior comfort now was, that all that uncertainty was at an end which disgraced the regime of Mr. Sheridan's house. The Manager of Covent Garden Theatre was really a man of business, who did not consider himself entitled to delay, much less alienate, the stipulated payment for which he had received the valuable labours of his performers. I never knew

a gentleman better calculated to be at the head
of a theatrical concern than the late Thomas
Harris, Esquire; and, fortunately for him, his
power was not a matter that could be disputed,
owing to a clause in the covenants of purchase;
during his life the management vested solely in
him—the stage manager acted under his authority. Mr. Harris's system of management was
built on the two principles of *variety* and *novelty*,
and he looked strongly to the commercial or profitable side of things. Perhaps he was not enough
aware of his partner's real value; but of Mrs.
Siddons he knew the exact importance—her wonderful talents, and the splendid train of admirers
which would now be the ornaments of HIS theatre,
and perhaps put a seal upon the doors of the rival
establishment.

The very *face* of his house was expressive of
his expectations. The enviable retreats of sixteen private boxes tenanted by the Northumberlands, the Devonshires, the Abercorns, the
Hollands, the Egremonts, and so on, taken at a
rent of £300 per annum, was a flattering earnest
of what his new connexion would achieve for
him. Added to this, the grace of high rank and
fashion, he was now about to place his theatre
first in the scale of reason, from the superior
power he possessed of presenting the standard
works of our great poets. The Apollo had not

yet sunk into the flaming ruins of Drury, but stood as if meditating his flight from a temple erected to his honour, but quite *unfinished* either within the walls or without.

It might have been expected that Covent Garden, proud of its great accessions in the whole of the Kemble family of tragic moment, would have opened with one of Shakspeare's tragedies strongly cast, Macbeth for instance, and struck the town with its full strength at first. But there were various reasons against it, which respected the feelings of the rest of the company; and on the first night the new management was contented to let the house, in all its beauty and improvement, speak for itself, and Mr. Fawcett bespeak the public favour to their new commander of the stage, by a liberal and well merited compliment to the services of his predecessor. Mr. Kemble, accordingly, made his first appearance alone in Hamlet, and Mrs. Siddons, like her brother, repeated her original *debút* in town, and acted Southerne's Isabella on the 27th of September, 1803.

There is sometimes a wild notion, that the audiences of one theatre are differently affected from those of another; and some persons seemed alarmed at the result to Mrs. Siddons of invading a region of rather lighter amusement than the stage of Garrick. But her own identity was not surer than the *feeling* she excited; and unresisted passion stormed every breast within her new sphere of exertion. If I am not mistaken, her *pathos* was even more profound than less; to which, indeed, her personal afflictions must have contributed. On the 6th of October she acted Lady Randolph; and her son, Mr. Siddons, was the Douglas—Mr. Kemble took the part of old Norval. This was followed by Elvira in Pizarro; but to his other vices that adventurer now added drunkenness, and his representative, Cooke, being unable to speak the part, her son read it, and read it so well as to gain much credit by doing the friendly office.

The present was the age of revolutions. The most surprising events had occurred on the stage of real life, and the mimic world followed the course which seemed to strike down all reasonable expectations. It might have been, supposed that Mrs. Siddons and her brother had now established their tragic supremacy so as to " laugh a siege to " scorn"—their proud citadel was taken by storm, and the assailant was an ignorant boy.

" Quoniam medio de fonte lepôrum
Surgit amari aliquid, quod in ipsis floribus angat."
Lucret. b. 4. v. 1127.

But the triumph of Covent Garden had not been complete even in their first season. One

might have imagined that Drury Lane Theatre
would suffer dreadfully by such a diminution of
its strength.   By no means.   Bannister took the
management, and his receipts averaged £242.2s.8d.
nightly through the season.   The causes of this
singular result were three.   The Caravan—Cin-
derella—and the Soldier's Daughter.   The first of
these had no greater principle than the making a
Newfoundland dog jump into *real water*, contained
in a tank upon the stage, to recover Julio, the son
of the Marchioness of Calatrava, plunged from a
precipice into the river below, on account of her
resistance to the passion of the Governor of Barce-
lona.   It was, what an afterpiece may very properly be, an ingenious trick, surprising by its
novelty.   It was repeated forty times during its
first season.   The *second* of these charmers was
one which secured us all originally in the nursery;
and now, mingling mythology with Mother-Goose,
attracted the largest *second price* to the theatre that
had been known.   It was repeated fifty-four
times during the *season;* or, to speak more cor-
rectly, as well as favourably, between the 3rd of
January and the 11th of June.   The *third,* a
comedy written by Mr. Cherry, and beautifully
acted by Mrs. Jordan, during its run on the first
season, kept up by either the Caravan or Cinde-
rella, brought in twenty nights performance the
sum of £7544. 14s. 6d.   Thus, to use a favourite

expression of Mr. Kemble's, " as it happens for " ever in theatres, a lucky chance *had* turned up " for them," and the Drury Lane people were NOT ruined, even with Kemble and his brother Charles, Mrs. Siddons and her most accomplished daughter-in-law—Braham, Incledon, and Storace, all at Covent Garden Theatre.

Here, though perhaps a little surprised, there was nothing that either Mrs. Siddons or her brother could regret—it is to the advantage of each theatre that its rival should flourish. It shews a full tendency of the public mind to the species of entertainment; the interest of the rivals forbids every thing like indolence; the best strength is put forth; the sphere of attraction is enlarged. But the peculiar mania which seized these islands for the performances of Master Betty, is a thing quite unexampled in its extent, and his measure of success was due only to the most consummate excellence in the art. Unquestionably, Mrs. Siddons, in the summer of 1802, when she acted Elvira at Belfast, never suspected that she was then inspiring a mere child with an irresistible passion for tragedy; and that, in two short years, the most accomplished actor of the age was to be eclipsed by this meteor, which dispensed with all our usual attractions at both theatres—

" And turn'd our SUN to *shade*."

It must have needed philosophy of more than common power, thus to give place to commercial advantage, and expect with calmness the returning reason of the town, enamoured of its own injustice, and elevating mere prematurity into prodigy.

There was one circumstance attended his performances which was visually absurd. I mean the palpable disparity as to figure and age;—the absurd contests in which this child was made to hector, and combat, and conquer what he could hardly reach. This exhibition surpassed the folly of former ages from its singleness. The little aery of young eyasses, the children of Queen Elizabeth's chapels, were at least unmingled with bulkier matter, the best of them was only an Iülus among his playfellows—comparative ages dispelled no illusion, when it was once admitted. But a Salathiel Pavy* among the Burbadges, and

* Salathiel Pavy had acted old men for three years with very uncommon skill, and died before he had completed his thirteenth year. Mr. Gifford, in a note upon the epitaph which Ben Jonson composed to his honour, observes, as he might be expected to do, the care taken of the *education* of these children of St. Paul's and the Royal Chapels—" they were opposed," he says, " only to one " another. Nothing so monstrous ever entered into the thoughts " of the managers of those days, as taking infants from the cock- " horse and setting them to act with men and women." They had a *minor* theatre for one

" Parvola, Pumilio, χαρίτων ἴα, tota merum sal."

Taylors, and Lowins of the Globe, what gallant of
that astonishing period would have endured for a
moment? By a contest with their matured com-
petitors, the children might seem, as Shakspeare
says, " to exclaim against their own succession;"
for we know that many of them grew up into
ordinary players, and admitted among men, gave a
delight more decorous, though less wonderful,
than that which they had excited as children.

As to the young Roscius of 1804, Kemble knew
exactly what was in him; and, perhaps, was not
displeased to see the fool multitude deserting,
even Cooke himself, for the youthful Betty. How
long the spell might be expected to hold; when
the stage should again be his own, and the hard
fortune to be supplanted, which hung upon his
exertions, be tired of farther persecution,—he
might, in spite of his philosophy, anxiously inquire. Mrs. Siddons had been (worthily I admit,)
long worshipped among the higher orders. What
scenes of pale and fluttering hypocrisy must have
been acted, when those who catch at every sort
of distinction were obliged to exhibit themselves
proud of following the boy Roscius, and hardly
able to avoid *decently*, before the GREAT WOMAN,
the hyperbolical nonsense, which all ranks indeed
slavered out, from morn to night, in his commendation. I do not feel quite sure, whether it
be not wiser to avoid the imputation of *envy*,

which sincere conduct is sure to excite; and, instead of attempting to throw impediment in the dance of folly around its idol, to assume that smile and good-humoured laugh, which, in the late Sir Joshua Reynolds, passed with the critical for derision, and with the simpleton for congenial admiration.

I have it from unquestionable authority, that Mrs. Siddons disdained at any time to *compliment* the young hero; and being convinced herself that the effect was delusive, maintained a cold reserve upon the subject, and heard the absurdities in society with much equanimity. That it might strengthen her wish for retirement is likely enough. But, however, we may learn to undervalue the public applause, it is difficult for one, on whom it has been long bestowed, to bear the dreary vacuity of private life. La Valliere, driven from the embraces of Louis XIV. by the superior charms of De Montespan, did wisely when she withdrew to the shelter of the cloister, which concealed, at least, the chagrin it might be unable to banish.

Mrs. Siddons was not called upon either to " pursue the triumph or partake the gale." Mrs. Litchfield was selected by Mr. Kemble to act with Master Betty. Her figure did not rise to the grand and commanding—but she had a very clear and perfect tone of voice, and that accurate knowledge of the business of the stage, which the occasion required. The list of Betty's characters during his first run was proper enough. The oldest character was Hamlet, who in the outset of the play is so young as to talk of going back to *school* again at Wittemberg, and yet, at the grave of Ophelia is proved to have attained his thirtieth year. The business of the play does not occupy a year. Perhaps Shakspeare suited the age of his character to that of its *representative*—a further indication may, perhaps, be found in an expression of the Queen Mother, during the fencing scene— " He's fat and scant of breath ;" circumstances which apply rather to the full habit of manhood, than to that youthful figure described as " the glass of fashion and the mould of form."

From this and a thousand other instances of the great poet's carelessness and want of revising his play as a whole, the assertion of his player-editors seems, I confess to me, entitled to the fullest credit ; " that what he wrote came from " his pen with so much *easiness*, that they scarce " received from him a *blot* in any of his papers." He very probably sent his works to the theatre for study, act by act, as he composed them, and trusted to memory for keeping them consistent throughout. That different printed copies of the same play are more or less full and perfect, proves nothing against this position : the printer exhibited, unauthorized, all that he could acquire at the time; when he augmented the copy he did so, NOT because the author had composed additional passages; but in consequence of his having found access to the *true and perfect* original, by which the deficiencies of his former publication were supplied. I disbelieve all *first sketches* by Shakspeare.

CHAPTER XXI.

REVIEW.—COMMENT ON IT BY THE AUTHOR.—AN EFFECT
OF LIGHT ON HER FIGURE.—REFLECTIONS ON HER LOSS.
—PORTRAIT OF HER BY LAWRENCE, AND ANOTHER FINE
LIKENESS FOR WHICH SHE DID NOT SIT.—THE AUTHOR
CLOSES HIS WORK.

THE retirement of Mrs. Siddons at this period
had a cause more distressing than the public
delirium—she had a long and dangerous illness,
that confined her to her chamber, and hardly
allowed her power to change her position; when
recovered she returned to Ireland, and performed
with her wonted energy and popularity. The
second season of the young Roscius lowered his
pretensions; but, having made his fortune, he
was now sent to college, and I presume the cultivation of his understanding did no great injury to
his subsequent performances on the stage. The
winter of 1806-7 once more beheld Mrs. Siddons
and her brother acting with undisputed supremacy,
and I do not recollect at any period to have more
enjoyed their transcendent efforts. The great
actress had become fuller in her person and more
majestic than ever. Her Volumnia, her Katharine,
her Lady Macbeth, were at their *nil ultra*. She
was no longer in danger of new studies, from
which nothing was to be hoped; but when she
chose to act was followed as the most accomplished of all actresses merited to be—as the

genuine interpreter of the inspired oracles of Poesy.

But a dreadful calamity was at hand, and the 20th of September, 1808, was marked by the conflagration of the theatre, which she so much adorned.

The modern stage affects reality infinitely beyond the proper objects of dramatic representation. Muskets are fired, with their wadding, to lodge, for aught anybody can tell, in some crevice; and at last, in the night time, the lurking pest bursts forth to the ruin of a stately building, and half its neighbourhood. The drum, that used to threaten with its empty ordnance the canvas walls of some fortified city, must soon give way to the real implements of war; and the guardsmen who nightly act the heroic troops of all times and nations, may march from their quarters to the playhouses, preceded by their own bands, and drawing their *field-pieces* to a boarded field of battle. The delightful odour of powder, mingling with that of *gas*, renders a theatre the most unsavoury place we can enter. Formerly, the painted *scene* was a scene of battle, whereon immoveable combatants suggested to the fancy of the spectator, and the prompter's troops behind contributed the vocal cheer to the shock of armies. We now fill the stage with something like a detachment; and in the midst of confusion and noise, two unknown champions occupy the front of the stage by a display of the broad-sword exercise, and the *sparks* of their courage alarm the drowsy musician in the orchestra, lest the blade itself should descend, and " mar the plea- " sure of the time" it was trying to *beat* to his music.

It is in vain to dispute the inference from all this absurdity. The million will always be governed by the eye. In proportion as by over attention to them the accessories become princi- pals, the writer and the actor vanish together. Their art cannot exist without the full triumph of that art. The " thoughts that breathe, the words " that burn" of the poet, inform the features, in- spire the tongue of the accomplished actor— together they have power beyond their originals, and the stage of Shakspeare and Siddons is more true to nature than history itself.

But the tide set now so strongly in favour of these improvements of dramatic exhibition, that after a decent interval of sorrow for their actual loss, and before the ashes of the late pile were well cold, the proprietors determined to erect an edifice of transcending magnificence, and turn their disaster into triumph. The first stone of the new theatre was laid by his present Majesty, then Prince of Wales, on Saturday the 31st of De- cember, 1808. Among the ladies who attended

upon this occasion Mrs. Siddons was placed,
where she could best see the important ceremony.
She wore a plume of *black* feathers, forgetting the
ominous foreboding of her own Isabella. The
rain descended in torrents, and Kemble would
not abate one jot of punctilio on such an occasion,
but, like King Lear, bareheaded, and in white
silk stockings—

" Endur'd the pelting of the pitiless storm."

Mrs. Siddons, who knew he had just left his
room, after a month's confinement, was perfectly
in agony at this exposure of his person. His
venerable partner, Mr. Harris, on that day, laid in
the foundation of a paralytic disorder, which conducted him to his grave. My superstition remembered the war of elements, that had commemorated the preliminaries of peace with France
a few years back; and would not countenance
the joy that looked so extremely like sorrow. I
shrunk away from the dreary scene, with a damp
upon my spirits, that I did not care to spread
among my friends. As to my dear Kemble,
through this whole business he trod in air. The
amazing structure—the vast patronage—the private boxes—the now unquestionable increase of
prices, filled his mind with not unreasonable hopes
of affluence and triumph. Perhaps, Mrs. Sid-

dons herself expected to be teased by the fashion‑
able world, to use her influence with her brother,
that their application for the luxuries of the new
theatre might obtain a friendly preference.

There was at this time but little expectation
that our great actress would herself act in the
new theatre. She really wished to retire. But
I must not anticipate. Scarcely did the solidity
of Mr. Smirke's edifice begin to shew itself in
progress, when the metropolis was called, by the
conflagration of the other house, to express no
common wonder and even alarm at the fate which
joined them in equal ruin. So speedy a coinci‑
dence, as it defied the doctrine of chances, and
the probabilities of life, so in the breasts of per‑
sons suffering by the system of irregularity at that
house, it begot a suspicion that the destruction of
Drury Lane Theatre was wilful. One person
was frequently named as the contriver of the
whole mischief, and he, certainly, was a man who
possessed the entire *means* in himself; but his
very accusers could assign no *motive* to such an
action.

It was on the 24th of February, 1809, that this
beautiful, light, and yet vast work of Mr. Hol‑
land, unfinished externally to the last, was con‑
sumed by fire. It was a more regular and splendid
conflagration than that of Covent Garden Theatre;
and exhibited by twelve o'clock at night the sub‑

lime, because terrible view of one unbroken body
of flame for the space of at least four hundred and
fifty feet. Some of the performers, among whom
was my friend Charles Mathews, at a personal
risque sufficiently alarming, thridded the suffocat-
ing maze of passages, and bore away their personal property. Mrs. Jordan found some kind
help in this disaster, and lost, I think, little or
nothing. Sheridan had used his theatre as a store
to deposit the spoils of office; and by this fire
was destroyed the whole of the furniture, which
adorned his house in Somerset Buildings, when
he was for a short time Treasurer of the Navy.
He was himself in the House of Commons when
he received the disastrous intelligence; and he
behaved with his accustomed fortitude. The
sympathy of the House would have led the members to adjourn, but he refused such a personal
compliment to his feelings; and only at the proper
time could be prevailed upon *himself* to repair to
the neighbourhood of his ruin, where he sat out
the last appearances of conflagration. When the
reader reflects upon the state of this great man's
finances, the little hope he could entertain of his
theatre's being rebuilt at all, or of its ever yielding
an income to *him* again, if it were—and is told that
neither his fortitude nor his pleasantry abandoned
him, he may suspect that WIT has a buckler more

impassive than adamant, and think him an object
of envy in every condition of his fortune.

There is a relation of circumstances to each
other, which is often only succession, sometimes
cause and effect. Whether Drury Lane would
have been safe had the Kemble and the Siddons
remained *there*, we can form no probable solution :
a glue-pot may boil over in one management as
well as another. But, as *they* were the positive
causes of Pizarro's being acted at Covent Garden
Theatre, the wadding of the Spanish Soldier in-
dubitably could not have lodged in the flies, had
there not been this call for firing his musquet;
and thus a whimsical friend of mine proved—that
the KEMBLES were the *cause* of this conflagration : but his argument has a longer train than he
suspected, and as properly includes Mr. Sheridan,
the writer,—Mr. Kotzebue, the inventor, and even
Pizarro himself, the conqueror of Peru. However sound the philosophy, on the present occasion it would be irreverent to proceed farther in
this chain of causes : but Wollaston has made a
noble use of this great position in the fifth section
of his work, to which I would, for the highest of
purposes, refer every reader.*

During the latter part of the season 1808-9,

* See Relig. of Nature, page 114 of the Edition 1759, 8vo.

while the Covent Garden company was acting in the Haymarket, Mrs. Siddons announced some of her characters in the bills for the last time; but she yielded to the interests of the new theatre, and accepted an engagement at FIFTY pounds a week; terms both complimentary and just. There was no wantonness here of seeing how far liberality would stretch; the precarious tenure by which such excellence was held, after the steady exertions of thirty-six years, might have justified something even beyond this remuneration.

In accompanying Mrs. Siddons through her splendid career, I have not often turned aside to consider other professors of her art, nor revived my own uneasiness at the progressive losses of the stage. But, during the temporary sojourn of the Covent Garden company in the Haymarket, a retirement took place, which, in the words of our memorable sage, *once more* really " eclipsed the " gaiety of nations, and impoverished the public " stock of harmless pleasure." I allude to the farewell acknowledgments of a gentleman whom I had the happiness to know, and long to esteem, the late unrivalled William Lewis, Esq. With a handsome fortune, the produce and the reward of unexampled diligence, steadiness, and principle, he determined to quit the scene while he was in full possession of its comic charm, and having for the last time indulged his spectators and himself

in unbounded hilarity, finished by the excitement
of their tears and his own.

It was on the 29th of May, 1809, that this
great comedian appeared in Michael Perez, the
Copper Captain of Beaumont and Fletcher, for
the last time. The comedies of his *own* time were,
perhaps, indebted to him for their success; but
they are not so highly rated as to allow of an
appeal to them as *criteria* of his talent. Rule a
Wife and have a Wife is likely to be a favourite
in all ages, and until it becomes an *opera*, which,
in other words, is until the characters make no
pretence of being acted *at all*, there never can be
a more diverting exhibition of this *original* than
Lewis afforded. It is delightful to me to recal
his eager gullability, his rueful change. The rich
description of the mean lodging, where in truth
Fletcher is all *but* Shakspeare, came from him in
all the perfection of the art; like the Don John of
Henderson, where even the words themselves derived an extended power from the way in which
they were spoken. I must instance in one passage, where the actor really equalled the author.

> " There's an old woman, that's now grown to marble,
> *Dried* in this brick-kiln, and she sits i' the chimney,
> Which is but *three tiles* rais'd, like a house of cards,
> The true proportion of an *old smok'd Sybil*:
> There is a daughter, too, that nature meant
> For a maid-servant, but 'tis now a monster;

She has a *husk* about her like a *chestnut*,
With *laziness* and living under the *line* here:
And *these* TWO make a hollow sound together,
Like FROGS, or *winds* between two DOORS that *murmur*."

But where he absolutely exceeded all expectation, even from spirits like his own, was in the first scene of the fifth act, where he meets with Cacafogo, who has been *cozened, too,* and by a *woman* also, (indeed the same woman;) the convulsive joy of his *laugh*, frequently renewed, and invariably compelling the whole audience to a really painful sympathy, was one of the most brilliant exploits of the comedian. If we ever die of excessive laughter, I should imagine such must be the expression of that uncontrollable emotion, where the FANCY lords it over the whole animal economy, and the strings of life itself crack under the dangerous enjoyment.

However his reign of gaiety was at length to close, and Mr. Lewis advanced to utter the only unwelcome expressions that his friends and admirers ever heard from him. It is usually ridiculous when the performer employs some versifier, uninterested beyond the sound of his own lines, to string the common-place acknowledgments and figures together, which he is to deliver to his patrons; and there can be but little variety thrown into similar thanks for similar benefits in either verse or prose. But there is a charm in even pre-meditation when it looks spontaneous, and the language of real life should sometimes be heard from the stage. On the present occasion Mr. Lewis spoke as follows :—

" Ladies and Gentlemen,

" I have the honour of addressing you for the " last time. This is the close of my theatrical " life, and I really feel so overcome by taking " leave for ever of my friends and patrons, that, " might it not be deemed disrespectful or negli- " gent, I could wish to decline it ; but it is a public " duty which I owe, and I will attempt to pay " it, conscious that I shall meet your indulgence : " for when I remind you that I have been thirty- " six years in your service, and cannot recollect. " to have once fallen under your displeasure, " my dramatic death cannot be met by me " without the strongest emotions of regret and " gratitude.

" I should offer my acknowledgments for in- " numerable acts of kindness shewn to my earliest " days, and your yet kinder acceptance of, and " partiality shewn to my latest efforts : all these I " powerfully feel, though I have not the words " to express those feelings. But while this heart " has a sensation, it will beat with gratitude.

" Ladies and Gentlemen, with the greatest re-
" spect, and, (if you will admit the word,) the
" sincerest *affection*, I bid you farewell."

> " Some natural TEARS he dropt, but wip'd them soon;
> The world was all before him, WHERE to choose
> His place of *rest*, and providence his guide."

Mr. Lewis had rather a spare habit of body,
but seemed always in possession of even florid
health, to which his daily walk for a couple of
hours greatly contributed. His figure, from his
deportment, might be deemed even elegant in the
scenes of comic luxuriance; when he exceeded
all the common bounds set to human action, he
never was vulgar, no—not for an instant. Where
all the manners are diverting, it is difficult to
sketch any in very bold relief; but he had one
peculiarity, which was the richest in effect that
could be imagined, and was always an addition
to the character springing from himself. It might
be called an attempt to take advantage of the lingering sparks of *gallantry* in the aunt, or the
mother of sixty, or the ancient maiden whom he
had to *win*, to carry the purposes of those for
whom he was interested. He seemed to throw
the lady by degrees off her guard, until at length
his whole artillery of assault was applied to storm
the struggling resistance; and the Mattockses
and the Davenports of his attentions sometimes
complained of the perpetual motion of his chair,

which compelled them to a ludicrous retreat, and
kept the spectator in a roar of laughter. In
short, whether sitting or standing, he was never
for a moment at rest—his figure continued to exhibit a series of undulating lines, which indicated
a self-complacency that never tired, and the
sparkling humour of his countenance was a signal
hung out for enjoyment, that it would have been
treason against human happiness to refuse to obey.

To write for Lewis could hardly be said to be
difficult. Fill his heart with generosity, and his
head with frolic—let him enter every man's
house, and inquire the concerns of every living
soul of both sexes—turn him loose to do all that
he fancies ; let him plunge into ridiculous disaster, and be relieved only by improbability—make
him, in a word, the harlequin of modern comedy,
and only take care, that the less mercurial personages of the play do not spoil any of his *leaps*, and
the business is achieved.

But all this was *personal* to the actor, and so
absolutely was this the case, that, because Lewis
himself was to be exhibited, the comedies were
never much varied ; and like an adventurer on
the greater stage, the hero only passed under
different names, but invariably played all his
old tricks. I have never seen the characters
of Mr. Lewis in modern comedy played by other
actors, and, therefore, am unable to state by

what still more grotesque achievements they laboured to compensate the certain want of features, and whim, and absolute *gaieté du cœur,* which so distinguished the lively original. Happily for the provinces they have their own humourists, to whose style they have been long accustomed, and in sending them the better actor we might not always benefit the new piece.

Among the conversational excellences of Lewis, was the power of telling a story *well.* He embellished the ground-work usually, I confess; but the additions were so rich and brilliant, that it was impossible to desire the narrative other than he left it. There was a something high and gentlemanly in his course of life; he never degraded himself in dancing after patronage; but looked to his art and his industry as the sole means of attaining an honourable affluence, and he attained it. He fortunately burst away from the ensnaring *property* of the great London Theatres, and consequently passed his latter days in comfort, and left his family wealthy.

The repose of Mrs. Siddons seemed now at some distance. She had agreed to open the new house on the 18th of September, 1809, in Lady Macbeth, and in dumb shew passed through the character, hooted and reviled by an organized body of rioters, demanding to be admitted upon the *old prices,* and thence called O. P's. This was a

second attempt on the part of the proprietors of
theatres to raise the rates of admission; and
their opinions upon this subject, like those of
other men, seem to have fluctuated with their interest.   In the time of that miserable statesman
Lord North, those gentlemen were applied to on
the subject of a tax upon the theatres, to be
covered by a slight addition to the money paid at
their doors.   Their answer was most decidedly
this, " that any alteration in such a matter, must
" inevitably produce the ABSOLUTE RUIN of their
" properties;" and so America escaped the armed
invasion of pantomime.   When we think of such
resources as these among objects of taxation, we
are apt to fancy there must be some mistake in
the history of later times, or that the term of a
heaven-born minister, was applied without much
licence to William Pitt.

It is not my design to go into the history of the
O. P. war.   My heroine was only *not* stricken
down by the careless hostility of the rabble, who
were inspired with a very remarkable hatred to
the house of Kemble.   Let me indulge myself
with the recollection of her brilliant figure on this
first night.   She wore a dress fashioned after the
bridal suit of the unfortunate Queen of Scots, and
was a perfect blaze of jewels in the stomacher of
the dress, as well as upon the hair and around
her neck.   Whether some exaggeration might

not increase the cost of this dress I know not;
but the theatre itself used to talk of some hundred pounds laid out, not only on that, but the
regal dress of Macbeth himself.

One may now venture to speak on this subject
with the freedom of history, and look into the
secret causes of so remarkable a failure. The
real fact is, that too much was attempted at one
time. The prospect before the proprietors was
an entire monopoly of the public. Covent Garden Theatre was to possess every enviable convenience, and display every kind of talent. The
fashionable world has only one species of amusement, at which they are not subject to the intrusion
of strangers—the Italian Opera. It is a very
dear privilege, and the space they occupy is little
more than the carriage itself contains which con-
veys them to it. By devoting one entire tier to
the nobility and gentry, the proprietors of Covent
Garden Theatre could offer to their patrons a box,
accessible at any time, with an anti-room, when
they chose to withdraw for conversation or re-
freshments; there was, besides, a general saloon,
for the occasional promenade of the privileged
orders, and every arrangement made to render a
public place of entertainment to *them* as select and
private as their own residences — they quitted
their boxes by exclusive staircases, and left

the theatre from doors equally devoted to themselves.

Such was the attempt now made to secure to the drama of our country those who it was imagined, from the privilege rather than the performance, had hitherto patronised the opera; but if a fondness for Italian music, executed in the highest perfection, was still an object of solicitude, our great proprietors, or undertakers, were prepared to gratify that passion also; they had engaged CATALANI *herself*, and were disposed to add the fascinating graces of the *ballet* to all the known captivations of either sense, or sound. Had they at first opened at the *old* prices, I am sure the other objects would have been carried. The *fashion* of life is essential to a theatre—if we do not envy, we *admire;* and it is not by his nature that man is revolutionary—he seldom owns entirely to *himself* the allegiance, he yet admits to great rank, great beauty, splendid dress, and services in the style of almost respectful veneration. If it be said that these high pretensions of the new theatre could only be triumphant by the greatest exertions on their part; that the splendid talent of Mrs. Siddons could not long be with them, and that a perpetual supply of novel excellence must maintain the ascendancy they had gained; they might fancy, indeed might say, that they had no rivals in the market—that the Opera House was embarrassed with debt, and Drury in ruins, never probably to rise again—that from their credit as merchants they could always obtain any sterling attraction, or object of caprice, and that, now they had secured the leading nobility of the land, it was quite certain that the gentry and inferior orders would chuse to *be* where the best company was assembled.

I remember, from the first, however, of the conflict, CATALANI was the grand theme of discontent; and we heard of NATIVE TALENT from the rioters, though they would not allow us to hear it from the stage. Poor Mrs. Dickons was ridiculously singled out for an object preferred to the great charmer. A finished singer she unquestionably was, and probably read music with facility that the lovely Italian would have needed to study; but we sometimes respect what we cannot love: the singer may be as true as the notes themselves before her, and more full of *graces*, though to *delight* may be for ever unattainable.

For a few nights the principal object seemed to be to riot, no matter about what. As the business proceeded, it acquired heads to reduce the whole to system, and the lovely elements of jacobinism covered the fronts of the boxes with placards by the foot, and added a band of suitable instruments to the discordant braying of their cham-

pions.　LAW was bound hand and foot in its own
forms, and could only refer the proprietors to " the
" coming on of time."　The lesson of Macbeth
had not been lost upon them.　Among the most
deadly weapons in the armoury of the assailants,
HYPOCRISY was soon discovered.　" The theatre
" was a licensed brothel, and the private boxes
" the impure styes of abandoned and titled sen-
" suality."　This happy thought absolutely ruined
the whole concern.　Gibbon has admirably expressed what followed such a hint.　" The coldest
" nature is animated, the firmest reason is moved
" by the rapid communication of the prevailing
" impulse; and each hearer is affected by his
" own passions, and by those of the surrounding
" multitude."　The ravers about indecorum, who
libelled the female nobility, by thus suggesting
impracticable depravity, were sitting with declared profligacy by their own sides; or walking
in the lobbies with the licensed traders in prostitu-
tion, insulting every thing decent in their own rank.
After sixty-seven nights of outrage, thin houses,
and exhausted spirits, the contest thus closed; the
price to the boxes became seven shillings, that to
the pit remained at three shillings and sixpence;
the private circle was opened to the public to the
full extent of the semi-circle, and the property
boxes became so limited in number as to defeat
entirely the object of their erection.

There was that respectful attention to Mrs. Siddons during this whole business, that through two volumes of trash, collected upon the subject, her name is not mentioned; they did not desire her to *act* where she could not be heard; and being out of their sight, the rioters had nothing to remind *them* of her existence. The entrance of Charles Kemble was a favourite signal to renew the assault. I have said that HYPOCRISY mingled in this business, and FANATICISM, as usual, was not far off. A layman of the church of Christ, alarmed at the destruction which *theatres*, it seems, brought upon pagan antiquity, on the 16th October, 1809, occupied the present "Times" with the most dreadful forebodings; and deprecates, that is, insinuates, the bringing the grey hairs of our sovereign with sorrow to the grave, by our persevering to foster those establishments, which even an Archbishop of our liberal church has called "the Devil's chapels." I quote but one sentence of his "drowsy hum," and hint with tenderness my apprehension, that the imagination is not absolutely clean, that expresses a devout alarm in the following terms. "Shall Christians *revel* "in licentiousness and debauchery? Shall these "associate with, or encourage by their presence, "the *most dissolute* of both sexes? Let those who "have cast off all fear of God, whose glory is their "*shame*, who, being past feeling, have given

" themselves up to *lasciviousness,* and to work all
" *uncleanness* with *greediness,* let THOSE frequent
" the theatre ; they act consistently: but let no
" one who enters that *sink* of *impurity* assume
" the name of a CHRISTIAN; nor dare to lift up
" the same heart, that has been entertained with
" *all manner of lewdness,* to that Being of infinite
" purity !"

It is not my intention to enter into the dispute
between the Christian and the comedian. My
charity, beyond that of Catholicism or Methodism,
can think the characters perfectly compatible,
and feel the value of works of taste, and know
their often unsuspected effect upon morals. But
in utter scorn of modern calumny, I deliberately
affirm, that the purity and utility of all specta-
cles must depend upon the presence of the higher
orders. I would not sully my page with even
the *titles* of productions at some minor theatres,
which are calculated for the passions, and suited
to the taste alone of the lower classes. There is
a gross ignorance or indifference in certain situations as to our public amusements; instead of
protecting such as alone have a tendency to *refine*
the manners, they allow them to be invaded and
impoverished, and overborne by every variety of
obtrusive bad taste, bad language, and still worse
principle. But I am drawn into the indulgence
of the feeling, excited while I am writing; and

return, therefore, to the peace established between the high contracting theatrical parties, on
the night of the 15th of December, 1809. Many
points were carried of great importance. "MA-
"GISTRACY may be defied,"—"CONSPIRACY may
" be *permitted*,"—" FIDELITY may be *punished*,"
—and " the GENTRY of the land be both *insulted*
" and *taxed* by the same description of orators,
" as represent the electors of Westminster, in
" front of the hustings at Covent Garden." The
unfortunate proprietors drank the " *Eisel*" poured
out to them, and swallowed as evidently a portion of the *crocodile;* and after *begging pardon,*
most humbly, for endeavouring to *preserve* their
property, and *discharging* one of the *most deserving*
persons in their theatre, they were suffered to resume the business of the season, and solicit the
public to revisit what had been so recently the
most disgusting of all houses.

Mrs. Siddons had opened the theatre on the
18th of September, 1809, and her *second* night
of performance was the 24th of April, 1810, when
she repeated her Lady Macbeth. Such an interval spoke loudly for the taste of a London
audience. Now, however, points of moment
having been adjusted, the great actress was
allowed to speak in the magical *chef-d'œuvre* of
Shakspeare without interruption, and the public
came again into the regular enjoyment of the

purest of its pleasures. She repeated this charac-
ter on the 30th, and on the 2nd of May performed
Lady Randolph, in Douglas, for the benefit of the
Theatrical Fund.

I notice, on the 23rd of May, one of the most
attractive performances of the season. Fawcett
selected for his benefit the play of King Lear—
he himself took the part of Kent, a character
which all who know him will be aware was
exactly suited to him. As, however, he was new
in it, Mr. Kemble rehearsed Lear with him; and
when it was done, drew from the " man of his
" word," an exclamation of astonishment at the
amazing power he had displayed. He frankly
told the great actor, that he had often seen him
at night, but never had thought him near his
present excellence; never had himself been so
moved as he then was. Mr. Kemble said, that,
however singular it might be, in Lear an audience
quite unsettled him; the noise of the box-doors
caught his ear, and routed all his meditated
effects; and he found it absolutely impossible to
do that at night, which he had thrown out during
the rehearsal in the morning.

The astonishing impression made by Garrick
in Lear, is well known; and the discipline into
which he brought his stage business,—I had
almost said his audience. In his small theatre
every individual could be well seen, and any

noisy intemperance was removed in a moment.
Conversation above a whisper was checked immediately, as indecent, while so great a man
was upon the stage; and the necessity of profound silence during certain scenes, introduced
the custom of stationing what were called *hush*
men, in different parts of the house, who, by
" *histing* along," as Milton has it, the " mute
" silence". in the proper places, begot an awful
attention in the audience, and left the full impression of his vast powers upon the suspended and
chilled spectators.

I believe nobody ever took less pains than
Mrs. Siddons, to second her efforts on the stage
by those ingenuous arts, which, if they assist the
performer, no less benefit the hearer. Audiences
like ours, are mixed up of such discordant materials: a positive or a vague desire of amusement in some; vanity in others, *with* the true
feeling of art, or without it; honest homely sense;
refinement, and its excess, affectation; with an
aimless hilarity, a restless joy; and much of a
coarse and sluggard notice, moved more by its
neighbours than the stage;—all this to be blended
and bound together by the eye and the ear, attributes a something like magic to the actor's art.

The last season but one of our great actress,
1810-11, she performed nearly the whole of her
characters; and never did she display greater

dignity and force of mind. The singular lot of this consummate artist was to possess some compensation through life, for every excellence that time could not but diminish. It would be absurd to say, that her Autumn excited the tears of her *April*, when her Isabella, her Shore, and her Belvidera, were in their prime, and in my time were neither equalled nor approached; but I may reasonably inquire, whether I myself have not lost more than the actress ever did? and allowing much for the operation of age, I may also take into the account, the frequent performances which I have seen of the same characters. But I incline to think that the Lady Macbeth, the Queen Katharine, the Constance, the Hermione, never suffered in the slightest degree, down to their very latest repetition.

The year 1812 was to be distinguished by the greatest loss of the tragic stage. The play-bills now, announcing the character of the night, with melancholy accuracy stated, that it would be the *last time* of her ever appearing in it; and it seemed almost a withdrawing of the character itself from the stage. After some little fluctuation about the farewell part, it was properly settled to be Lady Macbeth; and on the 29th of June, 1812, being her own night, she took leave of the public, after a very sublime performance of her greatest effort. Her nephew, Mr. Twiss, supplied the verses upon this interesting occasion, and shewed how successfully he could assume the tone of a popular poet, for whose composition, indeed, it might be mistaken. I preserve what constituted the personal appeal, because the lines are very flowing and musical, and extremely well pointed to the object.

> " Perhaps your hearts, when years have glided by,
> And past emotions wake a fleeting sigh,
> May think on HER, whose lips have poured so long
> The charmed sorrows of your Shakspeare's song;
> On her, who parting to return no more,
> Is now the mourner she but seem'd before,
> Herself subdu'd, resigns the melting spell,
> And breathes, with swelling heart, her long, her last farewell!"

Ad captandum, Shakspeare was right here;— but it was not by the charmed *sorrows* of SHAK-SPEARE, that Mrs. Siddons established her supremacy; and the oblivion thrown over the authors, who wrote her Belvidera, her Shore, her Calista, and her Isabella, covers very nearly all the TEARS she ever excited. " Be just, and fear " not," is the recommendation of Shakspeare himself, and the line, with strict propriety, and equal feeling, might have stood thus:

> " The charmed sorrows of your NATIVE song."

For Shakspeare services were to be performed

of a different cast, and in character infinitely
more sublime; and they were rendered by her
so as to become the despair of admiration.

As the audience dismissed the rest of the play,
when the terrible *night scene* of Mrs. Siddons
shut in, there was only to wait till she was ready
to address them, which they did with complimentary patience; and her brother came on the stage
to lead off that great partner of his toil; and by
whom alone he could have accomplished the dis-
tinguishing object of his management. The retirement from what has been the source alike of
fame and fortune, may be a graceful, but is commonly an anxious moment. Five and twenty
years earlier, the historian of the DECLINE and
FALL, at the close of the same month, had written the last words of his mighty labour. His pen
dropt a few reflections upon the state of his mind
at that moment, full of truth and melancholy
beauty; the reader may not be displeased to see
them here, and his fancy may apply them with
strict truth, to the noble actress, whom Mr. Gibbon had so greatly admired, and so constantly
attended while in London. " It was on the day,
" or rather night of the 27th of June, 1787, be-
" tween the hours of eleven and twelve, that I
" wrote the last lines of the last page, in a sum-
" mer-house in my garden." (At Lausanne.)
" After laying down my pen, I took several turns

" in a *berceau,* or covered walk of acacias, which
" commands a prospect of the country, the
" lake, and the mountains. The air was tem-
" perate, the sky was serene, the silver orb of
" the moon was reflected from the waters, and all
" nature was silent.* I will not dissemble the first
" emotions of joy on the recovery of my freedom,
" and, perhaps, the establishment of my fame.
" But my pride was soon humbled, and a sober
" melancholy was spread over my mind, by the
" idea that I had taken an everlasting leave of an
" old and agreeable companion, and that what-
" soever might be the future date of my his-
" tory, the life of the historian must be short and
" precarious."

Whether the great actress regretted or not the
stated calls to exertion, I know not; but her
kindness certainly, probably her taste, led her,
the year following, to act Lady Macbeth, for the
benefit of her brother Charles. In the year 1816
she performed Katharine once more, for the same
kind object; and had consented to repeat her
Lady Macbeth, on the 8th of June of that year,

---

* The classical reader may here suspect the influence of Homer
to have suggested at least as much as the lovely scenery before
the historian.—See the close of the 8th Iliad; but perhaps
the true reference may be to a similar passage in Dr. Johnson's
Journey to the Western Islands.—Works, Vol. 8, p. 255. Edit.
1796.

to gratify the Princess Charlotte, and her Royal Consort of Saxe Coburg. The Princess, though ill, at first imagined she should be able to attend; but her illness increasing, she was obliged to relinquish the design, and send notice accordingly to the theatre. At first the managers thought of changing the play; but conceiving that the public would suffer disappointment at not seeing Mrs. Siddons, she readily consented to act, and seemed to have lost little of her power in the four years of retirement from the stage.

One other exertion, a public reading, is attributable to a higher motive, the desire to assist a family suffering under the premature loss of the father of it, a man of no mean powers either as actor or author. It was in the month of February, 1813, that this graceful aid to the widow of Mr. Cherry was rendered by Mrs. Siddons. That lamented actor expired on the 7th of February, the preceding year.

I know distinctly that the sensibility of Mr. Cherry was so hurt by some of that flippant stuff, which dishonours the name of criticism among us, that he, who had restored prosperity to Drury Lane Theatre, by the Soldier's Daughter, died of a wounded spirit. I have at times heard something like a positive avowal from critics, " that they wrote bitterly without spleen, " that the public called for such amusement,

" and that depraved appetites required poignant
" sauce."

" The TEMPTER or the *tempted*, who sins MOST ?"

The public readings from Shakspeare, at the
Argyll Rooms, during two seasons, proceeded,
as I understood, from the two-fold inducements
of personal gratification and an important addition
to her income. I was informed, by Mr. Kemble
himself, that his sister was not in that state of
affluence, that she could live unemployed, without
some diminution of her comforts. I am quite
sure, that all the kind imputations of *jealousy* of
any other attraction, *avarice*, and *vanity*, were
NOT the motives to the exhibition; which remains
to be described in its style and its effects.

As to the style, nothing could be well more
simple and yet dignified. In front of what was
the orchestra of the old Argyll Rooms—a reading-
desk with lights was placed, on which lay her
book, a quarto volume printed with a large letter.
There was something remarkably elegant in the
self-possession of her entrance, and the manner
in which she saluted the brilliant assembly before
her. She assisted her distant sight by glasses,
which she waved from time to time before her,
when memory could not entirely be trusted, and

like the Nereïdes that attended her own Cleopatra—

" She made their bends adornings."

Mrs. Siddons divided the reading into parts for
convenience, and was the whole time standing.
She was led to and from the desk by a gentleman; but few gentlemen could gracefully accomplish the office. I would not persecute any
little beings, by naming them at the side of this
noble and seemingly inspired figure; but I *will*
remember that, one night, I had the pleasure to
see this duty discharged by her nephew Mr.
Twiss; and when he gently resigned her hand to
retire himself, his bow of affectionate respect to
his illustrious relative, was, to say all in a word,
fully worthy of the occasion, and highly honourable to his taste.

  The task to be sustained by the great actress
presented extraordinary difficulties. In the first
place, the plays of Shakspeare abound in *male*
characters—the comparative number of his females
is few. There is, therefore, an almost awkward
effort of an elegantly drest female to assume the
vehement passions, coarse humours, and often
unguarded dialogue of every variety of manly
character; and it is, perhaps, easier for the male
reader (at least, it was so to Le Texier,) to aspire

to the tender sweetness of the female character,
than for the lady (even Mrs. Siddons,) to assume
the passions or the follies, the agonies or the enjoyments of the other sex. The wish of Cordelia
to *unsex* herself, even for King Lear, could not
have been recommended to her imitation—all
that she attempted was in the strictest decorum,
fitted to her condition and her knowledge. I
heard her pass slightly over the lapwing Lucio, in
the Measure for Measure, and he had lost all his
grossness by the refinement of her delivery.

The reserve of her sex, too, greatly intercepted
the *variety*, which the great artist could unquestionably have bestowed upon these readings;
but such a *largesse* would have somewhat savoured
of *mimicry*, the lowest of all modes of representation, which requires but the mechanical part of
man, and copies not so much the passion as the
exterior manners. Such a style of exhibition is
incompatible with dignity, and he who felt that
upon the stage Mrs. Siddons was rather lowered
by comedy, was rather apprehensive than solicitous of those sallies of humour that burst from the
manly desk of Henderson and Le Texier. It is
said of Voltaire by an exquisite judge, " that in
" his own theatre his declamation was fashioned
" to the pomp and cadence of the old stage ; and
" he expressed the *enthusiasm of poetry*, rather
" than the feelings of nature." The charm of

versification forces something like this from every public reader of Shakspeare. The *witches* of Mrs. Siddons accordingly were poetical creations; the organs of destiny, the ministers of darkness, beings resolving " into air, into thin air," and whose language seemed to wander from that element alone, unimpressed, at least, by any organs that were human. She divined a meaning in the poet beyond his words; and it was not like a creature of earth's mould that she delivered the following lines :—

> " Double, double toil and trouble ;
> Fire, burn ; and, cauldron, bubble."

On the stage, where the Wierd Sisters are necessarily consigned to actual persons and positive habiliments, the charm is dispelled; for the imagination has no picture to paint, no mystery to develop.

However, I entirely concur with Capell in the following estimate of Shakspeare's witches. " With regard to the witches' *persons*, the poet's " notion is uniform: his witches are the witches " of his own time and country, without mixture " of Scaldic or of Roman ideas; bating that he " borrows the name of ' *Hecat*' or ' Hecate' for " the governing spirit, the ' *mistress*' of their en- " chantments, in two of his scenes; where the " personage she exhibits has no image of the

" classical Hecate, but of the state of modern
" witchcraft."

In the reading of *Othello*, the general opinion
seemed to be, that Mrs. Siddons threw her whole
force into Iago, a judicious choice; because
where the CAUSE is displayed in its utmost irresistible strength, the hearer's mind is as much
subdued as Othello's; and agonies, impossible
for mere reading to express, are admitted, because they are imagined. Upon the recognition
by the noble Moor of the *practice* under which he
had fallen, the exclamation, " O fool, fool, fool!"
seemed to express ALL *that* sense of rashness,
false inference, unguarded trust to appearances,
unbounded love, and measureless despair, which
fill his mind at the moment when it is uttered.
She has seldom been greater than she was at that
moment.

Upon these, and all occasions, Mrs. Siddons
was uniformly graceful. But she was not graceful by *effort*, and sacrificed nothing to become so.
In this, she widely differed from her brother, Mr.
Kemble. I cannot think, however, that HE sacrificed ENERGY OF ACTION to grace. He rather
sacrificed ease to attitude. and seemed fond of
personal display: he would be on the PARADE,
when not called into the field. Points of FORCE
he had a peculiar alacrity in seizing, and an amaz-

ing power in conveying.   It is by this salvo, that
I introduce the following anecdote, which I find
in the Quarterly Review of my life of that great
actor, No. LXVII. p. 216.

" There was also visible in Kemble's manner at
" times, a sacrifice of energy of action to grace.
" We remember this observation being. made by
" Mrs. Siddons herself, who admired her brother,
" in general, as much as she loved him.   Nor shall
" we easily forget the mode in which she illus-
" trated her meaning.   She arose, and placed
" herself in the attitude of one of the old Egyp-
" tian statues ; the knees joined together, and the
" feet turned a little inwards.   She placed her
" elbows close to her sides, folded her hands, and
" held them upright, with the palms pressed to
" each other.   Having made us observe that she
" had assumed one of the most constrained, and,
" therefore, most ungraceful positions possible,
" she proceeded to recite the curse of King Lear
" on his undutiful offspring, in a manner which
" made *hair rise and flesh creep*—and then called
" on us to remark the *additional effect*, which was
" gained by the concentrated energy which the
" unusual and ungraceful posture in itself implied."

The reviewer *himself* is entitled to every attention from ME : he will receive the few remarks
that follow in the cordial spirit with which I am

sure they are written. In the first place, then, I do not believe that any part of their delight, (a severe delight,) resulted from the concentrated energy of *introverted toes*, and *elbows pinned to the sides*,—however " unusual and ungraceful." There would have been MORE energy, aye *concentrated* energy, too, if the figure had been thrown upon its knees, and the hands *clasped*, and convulsively *drawn home* to the bosom; which, permit me to observe, WAS the energetic and graceful attitude of Mr. Kemble, when pronouncing that curse, which harrows up every heart. As far, however, as this Egyptian figure folded the hands, and pressed the palms to each other, I may be permitted to observe, that it was certainly neither unusual, nor ungraceful, but in fact exhibited the *common*, and *most natural* sign of supplication ; and this, in fact, was the reason for selecting the attitude in question.

In my opinion, the admiring theorists were overwhelmed by quite other forces. The " hair " rose and the flesh crept"* at the *agonized countenance* that glared before them; at the mingling

---

* When I read, in the Review, the words, " made *hair rise*, " and *flesh creep*," I could not but fancy the phrase to have wandered from the Minstrel of the BORDERS; whose hand also I recognized placing the " *single feather* of an EAGLE" in the bonnet of KEMBLE, or *Macbeth :* they were identified to me.

awful and *piercing* SOUNDS, that conveyed the execrations invented by Shakspeare.

> " Hear, NATURE, hear!
> Dear Goddess hear! Suspend thy purpose, if
> Thou didst intend to make this creature fruitful!
> Into her womb convey sterility!
> Dry up in her the organs of increase;
> And from her derogate body never spring
> A babe to honour her! If she must teem,
> Create her child of spleen; that it may live,
> And be a thwart disnatur'd torment to her!"

I think I can be quite sure, that while the GREAT EGYPTIAN uttered these lines, the hearers could be at *no leisure* to examine whether her arms had never quitted their bondage? or the feet recovered a position to which they were certainly more *accustomed*, energetic, as it must be confessed, they always were, in common with the rest of that dignified and perfect anatomy.

Nor are grace and energy of action at all *opposed* to each other. CONSTRAINT, AFFECTATION, MANNERISM, are the great foes alike to both. Through the whole range of my stage recollections, the most *energetic* things were at the same time the most truly *graceful*. Think of all the grand points, in either BROTHER or SISTER, and you will find the consent of grace and energy invariable. When the true artist is really UP to the great occasion before him, the ENERGY propels his frame to the *right position,* and that speaking index, the hand, announces the *graceful* triumph. Look at Mrs. Siddons herself in Katharine; " Lord Cardinal! To YOU I speak." Can you survey the energy, and overlook the grace? Look at the oath of the *trois* HORACES by David, and bow before the UNION of the two great principles.

But to close with the recitations, or readings, to whichever class the beautiful efforts of Mrs. Siddons are assigned. For the sake of any future exhibition of this sort, I will notice one happy effect, accidental or designed, (probably the latter,) which should invariably enter among the preparations of the apartment. A large red screen formed what painters would call a back ground to the figure of the charming reader. She was dressed in white, and her dark hair *à la Grecque,* crossed her temples in full masses. Behind the screen a *light* was placed; and, as the head moved, a bright circular irradiation seemed to wave around its outline, which gave to a classic mind the impression, that the priestess of Apollo stood before you, uttering the inspiration of the deity, in immortal verse. But such oracles have long been *dumb.*

" APOLLO from his shrine
Can no more divine ;
No *nightly trance,* or *breathed spell.*
Inspires the pale-ey'd priest from the prophetic cell."

Her noble figure, on such occasions, may be accurately conceived from Sir Thomas Lawrence's whole length of Mrs. Siddons, reading her favourite poem, the Paradise Lost. The picture was painted for her friend, Mrs. Fitz-Hugh, and is a very sublime effort of the great artist.

Perhaps I ought not to quit my subject without trying the effect of the PEN in delineating the person of Mrs. Siddons, and the charm that certainly accompanied her through every era of her public life. It is fortunately done to my hands by a FOREIGN WRITER of her own sex; and I shall annex it in the original language, claiming only the praise for first presenting to the British nation, so eloquent a description, and so admirable a likeness.

" Elle étoit grande et de belle taille, mais de
" cette grandeur qui n'epouvante point, et ne
" sert qu' à la bonne mine. Elle avoit le teint
" fort beau, les cheveux d'un châtain clair, le
" nez très-bien fait, la bouche bien taillée, l'air
" noble, doux, enjoué, modeste, et pour rendre sa
" beauté plus parfaite, les plus beaux yeux du

" monde. Ils étoient noirs, brillans, doux, pas-
" sionnés, pleins d'esprit. Leur éclat avoit je ne
" sais quoi qu'on ne sauroit exprimer. La mélan-
" cholie douce y paroissoit quelquefois avec tous
" les charmes qui la suivent. L'enjouement s'y
" faisoit voir à son tour, avec tous les attrais
" que la joie peut inspirer. Son esprit étoit fait
" exprés pour sa beauté, grand, doux, agréable.
" Elle parloit juste et naturellement, de bonne
" grâce et sans affectation. Elle savoit le
" monde et mille choses dont elle ne faisoit pas
" vanité. Elle avoit mille appas inévitable ; de
" sorte qu'unissant les charmes de la vertu à
" ceux de la beauté et de l'esprit, on pouvoit
" dire qu'elle meritoit l'admiration qu'on eut pour
" elle."

The reader will be delighted, I have no doubt,
with so fine a likeness, and require only to be
told the name of the fair and eloquent writer.
But it is with pride and pleasure I inform him,
that for this portrait, Mrs. SIDDONS never sat,
however striking the resemblance. It is the
sketch, still of one of the greatest, and best of
women—of Madame de MAINTENON, by her
friend Mademoiselle de Scudery.

I have now conducted this great performer
through the whole of her professional existence;
and, if I could flatter myself that I had fully

accomplished my design, have delivered to the world a MONUMENT to her HONOUR.

But no one can be more sensible than myself, that our WISHES are the children of the imagination, and that their execution must be bounded by our POWER.

THE END.

SHACKELL AND CO. JOHNSON'S COURT, FLEET-STREET.

SUPPLEMENT.

" THE desire to be lamented and remembered," says the excellent RAMBLER, " is often mortified when we remark how little concern is caused by the eternal departure even of those who have passed their lives with public honours, and been distinguished by extraordinary performances. That merit which gives greatness and renown diffuses its influence to a wide compass, but acts weakly on every single breast ; it is placed at a distance from common spectators, and shines like one of the remote stars, of which the light reaches us, but not the heat."

If any exception exist to the above reflection, the general truth of which is readily admitted, it may be found perhaps in such a case as the death of a great and admirable ACTRESS, whose excellence had become an intimate neighbour to our bosoms ; one who had so long been admitted the mistress of our affections, that a sort of kindred had grown up from the interest excited, and we sigh over the loss as of some portion of ourselves. Such, I am sure, was the feeling of many hearts among us, when the morning of Wednesday, the 8th of

June, 1831, announced that Mrs. Siddons had terminated her mortal career.

There was nothing in the mere event to strike or astonish. She had lived during 76 years, and her profession demanded great personal exertions through all the prime and vigour of her days. She had retired from the stage fifteen years, and since her retirement had been little in the public eye; or, if seen merely in her pursuit of air and exercise, at all other times devoted to her family, her studies, and a very select circle of old and beloved friends.

For a few days before her decease, the servant at her door presented, to such as enquired, a written bulletin of the state of the patient—not as an imitation of stately ceremonial, but that the fact to be known might be communicated in *correct* terms that admitted no misconception, and avoided noise. They generally represented her nights to be *restless*, and the mornings consequently to have arrived without improvement. Her medical attendants were Dr. Neman and Mr. Bushell, of Crawford Street, upon whose skill and friendly zeal she had the greatest reliance. I am perfectly informed as to the infirmity to which the frame of Mrs. Siddons was subjected, but I am not writing a clinical guide; and, when I speak of one of the sublimest forms of the Great Workman, avoid from taste and delicacy every unnecessary detail relating to " the painful family of Death."

A question naturally arose, whether the funeral of such a woman should be of a public or a private nature?

It was soon made known that the family had decided upon a private funeral for Mrs. Siddons. The great woman herself had said in the language of her ardent admirer Mr. Burke, that " she knew the partial kindness of her friends, but had in her life experienced but too much noise and compliment." Thus a first and strong inducement to this course was the preference the deceased herself had testified of an unostentatious interment. Be it remembered too, that the fortune of Mrs. Siddons, though the greatest name in her art, has been more than doubled by many professors of very inferior rank—and this is not intended as an invidious attack upon either *them* or the Public. Talent, like every thing else in the world, has at least its temporary value regulated by the demand for it in the market. This is merely noticed, that it may not be supposed her circumstances required and justified greater splendour than her relatives decided upon bestowing. Instead, therefore, of either a personal attendance of the great, or the acceptance of their carriages, (and those of very many exalted personages were offered,) it was settled that her hearse should be followed by two mourning coaches, with four horses each, containing her near relatives and connexions, and these by the two private carriages of Mrs. Siddons and her brother.

But there was a distinction which grew out of her profession not easy to be avoided; and the members of it chose to pay, at their own expense, the last tribute of respect to their great Queen. This might, it is true, have admitted of some selection. I should have considered a *deputation* from the two theatres, of such members of their companies as had either *acted* with her, or were honoured with her *acquaintance*, to be infinitely more respectful, than such a line as fourteen coaches, the mourners in which, by far the greater part at least, had no sort of relation to Mrs. Siddons but their mere employment in a theatre. But men err frequently in *delicacy*, with the best intentions in the world. There are some faces too upon the stage, that, if ever seen at funerals, should only be as those of the grave-diggers to poor Ophelia. It would be painful to pursue the subject.

The remains of the great actress were deposited in a coffin covered with purple velvet, with her name and the dates of her birth and death inscribed upon a brass plate. Thus :—

SARAH SIDDONS.
Born July 5th. 1755.
Died June 8th. 1831.

The original plate had the abbreviated *Mrs.* over the name. At the suggestion of her daughter, a second plate was engraved, omitting this unnecessary prefix; and the inscription stands simply as I have copied it.*

Every thing upon the ground itself being in readiness, on the morning of Wednesday, the 15th of June, the day week from her departure, soon after 10 o'clock, the procession began to move from her residence in Upper Baker Street. It consisted of the hearse with four horses, two mourning coaches and four—the *first* containing Mr. Charles Kemble, Mr. Horace Twiss one of her executors, and two sons of the late Mr. Henry Siddons:—the *second*, Mr. W. Meyrick the other executor, Mr. Stirling, and the two medical gentlemen before named; and after these, fourteen mourning coaches with a pair of horses each, containing gentlemen of both theatres. Two private carriages, agreeably to the arrangement before stated, closed the procession —her own and her brother's. They arrived at Paddington Church about a quarter before 12 at noon.

The ladies of the family were already privately in the church, concealed from the spectators. Her three female and two male servants also paid the last duties to their beloved mistress. The service was performed in his usual impressive manner by the Rev. Mr. Campbell, the present minister.

Mr. Charles Kemble, her brother, was chief mourner. His emotion was fully commensurate with his loss. There are few such sisters. There

---

* Mr. Nixon, of 123, Portland Street, Mrs. Siddons's Upholsterer, had the charge of the interment.

are supposed to have been at least 5000 people
present in the church and on the ground.   Mrs.
Siddons was long an inhabitant of the parish, and
her pew in the church, No. 28, close to the vestry
door, was an object of great interest.   At my time
of life, I may be excused for avoiding a crowd of
5000 people merely to view the body placed in the
sepulchre itself.   But on Tuesday, the 21st of June,
I visited the sacred spot which now shelters the
remains, and for more than an hour held communion with the solemn scene in solitude and silence.
Fancy itself could hardly form one better suited to
a mind of any sensibility.   It is a piece of ground
walled in and recently consecrated.   As you enter
the church-yard of Paddington, the path to the
right hand leads you to a sort of Etruscan gate of
stone, which bears for its motto the great consolatory principle of Christianity—

MORS JANUA VITÆ.

The beadle preceded to unlock the gate for me,
and, what was remarkable, he had been a guards-
man, and as a supernumerary had often attended
the great deceased upon the stage.   He particularly
named the play of Coriolanus.   He had, in a very
different office, preserved order also at her grave.
He led me up to the tomb.   It was then railed
round, and slightly painted : there is a plinth on a
ground step ; and a facing of marble is intended,
with the name and the dates of birth and decease.

My conductor then left me to myself with a permission to stay as long as I chose undisturbed—and I reposed myself upon the circular seat round a venerable elm. It has a companion on the other side of the small pathway, which separates the vault of Mrs. Siddons on the right from that of the late minister of the parish.

The new ground thus dignified is a square resembling some sheltered nook in a park; and this feature was aided by a few sheep, who were turned in there to pasture. It was a spot in which the contemplative " might think down hours to minutes." Her " *royal* Imogen" returned to my mind's eye, and I murmured to myself the promise of Arviragus :—

> " While summer lasts and I live here, Fidele,
> I'll visit thy sad grave."

A marble tablet is ordered in Paddington church itself. It would have been placed on the wall close to her former seat there; but as it is one of mere plaster, the place assigned is on the left of the communion table, where there are others, to which its form will assimilate.

As to any public tribute to the memory of Mrs. Siddons, the feverish state of all Europe is such, that the great soul of Newton himself, had he survived to our days, " might quit the world to mingle with his stars," and excite no other enquiry than how he had stood affected to certain forms of government, and what he thought of ecclesiastical property. But as Milton once said of the Muses, "I may one day hope to have ye again in a *still time*, when there shall be no chiding; not in these noises." At such a time, (I can *but* hope, at my age, to see it!) the public affections may be revived, and, properly directed, some cenotaph to Mrs. Siddons augment the illustrious names about the south entrance to Westminster Abbey : for the actual remains neither of Shakspeare, nor Milton, nor Gray, can there be found; nor those of her brother Kemble, yet more distant from such a tribute than her own.

There is an exquisite *medallion* of Gray placed by the fine taste of Mason close to the bust of Milton, —THAT I should greatly prefer as a model to any clumsy guess-work at a whole-length figure : it would cost less money and be infinitely more valuable—there are materials enough. She modelled, herself, very tastefully, and has left from her own hand, the conception she entertained of her countenance. Lawrence often drew and painted her, but I cannot think him very successful—he was struggling between nature and the ideal. His whole length, for Mrs. Fitzhugh, is a noble figure, but the face is not very like. Harlow succeeded, I think, entirely, in the Queen Katherine picture; but the attitude is too theatrical for sculpture, at least that which is to enter sacred walls, where the action of the figure should be less violent, and always in keeping with the sanctity of the tomb.

It was a matter of just surprise, for the whole week after her decease, to see how little the present writers for the press really knew of Mrs. Siddons and her family. They bestowed but *three* children upon her, all of whom she had survived; and thus passed over the living merits of the accomplished and excellent CECILIA, who had devoted herself exclusively to her mother's comfort, and was with her when she died,—and her brother GEORGE, who was Governor of Bencoolen, while we held that settlement, and is still one of the East India Company's civil servants at Calcutta. Some of his children are now in this country.

The family really consisted of two sons and three daughters.

HENRY SIDDONS—died April 12, 1815, at Edinburgh, leaving a family.

GEORGE—living in India, also married.

SARAH,
MARIA, } who both died unmarried.

CECILIA—living in Upper Baker Street, unmarried.

Having thus removed the real heirs of the departed, they bestowed her fortune benevolently upon her brother, Mr. Charles Kemble, and Mr. Horace Twiss, her nephew—quite undesired, I am sure, and quite unexpected by those gentlemen. As to her birth, the press quite luxuriated; 14th, 15th, and 1 believe 16th of July 1755, were named in succession: they were rendered impossible by her baptismal certificate, which was extracted for me by the Rev. Thos. Bevan, curate of St. Mary's, Brecon, on the 24th of April, 1826.

"Baptisms in the year 1755.
July 14. Sarah, daughter of Roger Kemble, a comedian, and Sarah his wife, was baptized."

Now it is usual for the birth to precede the baptism a few days, at least; and in the case of Mrs. Siddons, as we find, there was an interval of nine days. But it should be observed, in palliation, that in the getting up of our ephemeral literature there is usually no time for enquiry; and that accuracy is only the result of labour and evidence. The father of Mrs. Siddons was a Catholic; but she herself, like her mother " whose memory I bow to," was of the Protestant Church of England, and, in the company of her daughter, attentive to the performance of its public as well as private duties. While she resided at Westbourn, she constantly attended divine service at Paddington Church, where, be it observed, her pew was in the situation *least conspicuous*, close to the vestry-door on the left hand as you enter from the west door.

Her brother, in a few lines which I received from him, on the occasion of his loss, touches very affectingly upon her domestic character. " I know of no circumstances which can distinguish the latter days of my lamented sister from those of any other christian gentlewoman. Her private excellencies may be comprised in a few words—in all relations of life she strove to do her duty, and few will be found to have achieved their purpose better." It *is* the simple and unvarnished truth, written by one who cannot be mistaken—and at a moment when every thing like parade or consequence, if it ever could affect him, would surely be despised and rejected.

The latter days of Mrs. Siddons, however, have a distinction which I fear does not always attend the christian gentlewoman. I mean the *reverence*, as well as affection, with which she continued to impress her family to the last. In this view of her I can easily credit the exclamation of her daughter, who had been requested to occupy her vacant seat. "What! seat myself in my mother's chair!" It was their exact relation painted in a single phrase. Dignified self-possession was not only the constant habit of her character, but it was the soul of her professional excellence, and imparted the *ideal* by which she raised and governed whatever she assumed. "She kept her state, (says a profound thinker) in the midst of the tempest of passion, and her eye surveyed, not merely the present suffering, but the causes and consequences; there was inherent power and dignity of manner."

Lord Byron, we all know, in a style too fervid for philosophy, said the same thing, "that she was the *beau ideal* of acting: that her tones were superhuman, and power over the heart supernatural." But he aimed always at *intensity* in his language, and became frequently extravagant.

I have read somewhere that Dr. Johnson, speaking of Mrs. Siddons to a Dr. Glover, said, " No sir, on the stage, art does *not* adorn her. NATURE adorns her there, and art *glorifies* her." I have given place to the anecdote for the purpose of subjoining my opinion that Dr. Johnson never so expressed himself. All that he really did say of her, the reader will find at page 35 of the present volume.

I have always been anxious to ascertain what was really thought of Mrs. Siddons by people qualified to think about her, but am little disposed to notice the common gossip she has excited, whether favorable to her or otherwise. One ingenious gentleman assures us, that she spoke constantly in " *blank verse*," and that she had been supposed a lady of greater attainments than she actually possessed, for that she did not know the official sense of the French word *bureau.* He forgot that she had twice, if not oftener, travelled through great part of France, and could not be unacquainted with the Bureaux des *Postes.* But any absurdity passes that can hope to gratify the appetite for disparaging the eminent of either sex. In the hour of festivity, too, she has sung certain ludicrous songs, at her brother's house, and I dare say at her own—but the entertainment derived was from the *travesty* of her features and her mind. She was so little given to the *ridiculous*, that I remember she took a particular occasion of marking her dislike to what is called the *diverting* history of John Gilpin. James Boswell loved truth, and accurately related to myself what he heard. " Here," said Mrs. Siddons, " is a worthy and industrious citizen, who, although married twenty years, had never yielded to the natural desire of a day's pleasure in the country. At length, with very prudential arrangement, the family set off for the Bell, at Edmonton, in a chaise and pair. Mr. Gilpin, for himself, borrows a friend's horse, to save expense; but the unruly animal soon distresses his unskilful rider—his hat and wig are jostled from his head, and the home-made wine which he carried, by the shattering of the bottles, lays the dust upon the road instead of cheering the spirits of the party. When he arrives in sight of his family at the Bell, he is not permitted to *join* them—the horse, knowing that his real master had a house at Ware, decides upon going the whole of his accustomed route. At Ware the harrassed traveller arrives, and his friend refits him with good humour, and invites him to dinner. But here his *honour* is concerned, and he resolves, on his wedding-day to dine with his wife, cost what it will. So off he sets on his return, again to ride bare-headed upon a frightened steed; and never ends his torments until he reaches, not Edmonton, but London. And I should be glad to know what there is in all this for any *reflecting* creature to laugh at?"

Her brother John had a similar way of viewing things. I once sat by his side when a mimic in the company was, in profound darkness, imitating the return at night of a drunken German to his lodging, stumbling up a stair-case without light, treading upon the cat, and kicking the moveables in the apartment, getting off his boots with difficulty, and at length, after abusing his poor shivering wife, drawing the miserable coverlid over his shoulders, which, by its sound, seemed to give more wind than warmth. "I wish to heaven he would be quiet," said Kemble, "he absolutely makes my very heart *sick* with this wretchedness, which he displays to entertain me."

But such an estimate was to be expected from characters really *considerate* and never trivial; and the reader should not be refused the means of considering the further application of the great principle of ART before quoted, as it is shewn to govern even the real scene, and pronounce the conduct of the individual in life itself.

"Self-possession is the *ideal* in ordinary behaviour. A low or vulgar character seizes on every trifling or painful circumstance that occurs, from *irritability* and want of imagination to look beyond the moment; while a person of more refinement and capacity, or with stronger predisposition of the mind to good, and a greater fund of good sense and pleasurable feeling to second it, despises these idle provocations, and preserves an unruffled composure and serenity of temper."

The above remarks, for which I renew my acknowledgments, are a perfect clue, in the case of
Mrs. Siddons, to both the actress and the lady.
They are a history of her art and of her life, and
call only on recollection to support them. Her
place in society was assigned her by the general
feeling of her merits; and she was approached with
a reverence such as Dr. Johnson used to excite in
those who knew his talents and his virtues. In her
retirement she had not the slightest regret to have
resigned the applause of multitudes. Indeed she
strenuously avoided public notice: not that the
renewal of her efforts of exhibition was painful to
her, for she delighted occasionally in the most
energetic recitals from her darling Shakspeare, and,
to within a month of her last illness, evinced that
she had lost nothing of her power to terrify or
soften; but no spurious nonsense, on such occasions, was heard from the lips of Mrs. Siddons; lips
(to use the language of George Steevens,) " whose
matchless powers should be sacred only to the task
of animating the purest strains of dramatic poetry."

The only poet whom she could rank with the
bard of Avon, was the English Homer—Milton;
and of the Paradise Lost she was a very skilful and
even sublime reader. But I must here close the
fond estimate of her powers, however meritorious;
and, boldly expressing my perfect *despair* to see
them ever approached, resign the future to minds
of greater facility, or memories less extensive than
my own.

Upon the subject of the family property, I proceed to lay before the public the exact facts ; because on this, as on most other topics relating to this admirable lady, the greatest misrepresentations have been published, which she always disdained to correct.

Her husband, the late William Siddons, Esq. had for some time resided at Bath, for the benefit of his health, and, on the night preceding his dissolution, had a circle of friends about him—when his social and pleasant manners were even heightened by the improvement both he and they fancied in his looks and spirits. However, he died suddenly on the 10th of March, 1808. Mrs. Siddons at the time was performing at Edinburgh.

By his will, dated 28th December, 1804, he gives his freehold house in Great Marlborough Street to his son Henry Siddons, his heirs and assigns for ever.

He gives his leasehold house in Gower Street to his son George John Siddons, for the remainder of the term which would be unexpired at his, (W. S's.) death.

To his daughter Cecilia Siddons he gives £2000, at her marriage or attaining the age of 21, whichever should first happen. This is given in trust to accumulate in the funds.

The whole residue is given *absolutely* to his wife Sarah Siddons, and she is sole executrix.

By his first Codicil, dated 4th February, 1806, he adds £2000 more to his daughter's portion, upon the same trusts as the £2000 in the will; and also the Tontine upon the Bath Theatre ; but does not name the amount either of its cost or produce.

By the second Codicil, dated 18th November, 1806, he gives sixty volumes of the Classics, all of which he enumerates, to his son, Henry Siddons, and his gold watch, which is capped and jewelled. By a memorandum thereunder, the testator declares that he *had* given the books before stated to his son Henry.

There were witnesses to the Will, but none to the Codicils. Affidavits of their being in the Testator's handwriting were made to entitle them to Probate.

On the 2nd April, 1808, Probate of the said Will and two Codicils was granted to Sarah Siddons, widow, the relict and sole executrix. Personal property sworn *under* £20,000!

The Will of Mrs. Siddons has not hitherto been proved by her executors, who are her nephew, Horace Twiss, Esq. and her intimate friend William Meyrick, Esq. of Red Lion Square.

The residue absolutely at her disposal cannot, I fear, have been greatly increased by the efforts which she professionally made in the five years following the death of her husband. Indeed so scanty was the provision found upon her retirement from the stage, that Mrs. Siddons is understood to have sunk some part of her fortune to increase the income by annuity on her life. The residue is vested in the Long Annuities.

She bequeaths what there is in equal portions to her family :—

　　To the Widow and Children of her late son, Mr. Henry Siddons, one-third.

　　To her son George John Siddons, and his heirs, one-third.

　　To her daughter Cecilia the remaining third.

Mr. George John Siddons, a few months before the death of his father, married, in India, Miss Fonhill, daughter of Judge Fonhill, by whom he has a numerous family.

The reader sees, from the above incontestable statement, that the greatest performer during the last half century had never realised such an independence as to allow of any thing like *splendor* in her establishment. She lived as a gentlewoman, but, from necessity, with systematic economy.

Upon so great a loss, and the breaking up of an establishment endeared to her by so many touching recollections, Miss Siddons was prevailed upon by her sister-in-law, Mrs. Henry Siddons, to accompany her on returning to Edinburgh.—Change of *scene*, and *time*, are the only palliatives for a grief equally profound and unavailing.

J. B.

Lightning Source UK Ltd.
Milton Keynes UK
UKHW030807250223
417646UK00007B/750